The

ESSENTIAL
Paul Belasik

Also by **Paul Belasik**

Dressage for the 21st Century

ESSENTIAL
Paul Belasik

RIDING TOWARDS THE LIGHT

EXPLORING DRESSAGE TECHNIQUE

THE SONGS OF HORSES

Trafalgar Square Publishing

North Pomfret, Vermont

This omnibus edition first published in the
United States of America in 2001 by
Trafalgar Square Publishing
North Pomfret, Vermont 05053

Printed in Hong Kong

Riding Towards the Light first published in 1990,
Exploring Dressage Technique first published in 1994,
The Songs of Horses first published in 1999,
all by J. A. Allen, London, England.

Library of Congress Control Number: 2001094953

ISBN 1 57076 212 0

Exploring Dressage Technique: line drawings by Dawn Caronne,
Dianne Breeze (chapter openings), and Maggie Raynor (Chapter 6).

The Songs of Horses: illustrations by Dianne Breeze.

Jacket design by Carrie Fradkin

10 9 8 7 6 5 4 3 2 1

Preface to the Omnibus Edition

When I first wrote *Riding Towards the Light*, I showed the manuscript to one of my most important mentors, Henri Van Schaik. V. S. didn't like the book. He said, "You can't tell people these things, those 'mistakes,' you have to show them the ideals." I said to him, "But you went through these same kinds of trials and struggles." "Of course," he said, "But that's not for public consumption." I should add that one of the reasons I thought Van Schaik was such a great teacher was that he found nothing wrong in disagreeing with anyone; he actually liked it. So, if you asked his opinion you got it. If you had your own opinion that was fine with him, too. There was certainly no problem if it was different as long as you made a good case for yours, because he did not suffer fools gladly.

Judging from the worldwide reaction I received after *Riding Towards the Light* was first published, many people did want to hear about the "mistakes." I wasn't alone in my wondering about the failures that seem to guide my work more than any successes, and about my worthiness to live up to the classical ideals. So I thought I would continue my odd little journals offering an inside view about learning a classical art in the age-old phases of apprentice, journeyman, and finally, craftsman. From these phases came the material for the books *Exploring Dressage Technique* and *The Songs of Horses*.

I remember an incident on one of my visits to another important mentor of mine, the poet A. R. Ammons, whom I studied under. I was on my way to Archie's office and I stopped by a museum on the Cornell University campus. The museum has an open space in the middle that allows you to look up or down from any floor. When I walked in, I heard a strange, rhythmical, grating sound. I knew that the Dalai Lama was going to give a talk at Cornell in a week or so, and was not entirely surprised when I went to the center balcony and looked down to the lowest floor to see two young monks in Buddhist robes preparing a mandala. They had been laboring for weeks to prepare this elaborate sand painting. The grating sound came from running a kind of stick over the small metal ridges on a slender tin-like funnel. This skillful vibration shakes the different colored sands from the funnel in precise amounts almost a grain of sand at a time if necessary. The most exquisite, complex, precise, geometric art was being formed. This mandala was going to be used in a ceremony when the Dalai Lama arrived. It would then be brushed off into Cayuga Lake. There was never any thought of holding on to this art, it was part of a great tradition. It would be used in a rich ceremony and let go.

I then realized that this is what classical riding is all about. We have to learn to make riding pure again. Riding as well as you can is more important than all the analysis or accolades that are laid upon it afterward. So many riders sacrifice so much to get a moment of glory, and then they sacrifice more to hold on to it, and still more to try and go back to it again. Finally, riding becomes more of a strategy than an art form.

All too soon, my mentors were gone and some riders began to come to visit me, in a similar way. At first, I thought how sad, they have to settle for someone like me when I had those lions to sit next to. Now, I practice harder than ever so maybe these people will see something that will help them the way I was helped.

Each night I drag the riding arenas. There I brush my sand clean. For me there is no sense of loss, the feeling is more like one of absolution, since I still seem better at showing "mistakes." It is easy to let go of mistakes, but I'm also learning to let go of more cherished things, which is a much harder task. Why? In order to learn to live right now. Relish the joy or the pain of the phase you are in. Feel these things, after all feelings help you ride—not words, and riding a horse will help your feelings. I don't know why they let us ride them, but I am grateful beyond words.

Paul Belasik, 2001

Book One

RIDING TOWARDS THE LIGHT

An Apprenticeship
in the Art of Dressage Riding

Contents

I would like to dedicate this book to Henri Van Schaik. I know that I speak for many people of my generation when I thank him for cultivating in us an appreciation of the art in riding. Even more important for me has been his challenging insistence that we 'joust' with him.

Foreword

by
Erik F. Herbermann

ANY RIDER WHO has tangled at all seriously with the task of discovering the deep mysteries of horsemanship, will readily be able to identify with Paul Belasik's account of his journey through the bowels of an equestrian Hades in his search for truth about the horse. In this compelling and informative book, written in a delightfully frank style, Belasik shares his personal experiences of the unconventional and divergent paths he travelled. From masters of martial arts to masters of horsemanship, he sought out the common thread of fundamental values, and attempted to apply these in his own riding.

Important technicalities, such as the half-halt, balance, and the correlation of the seat and position and its effects on the horse, are all addressed with insight. I feel, however, that the most significant contribution is the thought-provoking philosophical dimension which will give readers a fresh perspective on riding, together with renewed hope and encouragement, and a sense of fellowship in the awareness that others too have made the arduous trek, and have known its doubts, and its joys and frustrations.

In today's highly technical equestrian world a book such as this one is very welcome indeed. It fills a considerable void, as food for the mind and spirit of man, as he discovers himself via the horse.

Preface

MANY YEARS AGO a monk was coming out of a monastery that was under the leadership of the great Zen man, Rinzai. Halfway across a bridge over a river, he met some monks from another Buddhist school. One of the monks stopped him and, referring to the river below, asked, 'How deep is the river of Zen?' The Zen monk, who was just returning from a session with Rinzai, a teacher legendary for his direct actions, without the slightest hesitation replied, 'Find out for yourself,' and began to throw the monk off the bridge. Fortunately he was saved by his two friends, who persuaded the first monk to stop.

To quote D. T. Suzuki: 'Zen is not necessarily against words, but it is well aware of the fact that they are always liable to detach themselves from realities and turn into conceptions. And this conceptualisation is what Zen is against. The Zen monk cited above may seem an extreme case but the spirit is there. Zen insists on handling the thing itself and not an empty abstraction.'[1]

With the tone of Zen's advice ringing in the air, I am going to try to recount my own apprenticeship in riding horses and particularly in the art of dressage. These words, apart from actual riding, are really meaningless. Perhaps they will mislead, or confuse, maybe encourage, but only the rider can enlighten him- or herself.

Dressage is from the French word for training. Above all, dressage is the systematic training of the horse to become stronger, more supple, and graceful. To a certain extent it is not an esoteric ballet-like endeavour, although it can look this way. Essentially it was born out of a highly practical matter. Namely, once a horse is mounted by a rider, its normal balance and centre of gravity are disturbed, to the point where the horse can prematurely damage itself with wear. Through systematic exercise and procedures dressage aims to remedy this imbalance, to train the horse to rebalance itself with the weight of the rider.

There is another element of dressage that cannot be glossed over. It is the pervasive connection it has with war, warriors and violence, primarily because of the horse's historic role in battle. At the Spanish Riding School in Vienna some of the most difficult movements

[1] SUZUKI, DAISETZ T., *Zen and Japanese Culture*, Bollingen Series, Princeton University Press, 1959.

[10]

practised today are living baroque representations of the evasive moves in battle – specialised kicks while in the air, controlled rears and so on. At Saumur in France, the famed Cadre Noir still perform ritualised battle movements in unison. In the bull rings of Portugal, exquisite horses perform spins, lifts, and passes with technical perfection, not technically perfect under the luxury of exhibition, but because improper execution may mean death.

Yet there is something in riding which is very close to the paradox which led the sword masters and Samurai of old Japan and martial artists of today to Zen. The most eloquent dressage masters have a common thread: their complete disdain for force. It is as if out of the roots of violence, subjugation and war, these few people seek harmony with nature. They try to create something ephemeral. It is art they can never finish. It is art that can't stand still. It is art that is alive. Art that must be watered and fed. In the last analysis it is really the art of living.

My own apprenticeship was no less subtle than the monk's encounter on the bridge. However, more often than not I was not the monk coming home full of balance from the lessons of a wise Rinzai; I was the monk being thrown off the bridge. I still don't know how deep is the river of Zen, but I know precisely how deep, dark and cold is the river water beneath that bridge, having been in it so many times. My apprenticeship covered about thirteen years. It involved traversing thousands of miles. It entailed thousands of hours of rigorous practice. It meant researching centuries of literature penned by old masters, and hours and hours of observation and lectures from new masters. Most of the time it was at the least puzzling, and sometimes it induced such mental upheaval that it pushed my personal life through vast changes. Yet, however much physical time and space I covered, I never even came close to the distance that it was necessary to traverse within the confines of the small sand rectangle, the perfect sand Zen garden, the dressage arena.

Prologue

I AM IN THE dojo of Shuji Maruyama. Mr Maruyama is a disciple of Uyeshiba, the legendary martial artist and founder of Aikido, and a student of Koichi Tohei, founder of the Ki-Aikido Society. Aikido, 'the gentle way', is an odd martial art. It has no offensive moves. It is an incredible awareness and balance. It will use the force of an opponent, move with it, guide it into a turn, or a spin, divert it with a psychic kind of timing until the attack is neutralised. Aikido is grace.

That *Ki* is in the centre of the word Aikido is not an

accident. This Japanese word for 'life force', or 'energy', is the blood of Aikido. In the human being it is centred in the 'hara' – a point below the navel. The closest western term is 'centre of gravity', but this is not a good equivalent. 'Centre of balance' might be better, as long as one does not limit it to physical balance.

I had been using *ki* breathing exercises for my riding for some years. I decided that Aikido could certainly enhance a rider's skills; after all, the dressage rider must train a horse ten times his or her own weight. Force is out of the question. Since I was already using some tenets of Aikido, I thought some more formal instruction would help. This was the second time I had come to Maruyama's training hall. In the evenings, after my riding and training, I had been working in several different dojos. Few were familiar with Aikido and most had drifted far away from the total balance that is at the heart of all martial arts. Maruyama's practice hall was different. It is close to Chinatown in Philadelphia, on the second floor of what looks like a narrow store front. One small door with a few pasted posters marks the entrance. This building is surrounded by short, once useful buildings, all similar. They seem to be held up as much by plywood windows and iron security bars as by bricks and plaster. On street level there are supply rooms, liquor stores, or empty spaces. People cluster on street corners. It has the look of a village at a remote outpost; the order of certain needs is clear.

At the top of a steep flight of stairs is a long, narrow room. There is a modest-sized office, then a small sitting area in front of the mats which go wall to wall to the far end of the room. The sitting area has a few chairs for visitors and a small table that is an unpretentious shrine. Maruyama was gone. He had returned to Japan with his family after sixteen years in America. He did return periodically, but his students, some of whom had been with him for the sixteen years, now run the hall. In front of the mats there is a row of shoes belonging to the people practising.

I have come to watch the practice again and to talk to one of the teachers. It is at least a sixty-mile round trip from my home, and this on top of my horse work. I am not sure that I can manage to attend three or more evenings a week. A woman is going to run the practice. As a few people warm up she walks alone to the back wall of the room. From a simple rack she chooses a bamboo sword and begins some slow movements which have their basis in *kendo*, swordsmastership. She is dressed in the traditional black skirt of advanced Aikido-ists and a white, heavy cotton, robe-like blouse, similar to those worn in other martial arts. She stands deep into the mat. It is easy to move her form five hundred years back in time to the Samurai in Japan. Her hair is like black glass. All her movements seem unhurried. They are smooth, uninhibited; so smooth at times they are very fast. Finally she changes her stance and brings the sword down from above her head in a quick slicing arc. It stops at waist level. For a moment it is still. She has met a certain spot. It has stopped without being abrupt. She returns the sword above her head and two more times she splits the air. Her movements don't seem threatening but there is no confusing what is in front of you. It is serious and commanding.

After the practice she comes over and sits down so that we can talk. She is gracious. She answers my questions. I tell her how impressed I am, but she is very humble. She is straightforward and serene. It is not my imagination. It is peaceful to talk to her. She frequently smiles. I tell her about my ideas of Aikido and riding. She seems ambivalent. At first I think that she is

[15]

sceptical. Then I realise that she is really listening. She simply doesn't want to make any presumptions. The more we talk, I see that she seems genuinely curious about riding. She almost suggests that she is envious of those who ride horses and live in the country. I assure her I am the envious one. Again she seems embrarrassed. As we continue talking something strange begins to happen. My talk about riding is coming very close to her talk about her own practice. One statement resonates with another, the way a tuning fork can agree with a pure note. There seems little else to say. Sometimes we just nod. A familiar feeling begins to grow inside me. This time I know what is happening. It comes on as a wave of melancholy. I know my apprenticeship is finishing. It is as if someone close to you has died. You are beyond shock and anger. You cannot arouse any more passion. You don't seem to care. The universe is pulling away. You are not sure whether to go on with it, but if you do you know it will be with far fewer expectations. Your ride becomes less ponderous. Since there seems to be less of yourself now; you are automatically less self-important. You are lighter. There is more room. You feel free.

I literally feel myself cracking. Deep in the primitive part of my brain there must be some memory, some programme of metamorphosis from ancient animals. The melancholy, the form with which I have become so familiar, certain that it was my only real self, is disintegrating around me. It is not fighting to hold on. It seems to know better than I do that it is finished. It has been the protective cocoon, until this new trans-mission, this new form, was possible. How do I know the time is right? What is it in this meeting that sets this off? Before I can try to explain, try to make the right sense of it, I have to go back to the beginning of my

[16]

serious riding, to what I consider the start of my apprenticeship in the art of dressage. If there was such a thing as a moment of fertilisation or conception in a course of my training, I know for me very well when it was. That is where I have to start.

Chapter One

The Seat

'PULLING THE CHIN IN slightly or making the back of the neck touch the collar will cause the sternum to come forward. This will produce a slight arching of the chest with the deep breathing that promotes posture and relaxation without a bad effect on the position of the other parts of the body . . . The position of the seat bones, as the base of support, vertically underneath the hips and the straight but supple spinal column enables the rider to protect himself against continual contraction of the muscles in the small of his back and his buttocks. It also protects him against fatigue because the point of support lies in the same vertical line as the rider's centre of gravity and he requires no effort to maintain his equilibrium . . .'

Waldemar Seunig[1]

'What is the essence of *zazen*?[2] Just posture, breathing and attitude of mind. In time, every gesture of life becomes zen, but the source, the origin, is simply sitting. The zazen posture is the 'right sitting' . . . Body – the trunk is straight. The pelvis tips slightly forward so the internal organs are placed naturally and the abdomen without tension . . . The head is straight, the chin drawn in . . . Push the sky with your head, push the earth with your knees. The elbows are not glued to the sides, but slightly rounded while the shoulders and arms fall naturally.'

Taisen Deshimaru[3]

A long creek flows in and out of high shale cliffs, along small beaches of grey sand and gravel. In some places the gorges are over one hundred feet deep. This old creek moves through the Tuscarora Indian Reservation on its way into one of the Great Lakes. A brown, smooth farm road follows the creek for half a mile before the water turns hard into one of the high shale

1 SEUNIG, WALDEMAR, *Horsemanship*, Doubleday and Company Inc.
2 *zazen* – the practice of sitting meditating in Zen.
3 DESHIMARU, TAISEN, *The Zen Way to the Martial Arts*, E.P. Dutton, Inc. 1982.

banks, spinning off into the dark shade as the road trails off into a rugged stand of pine trees.

It was on that dirt road bordering the creek and a fertile corn field that my first real introduction to the seat took place. A couple of days before, in a library, I had found a copy of a book on dressage by an Englishman, Henry Wynmalen. I had already been riding for a number of years, both in the American Western style and the English hunt style adapted by Frederico Caprilli, the Italian founder of the forward seat. Wynmalen's book fascinated me. He described the possibility of sitting on a horse in a way that a rider could follow every movement and be practically glued to the horse without relying on grip. I was mesmerised. No one had ever told me anything about this kind of riding. It seemed mystical. The descriptions of the horse's various movements were incredible.

I took Wynmalen's book and one of the two horses that my family owned at the time and went off to the road. It was a clear day. I had a flat, smooth English saddle, a typical old hunting type, with no padding beneath the skirt and built on a tree of a very flat contour. It felt like I was sitting on a wooden plank. I took the stirrups off and began to walk, then trot. The horse seemed to be trotting too fast and I kept sliding from one side to the other. Even though the road was perfectly straight, I could not keep my balance. Time after time I would slip so far over that I had to grab the horse's mane and pull myself up straight.

The horse became nervous from all my wrestling and clutching. We continued in this fashion up and down the road, again and again. The sun fired overhead as the trail of our dust rose above us. Up and then down again. Whenever my legs shook uncontrollably from exhaustion, I would stop and re-read Wynmalen, searching

[21]

for a clue in the writing, and then I would try again. My legs were rubbed raw and began to bleed. I kept at it. I became angry with myself, but still I continued until complete frustration took over. Finally, it was no use. It was too painful. When I had started at least I could stay on for a little while; now I was falling off every few strides. I had to stop. I was furious with Wynmalen. I looked at the black and white photographs of this frail-looking old man sitting to the trot. I thought it was a hoax. Exaggeration, rotten exaggeration. This old man beyond his prime, sitting there giving us fictitious images. Yet even when my rage with Wynmalen was at its highest, I knew one thing: somehow, deep inside, I felt (although I didn't even have one microscopic piece of evidence) that Wynmalen wasn't a liar. Somehow the old master had set the hook. I told myself that whatever it took, I would get this 'seat' thing. I would master it.

It is midnight and there is an early autumn storm in southern Pennsylvania. The rain is solid and feels even colder because we are leaving Pennsylvania and what has been, for my new wife and me, our first home together as well as our horse business. The lights of the stable reflect in prisms of moisture in the driveway. Our horses are loaded on the lorry. The motor is running. Occasionally they stamp a little nervously. There is the immediate pressure to get going. One of our best friends is there to help. It seems sad to leave. Why I don't have more doubts about this move, I am not sure. The dogs are crated in the car which my wife will drive. If all goes well, sometime in the next day we will arrive at our destination, a piece of land we have bought in the Adirondack Mountains. It is raining harder. There is nothing more to do. We have to go.

The Seat

At college I studied horse management as part of a pre-veterinary course, and in the riding school rode as part of an equitation programme. In the summers I gained more horse experience by working on various farms. After I graduated I tried to work with as many different types of horse as I could – carriage horses, polo ponies, hunters, and at racehorse studs, and event and dressage stables. The girl I married was also involved with horses. We worked together and eventually rented a stable and started our own business. I began teaching. We also both exercised and trained horses. If I could find good dressage instructors, then I tried to have lessons, but they were rare and expensive. I read everything I could find about horsemanship and dressage. By this time I had spent so many hours practising riding without stirrups that the seat seemed much less foreign to me. However, I kept at it. I wasn't anywhere near satisfied even though I could now stay on some difficult horses.

My wife and I worked hard and things began to improve. I was lecturing on horsemanship at a local college and teaching twenty to thirty hours of private lessons during the week. This left less and less time for my own riding. I couldn't believe it – here I was, running my own horse business, something I had always wanted so badly, but it could just as easily be *any* business. It was always business.

Years before, in college, I had hunted up in the Adirondack Mountains with a friend. I loved those mountains. My friend lived there so I asked him to look for a piece of land. One day in the winter, he called me. He had found a perfect place, and it was cheap. I went to see it and bought it. I thought we could start again, small, reshape the business – and ride. I didn't want to teach. I had too much to study. I just wanted to ride all of the time.

[23]

As I started to drive away from the Pennsylvania stable I wasn't sure if I would ever see this great horse country again. We survived the night with no breakdowns and I was convinced this was a good omen. In mid-morning, our little caravan drove through the small village of Ironville, where less than fifty people lived. It was still a couple of miles to the farm. The air here was so much drier, and in every direction we could see the peaks of mountains. I was excited. Finally we arrived. We turned the horses out into a wire-fenced paddock. They moved off a little unsteadily into the knee-deep grass. The other pastureland would still have to be reclaimed and permanently fenced. There was not even a barn. The house was falling into two feet of water in the basement. I had cut some trees on a previous visit. They were trucked and milled; now a fresh pile of lumber lay stacked in the dooryard. It would only take me time. I looked at my wife. I wasn't sure what she was feeling.

The stallions scream, partly in defiance, partly in fear. We are having breakfast and looking through the glass doors that face the southern slope of our mountain. From the dressage arena, bordered with white birch rails, the paddocks and pastures divide along the small brook, and run one third of the mountain to the end of the higher timber. There isn't any real cause for alarm. A black bear lumbers through the corner of one of the stallions' paddocks. He is certainly much more afraid of the huge horses. At this time of the day, deer and coyote can often be seen in the higher pastures.

Six years have passed since the move north and that long haul. They have been difficult years, marked by one drama after another. The new barn roof collapsed under a tremendous snow. Water froze for weeks at a time during the long, long winters. Our old house burned down in the middle of a winter's night. Everything was destroyed. We escaped with only the clothes we could carry. All my horse books were ashes. I injured my legs, pinned under a tree in a logging accident. Yet after each disaster we rebuilt and the farm improved. Horses were sent to us to be trained from all over. Our biggest customer was an independent breeder of German Trakehners. We broke many of the young horses and showed the stallions, even though I really didn't like it. I felt it was an interruption and, worse, I didn't like the attitude one seemed to need to be competitive. Through the work with the German horses I was privileged to meet and learn from many good German horsemen, and a couple of bad ones, and for an American at that time, it was an incredible experience. Even though we were reclusive it was a fact that on many given days during that time I probably had the chance to ride more German stallions than most other riders in America. No one then, though, I think could have foreseen the dramatic sweep that the German breeds would make across the USA in a period of a few short years. I read many more German texts and reviewed the popular German riding magazines every month. I pored over the riders of the past and those current. The forms of Loerke, Stensback, Staeck were as familiar to me as the forms of the ever-rising Reiner Klimke and Harry Boldt. With protractor and ruler, I dissected all these riders. I measured the angles of each one's knees and their backs. I calculated the seat in every fashion and matched it to the riders of the Spanish Riding School. Then, in my own practice, I had photographs taken and I compared myself. No master would have pushed me as I did myself. I seemed to be making progress. In spite of many flaws in posture, my seat was

[25]

becoming more and more effective, more influential and more demanding. When a particular horse went badly, I thought about it all evening. I wouldn't be able to get it out of my mind until I rode that horse again the next day. There were times when I rode the same horse twice. I was riding many hours, sometimes on very difficult horses. I loved working with young horses the most. I took some pleasure in the risk as well as the mystery of each one's potential.

My first wife and I did everything ourselves. The difficulty of the work forced me into equally difficult places with my personality. In order to accomplish the tasks, I needed a forceful intensity. This fierce energy was my ally, but it was hard to shut it off once I got it wound up. One typical day in one of the early winters, there was a problem with a valve at the bottom of a well which was about four feet deep and three feet wide. I had to get to the bottom in order to dismantle and repair it. It was below zero. There was no other way than to take off my coats and shirts, crack the ice on top and reach down, head first, into the icy water. I could not get myself to do these things with nonchalance. I would rev up the fire and bend any task to my will. The danger was that my will seemed to become ravenous once it tasted its own strength. It tried to control everything. With each success it became harder to control. My seat manifested this exact same force. Encounter resistance, strike it down. My seat was becoming more and more a weapon, and it began to concern me.

Sometime in this period, in all my calculations, I had convinced myself that my leg angle was wrong. I lengthened the stirrups as far as possible. This lengthened my leg and gave me the longer, elegant look that I wanted to see. It also tipped my pelvis forward as my thigh fell almost straight down. That this position was uncomfortable to me meant nothing. That it began to pull on the ligaments high up on the inside of my leg was simply the price I would have to pay. After all, I thought, many of the German riders were riding so long they pointed their toes below their heels. The great Theodorescu on his fine mare Cleopatra had his toes lower in almost every photograph. I was riding and training a horse that was closely related to her, a fact which enhanced the theorem. I spent two years stretching my legs until one day I realised I had trained myself into the perfect crotch seat. This is a fault that almost every single dressage book warns against. Yet only when the pain became debilitating did it occur to me that I was sitting badly. Finally, I raised the stirrups with relief. It took the better part of eighteen months for that ligament and muscle to heal to the point where I didn't feel it pull when I mounted a horse. My heels then dropped naturally; my back was released from constant torque and became flexible again. Previously, when I attempted to move my whole leg back further, I tipped my pelvis and arched the small of my back in a tight bow. Now it was easy to keep my leg under my body and my seat bones. I was more patient because I wasn't in pain and my aids were technically more accurate because they were freer.

During these years, I met a riding teacher who would probably have more influence on me than any other I would meet. I was working on a jumping book with a well-known horse photographer, Karl Leck. I sought the help of Dr Henri Van Schaik, who had won a silver medal in the 1936 Olympic Games in Berlin as a member of the Dutch jumping team, and who was now noted as a dressage teacher. I felt that he was a natural to review my writing. I sent him the work. He helped me and we became friends. Whenever possible I tried to have a lesson from him, but it was a five-hour trip to his home. I wrote to him, visited him and watched him teach as often as I could.

In the seat Van Schaik was masterful. A student will sit correctly, no matter how long it takes. If this means you can only walk a horse, so be it. Time seems to mean nothing to him and the student will not move on until the seat is right. To someone in a hurry, he will seem to be an enemy, and will drive him crazy. It was probably through Van Schaik's words and example that I began to put the brakes on my driving aids. He hated the term bracing the back'. He felt it was a poor translation of the correct position of the back even when it is being used as a driving aid. Yet it would take more time before I really knew what he was talking about. Maybe if I could have worked with him more . . . but probably the time was not right yet.

After around seven years in the Adirondack Mountains, my marriage dissolved and the business had to be divided. I stayed on alone to sell the farm. It was the only equitable solution. I needed time to think and readjust. I thought this break should be total, so, for the first time in all those years, I stopped riding. The horses were sold. I began logging for a friend of mine. I spent all day alone in the woods; sometimes I would see another person at lunchtime, just as often I would not.

Spring came, and then the summer. In the evenings I often ate my dinner at a table I had set up under a great old spruce tree facing the mountain that was now for sale. I mowed the empty pastures. Yet I was never lonely. All that time spent alone was important. When I wanted to be around people, I could go to them.

A strange thing was happening. The more proficient I became at my logging work and the more time lapsed since I had stopped riding, the more I thought about it. That summer was spectacular.

I worked for several more months in the autumn. I hunted a lot but I felt my sabbatical was ending. By Christmas I prepared to leave. I arranged everything with the estate agents and within a month I was riding again in Pennsylvania. The farm would be sold shortly afterwards.

On my way back to Pennsylvania, some cosmic cycle completing, I dropped in on an old friend who is an artist. She talked me into visiting a psychic she knew, a woman who was well known and respected by police departments and the like, for her special abilities. In the dark we pulled up at the woman's house in a rural community of upstate New York. The house was so ordinary that I felt comfortable. Before my arrival I had given her my first name and the time of my birth. When we walked in, she handed me a piece of paper. It stated my weight and height. She smiled as she told me that this was just for fun. When we sat down she became more serious.

She began by telling me that I was born under a triune of fire. I listened carefully – this is not something you take lightly when you have narrowly escaped your own death in a fire. Her insights went some way to explaining why I was never really afraid during that raging fire. I clearly remember looking at the charred remains the next morning, being totally possessionless. I felt free. This was a strong lesson in materialism. It is difficult to place too much stock in material goods once you have been shown so dramatically the temporary nature of things.

She talked for two and a half hours without a rest.

There were fascinating connections with riding. She told it all very factually. Finally she had an important story to relate. She told me of a group of Frenchmen who had formed a secret club. They used to design and build escape-proof traps for humans. Then they would put themselves inside these traps and secure them. They had decided that if the human intellect could invent a trap, then the human intellect could also invent an escape. They loved to place themselves in untenable situations and try to find ways out, just for the bizarre challenge of it. Although there was no emphasis in her voice, I couldn't seem to pass over the implication or the advice that seemed so obvious: that the biggest challenges we face are almost always self-made. The escape, therefore, must not be from the trap but from the dangerous process of building the trap for yourself.

The horse's steps are muffled in the soft footing of the indoor arena. The summer sunlight comes through one long open wall that frames a small valley banked by trees and meadow grass. The arena is set in a deep cut between two Pennsylvania ridges. Deer and fox often wander by. The arena is large and usually I have it to myself. I am riding the third horse of the day. This horse is stiff and quietly resistant. I am preparing it for competition for its owner. I ride the horse demandingly. It is now over ten years since I began riding full-time. I push the horse on. The day gets warmer. The horse is reluctant. I ask for more flexibility, for more action behind. My seat drops. I flick the spurs into the horse's flank a couple of times. No noticeable reaction. Some horses become ticklish from the prodding and will actually tighten their sides, freezing some of the motion instead of giving more. I know all these things.

I use more seat. In half an hour I'm wet. The horse

is getting wetter. I drive the horse on. If I get any yielding I hold it and ask for more. More determination, more resistance. We continue around the arena. A spectator might not even be aware that anything out of the ordinary is going on. We work through relatively simple movements, but without rest. I tap the horse with the whip again. I push on through lateral exercises hoping to loosen it, wishing it would give in. I sink my seat even further. I use my back for leverage. Van Schaik would be cringing. I attack a few times with the spurs. I know it is getting aggravating for both of us, yet in terms of technique there is even more I can do to pressurise the horse. I use more strength.

We turn through the corner and are moving straight along the long wall. I ask for more collection. I shorten the horse forcefully. In an instant, the situation explodes. As if in slow motion, like a great marlin breaking high out of the sea to free itself from the fisherman's hook, my horse rises before me. Straight up, straining, slowly shaking its head, twisting in desperate rebellion to free itself of the relentless force on top. The rise goes beyond the highest point and the horse begins to come over, out of balance. Like a great fish, it is falling backwards to the surface. All the horse is in front of me. There is no escape. We keep falling. As we hit the ground there is a horrible sound. The ground is unforgiving. I hear the horse exhale in a deep, full cough. Dust curls up everywhere around us. Enveloped in it, everything becomes still, fog-like. I am lying pinned against the wall of the arena. I have been spared. The horse lies there still and has missed crushing me by inches. Only my leg is trapped. I can see that the horse is alive, conscious. I am not frightened. I am not angry. The situation becomes liquid. I feel as though I am divided – one part of me is looking down at the scene from above. There is disgust and pity. I almost wish I were hurt.

The horse rises to its feet. It seems uninjured. I stand up too. I feel fine, and yet something momentous is building. Horses have reared with me many times. By now I have broken probably fifty to a hundred horses. There have been countless falls. However, before I was always trying to avoid them if they happened. They seemed to be accidents. This time I seem to have deliberately used all my skills and techniques for destruction. What was I doing? My feelings seemed to be bouncing between my different selves. Then, in an amazing process, it became clear to me what the seat was really all about. The Buddhists call it *satori*, an enlightenment, often set off by a dramatic incident. Like some struck monk, after ten years of deliberation, in the violence of the action, I see it all so clearly. Have I become this monster? Have I learned this skill to dominate, to force a proud animal into such anxiety? I look carefully at myself. I am wearing sharp spurs. My horse has whip marks on its flank. I take the spurs off quite calmly. I know that I will never use them again. I can see that I have to go back to the first day of my experience with the seat – that day, along the creek, with Wynmalen's book. Everything was wrong from the moment I gave the concept life. I had promised myself that I would master the seat and nothing had changed since then. I started out by trying to find Wynmalen's seat, then Podhajsky's and Seunig's, obsessively calibrating the seats of the new German riders. From that first day I had a goal, a target. I pushed it in every direction to give me the answer. I created a din of ambition. Increased skill brought me no closer to the truth of the situation. In fact, my dominating seat became a wedge, separating me from what I really wanted. My seat became insular and demanding in that it took on a life of its own. When you are talking all the time, issuing orders, you cannot hear. Never did I just listen. Never did I just sit and feel for myself what was going on. Hear the horse. In the absence of language and words, the natural world speaks in whispered feelings. I had to go back to the beginning. In the mind of the beginner, all things are possible. In the mind of the expert, few.

The quotes at the beginning of this chapter come from very diverse sources. They are worlds apart in culture, and in time. Yet their languages are almost identical, and there are many other examples. I do not believe this is coincidental. There are no coincidences in the postures of the seat – riding, *zazen*, martial arts. Posture is all-encompassing. Breathing is a path, and awareness is the result. If we inhibit awareness through contortions of the body or contortions of the mind, the results will be the same: a rigid being and, in riding, an inflexible seat. The correct posture alone has the power to open one's consciousness.

In the beginning I think it is important to concentrate on breathing. Not because breathing has magical powers of its own, but because it gives the mind something natural to do, without focussing its attention on conceptualisation, or too much thinking. It is well known in sorcery that if you want to manipulate someone, you need to control his attention. It doesn't matter if the subject's attention is centred on the sorcerer out of admiration, hanging on every word, or out of sheer hate or fear. Once the subject is occupied, the sorcerer can manipulate him at will. Breathing can free misguided attention – and to breathe well, you must have good posture. Furthermore only in an aware posture will you be receptive to the murmurs outside of yourself. If you are uncomfortable and tense, you cannot feel. After all, riding is feeling.

It is now my belief that a rider, properly positioned by a good teacher, can feel 'the correct seat' in his very first riding lesson. It might be, in fact it most probably will be, only for a fraction of a second in a whole hour's practice. How hard you try doesn't really matter. It may happen by accident. If the teacher adjusts and the rider allows himself to just be aware, the feeling will come back. Like a shy and curious cat, if you make a move for it, force yourself on it, it is gone. If you just sit quietly and wait, then sooner or later it will come sneaking back.

The horse will want to communicate with you through your seat. However, this is precisely the dilemma. Too many of us think we have so many important things to say, that the ego will not quieten down.

Imagine finding a great radio, call it Ego's Radio. It has channels to and from all parts of the world. You turn it on, and as you slowly turn through the dial mysterious and musical sounds of foreign dialects come out from all over the world. If you wish, you can begin the long, arduous study of these languages. The result may be that you will be able to truly communicate with these strange exotic people and learn things you may have thought were never possible. You may learn new perceptions and share different visions of life. Or you can turn one switch and broadcast – send your own messages out and leave it to others to learn to understand you if they so want.

In the world of riding, you will very quickly meet up with Ego's Radio. You must decide for yourself whether to listen or speak.

What I have learned is that the correct seat is never only a matter of the physique or its physical properties, even though they are essential. Many riders, even very skilful riders, never leave this plane.

However, if you study the seat *mushotoku* (the Japanese word meaning without desire for gain or profit), you can move towards a new plane that is much more profound: a way of perceiving, of being, of feeling part of and connected to the whole world outside yourself. With the right practice, the right concentration will develop, until you can hold yourself in balance on the horse, aware, in full power, without tension. This is the fundament of the seat – that it is a way of perceiving as well as influencing. The shy cat sits purring in your lap. The world of the horse begins to reveal itself to you, just by your sitting there correctly. The doors open. You are accepted, not tolerated. After that, nothing about the human world can be the same again.

Chapter Two

The Hands – The Longitudinal Field
of Balance

IN HIS BOOK *Piaffer and Passage*[1] Colonel Decarpentry
says about balancing the horse, 'never increase the pressure of the hands and legs at the same time'. In *The
Complete Training of the Horse and Rider*[2] Alois

[1] DECARPENTRY, COLONEL, *Piaffer and Passage*, Arco Publishing Co., 1975.
[2] PODHAJSKY, ALOIS, *The Complete Training of the Horse and Rider in the
Principles of Classic Horsemanship*, Wiltshire Book Co., 1967.

Podhajsky, writing on exactly the same topic, says, 'short action [of the reins] must be supported by the rider's legs pushing forward'.

Classical riding theory abounds with these apparent contradictions. The student of equitation must face them like quintessential Zen *koan*[3] riddles. The student interested only in the end result is in a terrible position. A wrong turn towards either master may ruin months of precious time spent training the horse. The student interested in the path or process is in a fascinating position. He may step into a new place, perhaps a place where Podhajsky or Decarpentry has never been. No matter where this student ends up, he will be happy for the chance to travel there on the back of a horse.

What Decarpentry and Podhajsky are talking about, of course, is the half-halt. A look at the half-halt may be a good way to look at the rider's hands. In a dull night sky you can often see the light of stars by not looking directly at them. The corners of your eyes are better at detecting this kind of light. Without harsh, direct scrutiny, the stars will reveal themselves.

The New England air is cool. The hills are green, but they are beginning to show small breaks of reds and rust colours. I have brought one of the young stallions to a horse trials competition. I feel a certain pressure. The owners of the horse will be there and several people who have mares to breed from will be watching him. He is still green in terms of performance. He has also been learning about his role as a stallion and sometimes it is difficult to control his libido. Still, I feel that he needs to be taken out in public. I want him to see other horses in a situation unconnected with breeding. If he

---

[3] Apparent dichotomies or paradoxes used as a system of meditative study to deepen a student's understanding.

can understand the difference, it will be easier to control him for the rest of his life.

After the dressage test, he is in second place. His performance was all right. He is aware of all the other horses and very curious about the mares. None, I hope, are in season. I keep him busy.

The cross-country phase is next. After walking the course I see no particular problems. In a few vantage points spectators are gathering; in fact, there are more people than he has ever seen before. In between fences I will try to ride him towards the crowd to make sure that he sees them and becomes familiar with their movement. Our time comes up. We are counted down in the starter's box, and we gallop off. At the second fence he raps his front legs hard on the obstacle, and wobbles on landing. In a way I am glad. I feel it may make him more alert on the remainder of the course. Just to make sure he understands that I'm not too happy, I tap him with the stick I'm carrying. Later on in the course I feel him lag in the middle of a combination. I use the stick hard, once, and he responds. He pulls me over the second element of the obstacle. It is fine; he feels aggressive and I would much rather have that kind of feeling. At the end he is clear and has made it under the time without really trying. After the scores are added up and recalibrated, he moves into first place.

The last phase is the show-jumping test. Unlike cross-country fences, which are solid and unyielding, show jumps will fall if struck; and each rail can cost penalty points. The day has dragged on. The competition is friendly and the organisation leisurely, but it is getting late. In this last phase the competitors jump in reverse order. Being first, we must go last. By the time we enter the arena it has clouded over. It is drizzling and near dusk. We begin. After the third fence with nine to go, we start hitting rails. Penalty points add up. The horse seems less and less respectful of the jumps, dragging his feet as he leaves the ground. By the time we cross the finish flags we have dropped back six or seven places. I am tired and disappointed. I contain my feelings. Everyone blames it on the light. I put it down to his inexperience but I know we have a problem. It is a long ride home. Over the hours, I go over the round again and again in my mind. Every bad move is painfully vivid. I can't seem to come up with an answer. I am baffled. I am not sure that I rode badly, but I am certain that I didn't have have him trained well enough. I run through more remedies trying to find some way to get him to start picking his front feet up. I wear myself out rethinking everything too far ahead.

A month has passed since the horse's competition. It is cooling off more. I am aware of winter approaching. There isn't much more time in this season to work outside. I have been schooling and schooling but I am getting nowhere. In a course of ten fences we still knock down three rails at least. If this problem is not solved, the horse will beat himself at every competition and, what is worse, may pick up a reputation as a bad jumper, which will limit his value as a breeding stallion. I know that many other trainers would adopt extreme measures of punishment for this apparent lack of concentration, making it decidedly painful for him to touch the rails anywhere. I am opposed to these measures. Somehow I feel they can't solve my problem, which is not only to correct the horse but to understand what is going on. Each day my frustration increases. I feel time is running out literally. I dread going into the winter without a solution.

On one particular day I begin my practice with this horse. The sun has softened the footing. The old turf is

[39]

firm but spongey, perfect to jump on. He is the second
horse of the morning. I start patiently. I try to ride him
lightly and freely. After the warm-up we begin working
through some jumping grids, combinations of fences
aimed at increasing the horse's dexterity. After a little
while he seems to stop trying. It feels as if he is deliberately reaching out to knock down the rails. I am thinking as fast as I can, when all of a sudden my will takes
over. I see a solid cross-country fence. This part of me
seems to have had enough. I start cantering towards the
fence. About ten strides from the fence I feel the horse
lag a little. He trips forward, trying to brake for the
fence. I take the reins in one hand and strike him hard
with the crop. At the same time I sit down in the saddle.
I am upright, almost in a dressage seat. I close my legs
hard, press the spurs to the horse's sides. In the back
of my mind I have a fleeting image of an explosion at
the fence like some crashing racing car, an elemental
chassis careening forward as pieces fly off, trailing
smoke and fire. Yet it doesn't have any effect on my
body. My determination fails to heed the warning from
my intellect. I drive the horse ever harder. The horse
scrambles a little, but miraculously yanks his front feet
up in time, even at that speed. I can't believe it. I ride
on to another fence without stopping. Ten strides out I
begin driving again. We are flying. This time he stands
back and sails. I take him into five more fences. The
harder I try to push him into the fence, the better he
jumps. I go back to the arena and jump five fences clean.
I stop and settle. I am mystified. My mind is quiet,
almost sheepish. It isn't raging with questions or solutions – it is speechless. I feel ambivalent. My will and
mind seem to be at cross-purposes, one subjugating the
other. There is a paradox here. When my intellect is
ruling, it seems deliberately to try to obstruct my will.

If it is left unchecked, it can increase the tension around me and inside me to such an extent that it freezes my body and prevents it from functioning. The idea of ferociously thinking up solutions stops me from finding one. When my will takes over, it couldn't care less about danger. To my mind this seems excessive and hazardous. My mind is fearful of my will, believing that it will always put me in very dangerous places. Yet at the times when I have faced my own death, the facts do not support this. When my house was on fire and a silent pall of black smoke was descending upon me, my intellect was calmly sleeping. It was some other part of me that perceived the danger and woke me a few minutes before I was smothered. Wasn't it my intellect and ambition that chose those paths which backed me into corners, where only a sheer burst of will could free me from the destructive tangle of my ideas? At those times when my will seemed excessive and irrational, whose fault was it really?

I wonder if I can ever merge the two or if they will ever do it themselves? It is troubling that as carefully as I think a problem through, I never seem to solve it until my will takes over. I can see very easily how successes can become connected with the force of will. I am leery of this connection between success and force. If it turns out that I become less interested in force, will it mean less interest in successes? Or will a new idea of success come into being?

I am also mystified because I know I have stumbled on to something important. It is fairly easy to explain physically what has happened. Intellectually one can describe some relatively simple physical laws. The thrust on the accelerator of a racing car shifts the car's weight over the rear driving tyres. The front end lightens with this transfer. You can flip a motorcycle over with a

[41]

similar burst of power. Isn't it the same with this horse? Maybe. But there is so much more.

A human being is fairly vertically oriented in terms of balance. The human's centre of balance is pretty well determined and set. We are keenly aware of this balance. It takes us a long time after we are born to accomplish the feat of standing and moving upright in balance. Almost all other animals move at birth in the same way that they will move as adults. Not humans. It is difficult to move upright over only two legs. The horse's centre of balance has a whole range along its longitudinal axis, which could roughly correlate to the horse's spine. In various phases of its gaits, its balance, like its weight, can shift from front to rear. When horse and rider join together to move as a team, this new union has a centre of balance that is different from that of either of its members alone.

What I had encountered that was so mystifying was this distinct shift in perception. I had shifted from my two-legged sense of equilibrium and balance to the perception of a four-legged's balance. I had become aware of and able to feel this whole longitudinal field inside which the horse can shift its centre of balance. Before my will took over I kept thinking about balance instead of feeling it. I thought that, to make the forehand lighter, I had to ride lighter and more carefully. The more careful I became, the more rails went down. The more the focus was on what I could do and on myself, the more I pulled us, as a team, off balance. It was only when my intellect and mind were totally frustrated and confused that a crack appeared for my body to take over, to get its chance. What did I have to lose? I was out of ideas. Now there was room for something new. Instead of dictating all the possibilities, I could listen with my whole body. I felt the answer.

[42]

Balancing, rebalancing and shifting the horse's centre of balance is the cornerstone of dressage. The half-halt is a technique for getting at the constant rebalancing that goes on with this longitudinal field inside the horse. If it is in the seat that the rider begins to find his own centre of balance and thus awareness, then in the half-halt this awareness will send the rider deeper into the horse, where he will be able to sense something of the horse's centre of balance. Ultimately horse and rider will come to a place where they will merge into something quite new: a place, a feeling, where the rider will literally be at one with the horse.

In true dressage this balancing is the practical reason for doing dressage. This balancing *is* dressage, and not the particular movements in themselves. In the introduction I said that dressage is not necessarily an esoteric ballet-like endeavour, although it can look like one. This is what I meant. You must look at dressage with more than your eyes. Movements executed without balance and transitions between them become simply strings of acrobatic tricks. In true dressage it is the continuum that is important. There is the most pragmatic of all goals in dressage – to help train the horse to learn to balance with the additional weight and mass of the rider on top.

The very best dressage riders become keenly aware of the balance of the horse. They never let the horse fall too far out of balance. This is so critical a feeling that in advanced dressage the rider is asked to prove that he has command over this perception of balance in the course of riding. The correct piaffe, a cadenced trot in place, is nothing more than a manifestation of moving this centre of balance backwards. In a very real sense it can be argued that the piaffe means nothing on its own.

[43]

Its whole reason for being is to see how horse and rider can move in the longitudinal field of balance.

Riders who are abrupt, pushing the horse from the legs into the hands, pulling with the hands trying to put the horse back towards the legs, falling in and out of balance during the movements, have to be considered novices to the art of dressage no matter what difficult movements are executed. In dressage it is always how they are executed, not that they are executed.

A great deal of literature concerning the half-halt uses explanations like 'lightening the forehand', 'lifting the head and neck', 'elevating the poll', and 'raising the forequarters'. A logical reading of much of this theory would imply something has to be done to the front end of the horse in order to lighten it. Yet the reality is opposite. Imagine you are sitting astride the centre of a seasaw at a children's playground, and there is a rope tied to the end of the seesaw in front of you, just as reins would go towards the horse's head. As long as you sit on the fulcrum it is easy for the board to move up or down. The board is balanced and you are not impeding it. Now slide forward a little and the board immediately drops in front of you. You are tipped forward, looking towards the ground. The tail of the board is high in the air behind you. You have the rope so why not just pull the board back up? You pull on the rope. You can of course pull on the rope forever. You will never be able to lift that board back off the ground until you move your seat back over the centre of balance. When you do, the board will be as light as a feather.

In true dressage the hands only work at refining the edges, adjusting something that is already relatively in balance. They can never by themselves put the horse back into balance, any more than a person can pull the seesaw back up to an equilibrium if the balance is tipped off centre.

A child walks along a balance beam. The aware coach walks beside her. The child begins to falter. The coach instantly reaches up and steadies the child around the waist, which is close to a human's centre of gravity. As soon as the child is in balance again, the coach releases. They continue. The child's steps become bigger, freer, with each repetition. The child can stay in balance for longer periods of time and eventually through the complexity of new movements.

Good half-halts work this way. The aware rider gives them to try to keep the horse in balance. The most important part of the half-halt is the release. If the driving aids and/or the restraining aids are applied to shift the centre of balance back further, they must be released the split second rebalancing occurs. Those next steps taken by the horse will always be the most beautiful. The balance is readjusted and the horse is freed of any restraints and the steps show this.

Back at the gym, the child turns and begins another pass. An expert gymnast comes into the gym. She begins to limber up. The coach notices her. His concentration lapses. The child before him loses her balance. The coach isn't aware. The child slips and falls off the beam on to the mats. She is unhurt. The coach apologises. He retrains his attention. The child climbs up and begins again. This time her steps are more tentative, short and tense. The child is mildly anxious. She is having a hard time staying on the beam. The coach holds her all the way across. The minute he tries to release, she starts to fall.

Bad half-halts work this way. If the rider lets the horse fall too far out of balance, the results will always be forceful and shocking. This kind of riding causes anxiety and a myriad manifestations will start to occur. Tension is insidious in riding. The rider has to do everything to limit it. If the rider can't release even the tense horse, then, like the unnerved gymnast, the horse won't be able to move without some psychological or balancing life-line.

Dressage literature tells the reader to load the haunches of the horse, using the half-halt as a tool to do this. However, it can only do this for a few seconds. If there isn't an immediate release, the horse's action will freeze and become unnatural. The horse will begin to try to lean on the reins for support. From there the hind legs will start pushing the weight forward instead of carrying it forward. If the rider is not fully and constantly aware, he can just as easily train the horse to be heavy and dull as he can to be light and free.

REIN EFFECTS

Many teachings in riding are very specific as to the number of rein effects that there are. Some will say there are five. Sometimes these different effects are clearly described and given names: for example, opening rein, rein of opposition, indirect rein. Furthermore, there has been great debate over whether the reins should be taut and elastic, or soft, loose, and semi-slack.

Why is there so much attention paid to the reins, and therefore the rider's hands, when universally all masters agree that the real controlling is done at the true source of power in the horse, namely the rear or hind end, and that excessive rein use will be harmful?

One obvious answer is that the young mounted horse does not instantly appear in balance. Like the child on our balance beam, the young horse will fall in and out

of balance and will be constantly readjusting its equilibrium along its longitudinal field of balance. The rider
can help to rebalance the horse with restraining rein
aids: not by pulling the horse back into balance, but by
slowing the motion for a split second so that the hind
end, in effect, can catch up. It is almost like damming
up a river; the power is stored behind the dam. In
applying this very brief rein effect, the hand must not
pull back to where it would have a braking effect. This
would only put the horse further on to its nose, much
as when a driver brakes in a car and the bonnet dives
down. Instead the hand is passive and poised, 'fixed',
for a moment, and the power bunches or pushes up into
it. The horse becomes rounder, with its hind legs up
further under its body, and rebalancing occurs. Again,
the moment this happens, the rider must free the horse
once more.

Another answer is that this infatuation with rein
effects is a man-made problem. In terms of my own
experience, I began to feel and see an obvious mistake
in my riding and training. Early in my dressage instruction and continuing through a lot of it, the term 'forward' was drilled into my riding style. It is an expression
of one of the most basic tenets of dressage, and for me
one of the most misunderstood. Forward riding has
always been described as animated, decisive action in
the gaits, impulse in spirit. (The opposite of sluggish,
aimless or wandering gaits and movement.) In my
attempts to satisfy the desire of judges and teachers to
see horses moving more forward, always more forward,
invariably I applied too much push or thrust behind by
using too vigorous and too constant leg aids. Because
this was coupled with the natural inexperienced timing
of an apprentice, I very often pushed my horses on to
the forehand instead of seeking an equilibrium over the

four legs, or even a little more towards the rear as in the collected paces. The result was always the same. The horse became heavier in my hands and not lighter. It took a very long time to learn to trust my feelings and to wait until the horse had mastered one level of animation before injecting any more impulsion. When I stopped chasing my horses forward, they automatically became lighter. If there wasn't enough movement, so be it. Until the horse could carry what was there, there was no point in pressing on for more.

In terms of the specific numbers of rein effects and their descriptions, I have found reality much different. Basically the hands of the rider can move: (a) in a vertical field parallel to the rider's spine, up and down; and (b) in a horizontal field, parallel to the horse's spine towards the horse's mouth and back towards the rider's torso.

In the three-dimensional space of intersection between these two fields, there is an infinite number of combinations and effects possible, and that is if both reins are applied symmetrically, which they almost never are. Therefore, you have infinity times two when you include unilateral rein aids as well. In my opinion on rein effects, there is only one feeling that really needs to be mastered. It is the feeling of heaviness or lightness. If the reins are becoming heavy, an alarm should be sounding off in the horseman's head, and it should not go off until they become light.

When I first started riding one of the greatest compliments one could hear was that so and so had 'good hands', 'light hands', or 'quiet hands'. It was conversely very bad to have active hands. It is now my feeling that the novice rider should be allowed to move his hands around. This is the only way to develop the dexterity which will eventually translate into educated touch and real finesse. If the novice rider is constantly forced to

[48]

keep his hands immobile, I believe they can turn into dead hands, with little capacity to feel and even less, to effect. If you take a pen in the hand opposite to that with which you write and you try to sign your name, you immediately become aware of the ineptitude of the one and the practised dexterity of the other. The more practice, the more facile. If you want to see fine, co-ordinated hands, you have to let the novice rider move his hands up and down, forward and back, deliberately encouraging him to move them and not keep them dead still. In this way as dexterity improves, so will feel.

'A lot of riders know inside rein, outside rein, but they do not know how to work all those degrees between nerves and relaxation. . . .'

Nuno Oliveira

Chapter Three

The Legs – The Lateral Field of Balance

'IN HIS USE OF language, La Guerinière was not very disciplined and this provoked misconceptions and caused Parocel, his illustrator, to draw the wrong diagrams.'[1]

H. L. M. Van Schaik

'Unlike the writing of his predecessors, his [de la Guerinière's] book is clear and easy to understand. He based it on simplicity and facts in order to be completely understood by his readers.'[2]

Alois Podhajsky

In modern riding few movements or theories about movements have captured as much attention or stirred as much vitriolic argument as the shoulder-in and leg yielding. These two movements are predominately controlled by the rider's legs and have an effect on the horse's legs and body. Since they have been argued by some of the most outstanding horsemen and trainers, I think if we look at these movements something important may be revealed about the use of the rider's legs.

I came across the dilemma of leg yielding and shoulder-in again and again through various literature during my apprenticeship, and more importantly through two riding masters who taught me and who were diametrically opposed on the proper execution of the shoulder-in. Once again no amount of mental gymnastics could free me from the confusion of these two schools of thought, especially since either man could execute perfectly the movement in question. It was only after years

[1] VAN SCHAIK, H. L. M., *Misconceptions and Simple Truths in Dressage*, J. A. Allen, London, 1986.
[2] PODHAJSKY, ALOIS, *The Complete Training of Horse and Rider in the Principles of Classic Horsemanship*, Wiltshire Book Co., 1967.

of my own practice in the dressage arena that I began to feel an answer to this riddle.

We know from reading historical literature that during the time of Pluvinel, trainers used forms of leg yielding. Pluvinel, who invented the use of pillars, used to work a horse around a single pillar in a side-stepping fashion. Pluvinel pushed the horse sideways while its cavesson was attached to the pillar. The horse's spine was relatively straight and both its front and hind legs criss-crossed. The horse performed this kind of circling traverse around Pluvinel and the pillar. Similar work can still be seen today in Portugal but without the aid of a pillar: a trainer stands near the horse's shoulder holding the reins in one hand and with the other pushes the horse sideways with touches of the whip. The horse is worked first one way and then the other. This exercise sensitises the horse to signals of touch on its sides and teaches it early on to move away from even a light touch on its side. This is not totally natural for the horse: often ticklish or belligerent horses will lean against pressure instead of yielding to it. If the horse learns to use its considerable strength against the will and signals of the rider, no rider will ever be able to work with it, since in the end no human rider can overpower a horse ten times his own weight. So these early lessons are very critical psychologically, much more than physically. These movements of leg yielding, either unmounted or mounted, have always been fundamentally loosening, warm-up-type exercises, and they are the first lessons the horse learns about the rider's legs.

In approximately the 1730s François Robichon de la Guerinière was credited with inventing or creating the shoulder-in. This movement could be performed along the wall and looked similar to leg yielding, but with a very important distinction: the horse's body had lateral

[52]

bend. Its spine was curved deliberately, by pressure from the rider's inside leg. With one side of the horse's body constricted around the rider's leg and one side stretched out along the outside of this curve, this exercise had obvious gymnastic value. Here was an exercise which could attack the one-sidedness with which all horses are born. This one-sidedness is probably some manifestation of a split brain, analogous to right- and left-handedness in humans. The shoulder-in, moving forward and holding a sideways curve at the same time, gained even more gymnastic value by playing off these apparently opposing sets of directions. Finally this enigmatic movement had the ability to rebalance the horse towards collection, which lightened the horse in the hands of the rider.

What happened over a period of time was that two distinct schools of thought grew from the creation of the shoulder-in. One developed into the modern shoulder-in as described by the FEI, which has a strong Germanic tradition. In this movement the haunches are straight and the bend develops from the straight haunches towards the horse's ears. The horse leaves only three imaginary lines of tracks because the inside hind leg and the outside front leg move in the same line. The second school of thought prefers a shoulder-in on four lines of tracks, similar to engravings that accompany la Guerinière's text. It can be seen being practised at many classical riding schools in Europe. In this shoulder-in the horse is also bent along the spine, so it is not like leg yielding, but the haunches are not straight like the modern shoulder-in.

I came first to the shoulder-in under the influence of the Germanic theory, especially put forward by Steinbrecht. My own masterful teacher of the time was in full agreement. It was insisted that this theory and practice was the real essence of la Guerinière's shoulder-in, and my teacher could precisely quote the French script. The essence was the loading of the haunches, especially the loading of the inner hind leg. The haunches had to remain straight with the bend starting approximately at a point in between the horse's hips and curving forward towards the head. The horse would leave three lines of tracks, with the inner hind leg and outer front leg travelling along the same line. It was argued that only this kind of shoulder-in could truly collect the horse and gymnastically enhance it, by virtue of making the inner hind leg step up under the curving body. If the rider let this bend out by releasing the pressure of his outside leg, which was behind the girth and behind his inside leg, the haunches would then turn out. The horse's spine would automatically then straighten out a little and the hind legs would begin to side step. The theory reasoned that if that happens the horse escapes the true loading of the hind legs, which is what develops collection and lightening of the forehand, and the exercise becomes more like leg yielding which was always considered to be a loosening exercise and never a collecting one. When sideways movement takes precedence over forward movement, the driving force[3] exerted by the hind legs is interrupted. In the worst case, a full sideways traverse, the hind end loses almost all power for propulsion.

In this kind of shoulder-in it was always explained that although la Guerinière clearly stated that the hind legs should cross over, he really meant that the legs and feet cross past each other. The engravings that accompany la Guerinière's text do not bear this out

---

[3] George Pratt Jnr's remarks on gait analysis: This driving force depresses the hindquarters and lightens the forehand with torque around the centre of mass of the horse through a very complex series of muscular contractions throughout the whole hind-end system.

because they clearly show four lines of tracks. These engravings were not considered to be definitive because they were not made by la Guerinière himself.

Later in my apprenticeship I had the opportunity to work with another outstanding master who held the opposite opinion. He was convinced that when la Guerinière said that the hind legs should cross over, he meant cross over and not cross by, as they do in every normal stride. He was equally convinced that the engravings were correct and were further proof of the text. The true classic shoulder-in was to be executed on four lines of tracks with bend in and along the spine, but not straight haunches. Furthermore, he always maintained that there is no problem with escaping haunches if the rider is aware.

There they stood in front of me, like the two Japanese swordmasters: neither had a weakness, and yet a loyal student can feel double the weakness for both of them. I continued to study and practise and eventually two curious things happened. One was that I began to feel that the weight of the evidence was against my Germanic teachers concerning their claim of inheritance to the classic shoulder-in of la Guerinière. It simply took too much intellectual reaching to arrive at a straight-haunches, three-track shoulder-in out of la Guerinière's text. He clearly speaks of criss-crossing hind legs as well as bending of the spine. It has been pointed out to me that *chevaler* (in ancient French) is criss-crossing, and that la Guerinière repeatedly speaks of *chevalen* – which is to criss-cross or to straddle with the hind feet, and this simply cannot be ignored. Furthermore, to denounce the engravings as inaccurate would not make sense, since no less an authority than la Guerinière himself endorses them in the preface of his book *Ecole de Cavalerie:*

[55]

'Not only did I make a point in giving clear, neat, precise definitions, but in order to make them more comprehensible, I added to this work boards which will ease and lift the difficulties. In those matters, what is exposed to the eyes becomes infinitely more sensible than all what is described – whatever art is used thereto. It is after the originals, and under the direction of M. Parocel, regular painter to the king and his Royal Academy, whose reputation in this genre is generally known, that the different airs of Manège which figure in the second part, were engraved. I also set diagrams in order to show the proportions of terrain that one should observe in the different ways to supple and work the horse.'[4]

The second thing I found happening was that although I felt the four-track shoulder-in was the true classical shoulder-in, I found the three track shoulder-in to be a better gymnastic tool. I began to believe more and more in the superior gymnastic value of the modern shoulder-in. However, I also realised that it is difficult to demand it of a green horse.

As I rode in my practice I saw a recurrent problem in a simple but elegantly difficult exercise. I would ride down the centre line of the arena in shoulder-in and at about the middle I would turn off into an eight- or ten-metre circle. When I returned to the centre line I would continue in the shoulder-in down the remainder of the centre line. It was always at the moment when I returned to the shoulder-in that the exercise faltered. Unless I had a firm outside leg towards the haunches, the haunches would invariably slip out. They would lose their straightness. The horse would begin taking criss-crossing,

[4] *Ecole de Cavalerie*, La Guerinière's preface, as translated by Jean-Claude Racinet.

[56]

traverse steps behind. As the horse took sideways steps behind, it would automatically lose the forward driving power that comes most efficiently from straight square haunches. There is a simple inverse relationship between driving force and sideways movement behind. The more sideways, the less drive. This follows true to gait analysis which describes the driving force as depressing the hindquarters and lightening the forehand with torque around the centre of mass of the horse.[5] One can then see why leg yielding would have a deleterious effect on collecting up the horse, and conversely why the modern shoulder-in with its straight haunches would have a distinct physical advantage in working the horse in collection and lightening the forehand. Here, while working in a bend, the trainer tries not to disturb the power thereby training for flexibility and strength.

It seemed true, as Steinbrecht had said, that escaping haunches would drag behind as it were, instead of creating the drive which fosters collection. However, the more I practised this exercise and its variations, the more I realised how difficult it really was to execute. By this time I had trained more than fifty horses to do the shoulder-in and I found it to be impossible for a green horse who had not mastered some collection. Whereas I could do leg yielding from almost the first day in the saddle, there was the rub. It seemed that his modern shoulder-in was as much a verification of collection as a path to collection.

It was during these practices that it became clear to me that leg yielding, la Guerinière's shoulder-in, and the modern shoulder-in were simply a continuum of lateral exercises. Each of my young horses went through

---

[5] George Pratt Jnr's remarks on gait analysis.

[57]

all these stages and probably many in between. Some horses progressed quickly, the stiffer ones more slowly.

It also became clear to me that simply forcing the horse into the position of the modern FEI shoulder-in was certainly no guarantee that the horse would be collected. If the horse were pushed too early and forced into the bend, it could become cramped and the hind legs would stiffen and lose all their freedom of reach and drive. So it looked as if Steinbrecht's worst fear of dragging haunches was to become another of those incredible paradoxes. The position of the modern shoulder-in is supposed to ensure collection, and yet if it is assumed too quickly, too early, it can also lead to dragging haunches by restricting the horse's movement.

A further paradox I found was that leg yielding was only supposed to have limited use and effect as a loosening exercise. Yet I found a few steps of leg yielding even at the walk could free a heavy horse from the rider's hands by distracting the horse from its fixation on the reins and bit and transferring its attention to the rider's legs without the added confusion of forward impulse. In these cases it curiously worked like the best collecting exercise in freeing the back of the horse and encouraging it to step lively again.

In the end I found my awareness had to focus on feeling the horse under me. I had to feel when the bending was too much and was killing forward impulse, or when there wasn't enough bend and the horse was just lying on my hands. The rider cannot separate the concept of a lateral exercise from the actual lateral riding, or he will begin to get an image in his mind of what a correct lateral movement should look like. A correct lateral movement is a matter of feeling. What is even worse for those who must pin it down, is that a correct lateral movement may change. Since it is a gymnastic exercise, what is good for the horse one day may not be good enough in a few weeks. The rider has to be careful not to strangle the movement by some conceptualisation which determines forever the exact placement of footfalls or exact angulation.

Finally, how does one account for the vitriolic rebuttal and counter rebuttals that have occurred over the years on this subject? Is it just a matter of racism or nationalism? Certainly one cannot minimise the political trauma that the various national schools of riding underwent, especially when dynamic and flamboyant horsemen appeared and reappeared on the scene. The effect of Baucher, for example, could certainly fill an interesting book. There were also complex cross-overs between individuals belonging to certain so-called national schools. The more modern world alone was responsible for the breakdown of strong regionalisms. Although I have always felt that these were factors, there was something more important under all of this. After all, some of these men were masters of high integrity. Most were careful masters, regardless of the school of thought that was always specific as to how their lateral work should be done. There is universal attention to detail. This attention to detail opens a 'Pandora's box' in terms of opposing viewpoints. Yet both schools of the shoulder-in know very well that if lateral movement in the horse does not have its basis in the rider's seat and legs, then imitation flexibility will come from the rider's hands. These kinds of riders will pull their horse's heads from side to side trying to create some suppleness. This is why I think there is so much attention paid to the detail of lateral work. Every exercise has in it a potential to build but also a potential to destroy if abused or overused. I believe this is what most knowledgeable masters

[59]

live in fear of, to see lateral work degenerate into abuse, because the principles behind it have been lost.

If these exercises are used incorrectly they can cause irreparable damage. Today, as in the past, we can see a lot of riders pulling their horse's heads from side to side or riding on circles bent to the outside. There are many variations of these invented exercises. However, there comes a point where they become contraindicative in that as they push a horse against the normal flexion and extension of a joint, they create a tension instead of suppleness. Exercises of counter bends etc., in opposite direction to movement, have an incredible potential for harm. In bending a horse's joints against their normal flexion and extension they create pain, which the horse in turn instantly feels and resists in order to protect itself from hyperextension which could damage ligaments, tendons and even bone. The horse's normal action will be very quickly paralysed, and what some riders feel as increased activity is a circussy stiffening, which will only lead to more stiffening and eventually collapse. Anyone who has ever been in northern woodland after a heavy spring snow has seen beautiful white birch trees bent in unnatural loops, leaning at freakish angles, as a result of being sprung by the inordinately heavy, wet snow load. The plasticity of these trees was pressed beyond a point of recovery. Once matter like this is pressured so severely, either all at once or with frequently repeated smaller overloads, it will weaken to the point where it cannot recover. I am convinced that all knowledgeable masters are familiar with this phenomenon and have seen horses broken past a point of elastic recovery. It is a sad and permanent sight and I believe it is the real motivation behind the attention to detail in lateral work.

In my own experience I have seen some Western horses being trained for pleasure riding in the western

United States. These horses had their heads tied to their hocks with a rope rig in an effort to make them surrender in the neck. They were also subjected to very long shank bits and riders with long split reins pulled their horse's heads from side to side. The result was the total and complete destruction of the horse's natural movement. They were incapable of decisive forward motion in a straight line. They were so rubbery that the bridle and bit had no connection to the back or the haunches. They were ruined like the birch trees. I don't mean to cast aspersions on all Western riders or riding, because I have seen good Western riders and things in so-called dressage practice which rival the abuse of exercise, but it was there that I became so clearly aware of the dangers.

I began to understand the reason for the specific writings of many of the masters and their carefully worded warnings. I was not so much concerned about converting a rider to one school of thought or another, but to convert the rider to any school of thought with a harmonious plan, not any whim or twist. Above all, I now see the great debates on leg yielding, la Guerinière's shoulder-in, and the FEI or modern shoulder-in as allegories, seemingly different but always illuminating the complete disdain of force. They were attempts to speak out, over and over again, that all exercises – and in this case lateral exercise – must work on developing the normal extension and the flexion of a joint or cluster of joints. This will require of the rider a knowledge of anatomy so that he will never work against a joint's normal bending.

Partially because the horse is a quadruped, it has the ability to negotiate very tight circles while remaining relatively perpendicular to the ground. With lateral flexibility in the back and spine enhanced by systematic lateral exercises, and the power to constrict one side of the body while extending the other, the horse is capable of acute lateral circles and turns as long as it keeps its balance upright over its feet.[6]

By comparison, imagine you are riding a bicycle. You need to make a sharp turn so you turn the handlebars and lean into the direction of the turn, tipping the bike on to its side. All of a sudden you realise that the ground is loose gravel, the tyres begin to slip. In a flash you have fallen straight down on your inside shoulder. Anyone who has ever seen a bicycle race in one of the great velodromes with their highly banked walls, realises the limitations of turning a one-tracked creature.

Poor riders can have a similar kind of effect on the horse, nullifying the horse's lateral agility. The mounted rider sits above the horse's natural centre of balance. If the horse is already negotiating a tight curve and the rider leans further into the curve, it can upset the horse's lateral balance drastically. The horse becomes insecure in its vulnerable unbalanced position, and will often take strong rapid, scrambling steps in an effort to re-centre itself and the 'out of sync' rider over its feet. The best riders are keenly aware of the horse's lateral field of balance and over a period of time become so attuned that not only are they not a hindrance to the horse but also in some cases they help maintain even better balancing by acting very subtly as a counter-weight in the most difficult turns.

Through the practice of turns, changes of rein, and especially the lateral exercises, the rider must learn to feel and then to be able to become one with the horse. He must enhance instead of impede its lateral balance.

[6] For background information see, 'Kinematics of the Equine Thoracolumbar Spine,' H. G. G Townsend, D. H. Leach, P. B. Fretz, *Equine Vet. Journal*, 1983, 15(2), pp. 117–122.

Ultimately the pair will be able to perform a movement like a canter pirouette, wherein the horse canters into, around, and then out of the smallest of circles without any loss of the canter rhythm, without leaning or falling over, and without pivoting off frozen hind legs, proving that horse and rider have mastered the lateral field of balance, and not a turning trick.

As I continued riding, the efficiency of my legs depended greatly on the security and balance of my seat. Only when I could sit in balance without holding or gripping with my legs, did my legs then become free to signal and feel the horse. Once they became free, I had to consciously develop their dexterity, especially on my left side which was my stiffer side. The added difficulty was that more often than not, I would be matched to the horse with my weaker, less flexible leg on the stiffer side of the horse, and my more agile leg on the more flexible side of the horse. There was a tendency often to ride unconsciously towards my strength instead of developing my weaker side into better overall balance. I had to make a strong effort in the beginning to practise all the lateral exercises until both sides felt similar. This usually meant much more practice on the stiffer side.

I believe it is helpful to begin to practise leg yielding and simple lateral exercises even before the seat is fully trained. I think they can accelerate the process of learning balance, because in an effort to move the legs independently, the legs will automatically have to release some of their grip. This will help to loosen tension and settle the seat deeper, sooner.

Once the dexterity of both legs is comparable, the legs must then get practice working together through frequent changes of direction and frequent changes of exercise. Like two hands playing a piano, both legs may act independently but must yield a coherent and complementary musical whole. At that point the rider can lose consciousness of the instrument, in this case, the legs, and be aware of the action they can produce – the immediate music. Something mysterious will happen to the western concept of time as one's awareness settles solely into the present action. The rider will be absolutely free. Free of any cumbersome past and devoid of future expectations. It is like stopping time, and the effect is just as rejuvenating.

Chapter Four

So Many Masters

BEFORE I MET MY first wife she had travelled to Ireland to study with Ian Dudgeon at his riding school. She talked with admiration about a horsewoman she had met named Sylvia Stanier. Later it was to happen that I would see Miss Stanier's writings and use her fine treatise on lungeing. I remembered reading in one of her introductions a thank you to Mr Oliveira. Over a number of years I kept finding or hearing references to Nuno Oliveira, and always from horsemen and -women who themselves were outstanding. I wanted very much to have the chance to experience some other schools of classical horsemanship, and to broaden my education beyond the German tradition I had been following. So when the chance came for me to go to Portugal to watch and work with Nuno Oliveira, I took it.

It is winter and it is dark. I am sitting in the dining room of a small hotel in a little town in Portugal. I am the only guest. There are at least thirty place settings. All the bowls, plates and cups are turned over so that they won't collect dust. Only mine are upright. The woman who runs the place gestures to me to come to the kitchen to see if I like what she is cooking tonight. We have to pass down a narrow corridor. On one side of the corridor is a row of opaque windows. I can make out the shapes of leaves from plants pressed up against the glass. One of the windows has a pane of glass missing at the bottom. As I pass it, the woman's watchdog rams his snapping, growling head through the frame. Finally in the kitchen, I agree to whatever she is cooking. On my way back to the table, I stay close to the wall, but in a second the dog's head shoots through with renewed fury.

Ever since I arrived a few days earlier, I have had a terrible cough. The weather is not extremely cold, although it is frosty at night; but it is very damp. The hotel has no visible means of heating. There is no heat at all in my room. In the room there is a bed and a chair. On the wall there is a calendar from some year gone by. On the chair, as part of the decor, is a large doll. It is the kind of doll that has its eyelids on rollers so they can move up or down. After a while I have to move it. I cannot stand the constant staring, day and night. It becomes eerie. I am always waiting for it to blink.

My cough seems to be getting worse. I sleep in my clothes but still I can't get warm. Everything is wet. My only relief from the night's coughing and freezing spells is some heavy port wine the woman stocks in the dining room. In the middle of the night I think about dying in a place like this and decide I don't want to get much sicker.

After a week, I feel I have to find another place. I cannot get the taxis to drive me over the rough dirt roads to and from the school. I decide to seek new lodgings.

There is a very small village nearer to the school. It has a few houses, and a public well on the main road where herds of goats come to be watered. It feels very isolated. A young woman has some rooms for rent. She is pleasant and when I see there is a portable heater in my room, I am sold.

Each day, as I walk from the village towards the school, the opera music that fills the riding hall can be heard long before I can see the school. Every day I arrive early to watch the youngest horses in training. Later there is the morning lesson and then lunch. After lunch there will be more training until the later afternoon lesson. After the final lesson the students are usually all invited to the small cottage near the riding school. In its library-like office, everyone is offered some port and the day's work may be reviewed, theory discussed, or the Master will simply recount some fascinating story about horses. Afterwards I walk home under the night sky, and then read and study Baucher and Beaudant.

I have been very lucky. Since I arrived here, there has been only one other student, a man from Paris. Thus we get full attention in the lessons. Even though there are very few words of correction, the horses begin training you instantly. You are allowed to try, and to make mistakes. Each day you are asked to do grand prix movements, over and over. First the horses do them for the voice of the Master. Later you follow more closely and become bold enough to ask for them yourself – always quietly, never with the physical straining that you can see in other schools of riding.

As I become immersed in observing and riding these horses, my scepticism changes to wonder. Some beautiful work is being carried out in an entirely different manner. When I say different I mean different, not only in terms of style but also in the actual structure of the training. Horses barely broken to saddle are being taught the ultimate movements of piaffe and passage and flying changes. This is almost the exact opposite of what I am used to, and yet it works.

As I continue to ride and watch these horses daily and compare the training of the young Portuguese horses to the training in the Austro-Hungarian, or the best German schools, an old, moth-eaten debate surfaces. As if some rag or garment lifts itself up and begins to move on its own, I am forced to reconcile the impossible. It is not pages of a book discussing some esoteric semantics that I am facing, but a living, breathing problem. How will I accommodate the two schools of thought concerning 'riding in lightness' on a slack rein, and 'riding in lightness' on a taut, elastic rein?

There is at least one key elemental difference in the training of the youngest dressage horses in the

[68]

Portuguese school and those of the Austro-Hungarian or better German schools which are quite similar. The youngest horses in Portugal are very quickly fitted with a full bridle and then ridden on a semi-slack or loose rein. The youngest horses of more central Europe are never fitted early with a full bridle and are always ridden in a snaffle with taut reins. This simple point regarding equipment exposes an underlying paradox. However, the imagined paradoxes may not be paradoxes after all.

When the young horse is fitted with a full bridle, it is reluctant to lean into it. The danger here is that the youngster may fear the bit and stay behind it. But the problem with being behind the bit is not only the visual picture that we see, where the horse's nose is pointed towards its chest and its face is behind the perpendicular line drawn to the ground – this is just an outward manifestation. The important issue or danger is that the horse loses the connection from the rider's hand and leg to the bit and thence to its legs. The rein aid does not go all the way through the horse's back, so there is a gap between the driving power and regulating it. To use a bad analogy it might be like driving a car with a bad clutch. The accelerator roars, but when the clutch is let out to move the car forward, it just slips; it won't catch and move off. Finally it slides less and less and the car moves. Likewise, to stop, the clutch is depressed to relieve the forward drive, but the car keeps going forward. The brakes have to be used to choke off the forward driving power. The car is dangerously late in all its responses because this gap has developed. In the horse that is behind the bit, the head carriage will be false, and the back of the horse will be hollow with the hind legs out behind the horse's balance, not underneath it for immediate response. An easy test to feel if a horse is behind the bit is to send it forward in an extension.

If the steps do not immediately elongate, if the horse does not stretch through the back, then the horse is categorically disconnected and is behind. It is afraid to move through the bridle and is not round.

A very serious mistake of observation can be to assume that because the reins are semi-slack the horse is not up into the bridle. Unless one has truly felt horses that are behind, you can make this mistake quite easily. Instead of 'seeing' (that is, perceiving) the whole horse in its totality – the back, the transitions, the engagement – the novice may just 'look' at the reins. One has to pay attention to the horse's back and the illusive quality of roundness. True exponents of the Portuguese style, riding with 'lightness', are always checking their young horses to see that they come energetically forward from the rider's legs, and they are not leaning on the bridle but will hold themselves in balance. This riding style is particularly harmonious with the types of horses ridden there because they are muscular, with a higher action and a predilection towards early collection. The modern mastery of these riders is clearly proven when these horses are seen to extend their movements with true forward stretching, something they rarely practised in baroque riding. When a dressage horse is ridden through transitions of longitudinal balance – extension and collection – on the lightest of rein aids, it expresses the highest kind of dressage.

When a horse is trained in the snaffle in the manner of the Austro-Hungarian school or the better German schools, the trainers are so concerned with forward riding that some concessions are made in the beginning in terms of sacrificing lightness. Here the young horse is asked to drive off each hind leg powerfully and return it way under its body, to swing freely and engage well. A wave of energy is thrust right up the horse's spine

[70]

towards the head, lifting the horse's centre of mass and lightening the forehand. The horse's whole back swings and the shoulder reaches out. The correct appearance is one of a well-timed, not fast, full swinging gait with good use of the legs, and with the horse moving through the bridle.

Any hollowness in the horse's back will slice this power wave in two. The horse will be disconnected from front to rear. These trainers will avoid hollowness at all costs, hence the mild snaffle and even some indulgent leaning by the young horse. These horses are taught to feel that they can always move forward. They learn never to fear engaged movement. In this school of riding, collection will develop from gradually mastering control over the forward impulse, training carrying power into the step. If the horse is used to stepping way under the body with free, swinging steps it seems logical that it shouldn't be too difficult to move its centre of balance backwards over these engaged legs and thus free the front end.

However, there is a large danger in this method of training. If a horse is allowed to lean on a mild snaffle or stretch into it while driving forward for too long, it can induce too much thrusting power and no carrying power. The horse can grow quickly accustomed to travelling unbalanced, too far out on the forehand. The back of the horse will become stiff and long, and when it comes to the time to collect the horse, it will be inflexible and unable to shorten its body longitudinally. The rider will have to pull harshly on the reins to get the horse to tip its centre of balance more towards the rear. The irony is that the rider, in an effort to avoid the disuniting factor caused by hollowness, creates a different paralysing stiffness in the back that is equally troublesome.

[71]

The mistake of observation here is to think that the mild bit is equal to mild riding or lightness in the hand. It may very well be that the horse is pulling much harder and causing much more damage to its mouth in the incorrectly used snaffle than it would in a more severe bit, or a correctly used full bridle.

To make the patent statement that the full bridle is more severe than the snaffle seems myopic. Do I mean it is more severe just hanging on the wall? Obviously I am talking about in the horse's mouth and connected to a rider's hand. That is where the trouble begins, because the next question must be, in whose hands?

The best riders of the snaffle school of training never seem to equate 'long and low' with long and heavy. These riders are aware, from the earliest training, of the tempo and balance of their horses. Stretching does not always mean leaning. By using frequent changes of tempo and transitions, these riders are constantly teaching and testing the young horse to seek its own balance. Very often these riders will drop the reins on the leaning horse. In this initial gap the horse lurches forward, as if a crutch on which it had been leaning were kicked out from under its bearing. Soon, however, these horses begin to try to hold themselves up instead of relying on this unreliable support, the smart rider's hands.

In an effort to seek some reconciliation in the old semantics, I am in a funny place. The closer one gets to the world of action, the fewer differences there seem to be among the best riders. Riding in lightness seems to be more universal and more true. In my mind's eye I liken it to a map with a circular road on it. There is no point in rushing to the end, because it is only the beginning where you have already been. If you ride lightly enough, you may come free from apparent diversions,

[72]

inevitable destinations. Regardless, it is the riding, not the road.

Perhaps there is an element of pragmatism in the choice of these bits. In the rounder breeds, like the Andalusians, Lusitanos and Lipizzaners, there is less worry about hollowness. Therefore, the full bridle is less ominous. The longer, flatter horses of more central Europe have greater facility in the extended paces. With their great reach they are more susceptible to hollowness in the back, hence perhaps the popularity of the snaffle. Whatever the historical reasons for this equipment it seems clearer to me that it has little to do with 'riding in lightness'.

A month has passed by. The school is still not busy. A few different Europeans have come in for a couple of days, and have left.

This weekend two women from Belgium are here, and on this day a well-known trainer from France's elite cavalry school, the Cadre Noir, is here to ride some horses and visit the Master. He watches the lessons and some of the practice with as much intent as anyone else. This evening we are all going out to dinner as guests of the Master. This will be only the second time in a month that I have been out of the tiny village.

It is raining. We all drive in different cars. I go with the Master and his wife; his son drives. I do not think Mr Oliveira even has a driver's licence and as far as I can tell he has no interest in mechanical things, other than his stereo which brings him, above all, his beloved music of Verdi. We are driving in the dark. I have no idea where we are going. It seems we must be getting nearer to the ocean. I swear I can feel the air off the sea. When we arrive we are the only people in the restaurant. There are familiar seafood decorations and the fish looks like it will be good. The meals come slowly. Much of the table conversation is in French although the Master makes several interruptions with political questions in English about the United States. Before much longer, the conversation is thickly into horses. The Belgian woman next to me tries to translate as much as she can. Finally the subject of the Spanish Riding School comes up, and there is criticism of its current work. It is not malicious, though perhaps some is motivated by nationalism. Some of the objections are very technical, like the angulation of the half pass; some are more encompassing, like objections about lightness. The feel of this discussion is so familiar to me it begins to set up an eerie kind of *déjà vu*. The resonances of the language have the same physical sensations as a kind of motion sickness. It is literally making me feel ill. My head is turning my stomach. There is an antagonism inside me stirring around. I finish the meal, but I feel cold. Something continues to irritate me. I would prefer to go out, to be alone. The rest of the evening is pure discipline. I wait it out. When I am finally back in my room, I think about it all night.

The next day is Sunday. There is no riding at the school. I hitchhike a ride to the coast, to a small fishing village and resort. The shops are all closed, but I feel better just wandering through the streets. I am still unnerved by the conversation the night before. If I were at the Spanish Riding School, I wonder, would I hear similar criticisms of other schools? What is it about these obvious and even understandable loyalties that keeps turning and folding my stomach over, again and again? There is something else going on. I follow one of the narrow, steep streets to the floor of the harbour. All the dories are docked on the shore. A couple of fishermen are there, but although they are tending the boats they are not dressed for work. From this harbour I see an old white hotel that sits on a point that juts out into the ocean. At the end of the point the high surf is breaking over the rock. White surf slides in all directions, cleaning the smooth grey stone. I decide to see if I can get closer to that closed-down hotel. After a twenty-minute walk I am on the street that goes down to the hotel. Off to the left I see a beautiful sandy beach, backed by a wall of rock that rises straight up at least one hundred feet. I find my way down to the beach. It is deserted. There is too much cold spray. I am getting wet and cold. I look up to the top of the cliffs. I can see a road and some houses off behind it. I think it will be nicer up there. After a climb, I sit down on the sandy grass and, in the full sun of the afternoon, look out over the Atlantic. To the right the surf curls up on to the point where the hotel is. I am certain that in a storm the water must reach right into the building. It must be incredible. I wonder if it is ever open?

Below me the beach fills the quarter mile or so of the cove; beyond that I can see miles of the coast of Portugal. Even way up here I can feel damp spray from time to time as it is lifted up the face of rock by the wind and the heat. I look out over the ocean. The waves roll steadily. I think of the potential of each wave. I see it travelling right across the Atlantic to the east coast of America. In my mind I see the eastern shore of the United States. Soon the problem retakes the forefront of my attention. I keep asking myself, over and over, how can all these masters be wrong? Who is doing it right? The afternoon passes. I wonder where I will have to go next to see and learn to do it right? The question seems to tie itself to the rhythm of the waves. The noise of the sea muffles other sounds. I feel my own voice come up again. It is pushing me, prodding me every

[75]

time I seem to get sleepy. I begin to get the feeling that if I look hard enough I will be able to see America. I feel a pull by the waves both in my stomach and in my concentration. Something is trying to break out. I run through all the teachers I have known, the statements of many, the different schools of thought. Each master appears before me in a stylised portrait. How can they all be wrong?

Then, almost at dusk, in all its ridiculous simplicity, I feel the answer. All the tension is gone. Nothing obstructs me from America. In one step I have returned home for a moment. These masters are not all wrong. They are all right! There are great piaffes in Portugal, but there are great piaffes in France, Russia, England, Spain, Austria and Germany; and there are great piaffes in America. How could five, ten or fifteen horses be trained differently and independently, yet all be doing the exact same movement correctly? It is now clear to me that different paths can lead to the same result. In western education we are so steeped in our precious scientific method that it seems inconceivable that there could be more than one correct answer for a question or problem. In reality there are all kinds of correct answers simultaneously existing side by side. You can take your pick. They will all work if correctly applied. There seems to be no such thing as only one correct answer, but there is only one correct way of answering.

I feel an instantaneous and tremendous relief. I understand the source of the antagonism during the dinner conversation. My own choice of loyalties seems liberated. It is simple. I don't have to choose. I can accommodate them all. There is infinite room. I realise a very important phase of my apprenticeship is complete. It is time now for me to try my own way. There will be room for this American's way as well. I will have to do it myself. I have to find my own path in order to have any chance at completing my training. I look out across the ocean. It is almost dark. I know what I have to do. Within one week I am flying back to the United States by way of Montreal, Canada.

While the quiet plane is streaking through the dark, my mind is filled with images of Oliveira, and his complete mastery. I am in awe of his artistry and skill, his control on the lightest of aids. One particular incident comes to mind.

At one end of his indoor school is an observation room. It has windows along its entire length so quite a few people can observe at once. From the windows there is roughly an eight-feet drop to the riding-hall floor. On this particular day the weather was terrible, and it happened that I was the only person in the observation room and Nuno was the only person riding. He was working a young grey stallion through some lateral work at the trot, and in the last few days he had been teaching this young horse the flying changes during the canter work. Very quickly the sky became dark. His methodic work continued quietly. The air became so still that it was easy to hear the horse chewing the bit even when it was at the farthest end of the school. Suddenly, in one flash a storm erupted. Lightning crackled and sheets of hail-like rain pounded the thin metal roof of the arena. The grey horse exploded and began blazing around the arena in half spins and huge leaps. As they passed in front of me, the horse caprioled right up alongside the windows. Oliveira was inches from me, flying through the air. The thunder crashed and the roof sounded as though it would collapse at any moment. The horse became even more frenzied, and went tearing around the hall again. Mr Oliveira's face was turning deeper and deeper shades of red. I was

certain that in another second he was going to be
thrown, and thrown hard. Oddly enough, what was
going through my mind was what I should do if that
happened. There is no entrance directly from the observation room to the school. You have to go out the back,
down a flight of stairs outside, then enter the school by
a side door. It would take for ever to get to him and
his horse. I thought about jumping from the windows.
It wouldn't have been a big jump; however, this place
was like a church and I wasn't sure what would happen
to me, no matter what the reason, after such a breach
of protocol. I was half standing when the horse and
Oliveira went by again, as much in the air as on the
ground. Amazingly, throughout this performance his
position hardly moved. He sat bolt upright. Only his
extremely flushed face and his surprised eyes revealed
his effort to stay on board. Finally, after what seemed
like at least three or four full minutes, he settled the
horse down. The storm eased and my own pulse began
to recover. When Oliveira worked he hardly ever looked
up to the observation room. But this time after he had
the horse calmly walking, he glanced up towards me
and smiled. I thought that deep inside it had been fun
for him. I couldn't wait until the evening after work
when I could go to his little office for some port and
conversation with him. As the day went on and I
thought about it, I was more and more impressed by
the fact that he never admonished the horse but only
comforted him.

Later that evening a couple of people showed up at
his office. The small room was filled with books and
photographs of some of his horses. A small kerosene
heater glowed red as it wicked off the dampness. As he
came in I was first to go to him. I told him I thought
that that was some ride today. This time he laughed. I

asked him very honestly if he had always had the amount of patience that he seemed to have so much of now. He looked at me squarely, and said, 'Of course not.' He told me he had done all kinds of crazy things when he was young, but that he had been riding for a very long time, and that it gets better. It was clear to me that he was emphasising the practice and not to worry. That it would come along by itself.

Now on the plane I think about patience and wonder if it isn't the greatest gift a horseman can receive. When I see the mountains of Canada, I feel very strong. I am only miles from my old Adirondack farm when we rest at the airport. I feel good, and yet I am apprehensive as to what will happen next.

Chapter Five

Technique and Poetry

'I WANT TO MAKE SURE they're not so concerned with technical precision that they'll miss the poetic content of the music. On the other hand they can only illuminate the poetic content when they're able to forget about technique entirely.'

Jorge Mester, on teaching a conducting class at the Juilliard School of Music in New York City.

When a rider/trainer begins to work with horses without the aid of a teacher's guiding eye, the limits of his technique quickly surface. For me it was no different. I constantly questioned my own technique and form. It seemed as if I would have to come to terms with the fact that I might never have the technique I thought I should have. If technique were all that mattered and I might never have enough, I was going to have a hard time not seeing this as a complete failure.

I began to review my feelings about technique. I knew that technique could always be improved: there were small flaws in many of the masters. Yet a perplexing phenomenon was that as many masters became older and lost a certain amount of physical strength, ability, hand–eye coordination, and many of the things normally connected with technique, these masters did not become worse riders and trainers: they usually became better. That fact alone made me suspicious of making technique the end-all. However, in riding the expression of the music in the riding (or the art) is incomprehensible without considerable riding technique.

Imagine a horse and rider cantering on a true canter, that is, cantering on the right lead when going to the right, and/or left lead when going to the left. The difference in leads in a general way corresponds to left-handedness and right-handedness in human beings. Every stride of the canter of a given lead has three beats: a single hind foot strikes the ground as the first beat; a diagonal pair of legs strikes at once for the second beat; and finally the lone remaining foreleg strikes for the third beat. At the end of this sequence there is a moment of suspension, and then the pattern is repeated. In high school work and at upper levels since the time of Baucher, one canter exercise has been to deliberately change from one lead to another during the moment of

[81]

suspension. This amounts to a kind of instantaneous symmetrical change along the axis of the horse's spine. In the highest tests of riding today, not only is it demanded that the rider be able to control the number of these changes, but also the intervals of strides between each change. For example, the horse and rider may execute four complete canter strides on the right, do a flying change in the moment of suspension and continue with four strides on the left, flying change back to the right, etc. This exercise can be increased in difficulty by doing the flying changes after every three strides, or two, and finally after every single stride.

There are two main methods that I use to teach the flying change. Each has its good points and I use whichever one seems to fit the horse better. One way is to circle the horse at canter. As I complete the circle, I make a downward transition to trot. I change the bend to the opposite direction, strike off on the opposite lead and circle in that direction. When I come back to the middle, I go back to trot, change direction and go off again on the opposite lead. As the horse becomes more proficient, I reduce the number of trot strides until, when I feel the horse is ready, I skip the trot entirely, asking with firm aids to change leads from canter to canter, through the flying change. Since this method is carried out in the open, away from any wall for support or guidance, some horses will swing out sideways too much.

Under the other system, I canter down the long side of the ring or arena, and about half way down, I start a small circle. Instead of completing it, half way around I head back to the wall on a small diagonal. When I return to the wall, I will be counter-cantering and about to ride through the corner of the arena. Just as I approach the corner I ask for a change. Often the horse obliges because it prefers to return to the true canter. Also, the relief from the extra stretch of the counter-canter is welcome. This method has the benefit of being next to a wall when changing, which helps to keep the horse straighter.

As soon as I began to teach horses flying changes it became very apparent why it was so necessary to teach the horse straight strike-offs in the beginning, making sure as a rider to use both legs to execute canter departures. I quickly saw how, by using one leg more strongly, be it outside behind the girth or inside on the girth, I could unconsciously develop a slight swing in the horse's body, away from the stronger leg at the moment of the strike-off. In the flying change, and even more so in the multiple flying changes, the horse could sway from side to side, and any time the horse deviates sideways it will automatically be less forward, and obviously less straight.

I am trying to teach an ex-racehorse the flying change. This particular horse is presenting some new problems which I have never faced. He is properly prepared in that he will strike off quietly and accurately on either lead in any direction. His counter-canter is confirmed. Everything is in place.

As I begin the flying changes a pattern quickly develops. Whichever system I try, if I ask too vigorously for the change, the horse leaps up into the air practically in a capriole, my back is wrenched by the great twist and kick, and when we hit the ground we are off and running. When I tone down my aids and ask gently, the horse seems to get lazy and changes first with his front legs and then late with his hind ones. It is very smooth and therefore very hard to feel, but almost always incorrect. There does not seem to be any middle ground.

[83]

At least a month goes by. I am essentially working alone and it is getting frustrating. There doesn't seem to be any progress. The changes are either calm and late, or they are wild. More time passes. I am in one of those training caves and there is no teacher to guide me out. I am stuck. The knowledge I have acquired up until now is not adequate. I have to find something new.

I decide to go to the indoor riding school. It has a large mirror in the middle of the short wall. I ride across the arena. I check my position and go through all the fundamentals. Straight, simple changes. I check myself to see that I am not crooked. I tell myself to stay calm, to give myself a chance to work through it. I try to be aware and feel what is going on. I decide to canter a series of serpentines. My intention is to try to change at every change of rein in the middle. At the time this is no stroke of training genius, but I do have two reasons. The primary one is that I will be able to see the changes in the mirror – if the changes become too smooth for me to feel, maybe I can see something in our reflection. The second reason is that I am hoping to use anticipation in a productive way. If the horse knows the change is coming every time we cross the centre line, maybe he will get a little ahead of me. Even if he changes before I ask, it will be a step in the right direction. There is a risk, however, that the obedience I have in the counter-canter will deteriorate if I do manage to get him changing every time. How am I going to make him hold the counter-canter in future? I decide to deal with that later.

On the first day indoors, we carry out a whole series of changes. When I feel the horse tiring, I quit. None is really correct, but I stay calm. I tell myself to wait. I listen intently. A few days pass. I am getting nervous about doing so many changes incorrectly. I am not sure

[84]

how much longer I can be patient before I start trying something else, but I continue. More time passes. The changes still have not improved, but some related things have surprisingly begun to change. I have found that simply by doing the serpentines and asking for the changes in the middle of the shorter width of the arena, the horse is reluctant to take the wild leaps he would take if we were out in the open. The walls of the arena seem naturally to contain him. Even if I ask fairly strongly, the horse immediately faces the opposite wall of the arena and then a short turn into the next serpentine. Without the wild leap, I am less protective in my own position. I soften my seat, and sit deeper. The result is a much better feel. Furthermore with this natural confinement I find I use much less hand to control the horse. As soon as I let go with my hands, the gait becomes freer and the balance shifts more towards the rear, as I send the horse forward with my seat and legs. The immediate turns at the wall into the next loop of each serpentine emphasise the change of bend and this seems important to this horse. He seems much less confused when I make sure the bending is consistent and deliberate in both directions. I cannot be too straight. The turns have an added benefit of collecting the horse, thus balancing him more towards the rear. The more days I spend going through the pattern, the more I learn about changes. Very soon for the first time, the percentage of correct changes begins to increase. I can ride with less hand and the result is more lively steps; the changes automatically become straighter as the horse goes more forward and less sideways. With the balance better shifted off the front, the changes are much less likely to be late. The more relaxed the horse is with the habit of the exercise, the easier it is to do the changes. Soon they are so good that I try some along the wall, where I can work on straightening them even more. It is clear now that although there is still a lot of polishing to do, the horse understands what I am asking.

My ideas on technique seemed to be settling somewhere in between those who said 'since technique is obviously separate from art, if you are interested in art then forget technique', and those who obsessively drilled their scales and movements of technique for the sake of discipline alone. These great technicians seemed to be crying out in strange ways for some release from their inevitably declining skill.

When I went into that indoor school I had my mental processes backed into a corner. I had no plan. I went inside with the idea of opening up my practice. What I really discovered was not so much how to teach one horse the flying change; instead I learned the power of the double-edged sword of technique. First, in order to 'understand' any problem with a horse, I found I needed good technique to feel what was going on. Then, practically simultaneously, the other edge of technique made me act on what I had perceived to effect the ride. As soon as I saw this, I sensed the urgency of good position. Good form is not some esoteric exercise, some historical theatre. No. It is very, very practical. It is language. If, as a rider, I cannot keep my legs in place and also have good dexterity, it will not matter how much I know about the difficulty – I will never be able to have any effect on it. I would not like to claim that these specific exercises had any magical qualities: my point is almost the opposite. I have begun to see that it is often more important *how* an exercise is done and not what *is* done. In repetitions the troublesome subtleties can surface as the rider feels them over and over. I think it is fair to say that a good teacher could have saved me a lot of

[86]

time by pinpointing difficulties from the ground, but the interesting thing was that the spirit of the movements was beginning to reveal itself to me up in the saddle and perhaps equally important, I was beginning to be able to influence it. Travel along the road was beginning to go both ways.

When, as a rider and trainer, I rode into the dark recesses of training problems without the guiding torch of a teacher, it was the discipline from my constant practice of technique that kept me from panicking and running in every direction looking for a way out. I simply continued to ride every day, trying to remain as open and calm as possible, and inevitably, although sometimes after a long time, I saw light and a way out was revealed. After each time I grew less afraid of the dark and I let the answers find me. It was the discipline achieved from the practice of technique that eventually could give me some freedom to go into the unknown without the paralysis of fear.

Good technique probably best manifests itself in the rider's form on a horse. Only in the proper form will the rider be able to perceive what is happening as he rides, especially if he rides into problems. Only in good form will the rider be able to effect a correction. Good technique is simultaneously reading the situation and acting on it. In the end, good technique can allow the rider freedom. If the rider never ventures beyond the technique, then the rider, even if a supreme technician, will leave a heavy stamp. Horses trained in this way will not likely step out from under this total and constant manipulation and submission. If the rider uses the technique to help let go, then new original solutions can be found. All the time one can tap the unconscious, and horses will take steps on their own. Their exhibitions become artistic presentations. One has to be warned that unless the practice is flowing and not fixated, it can degenerate into a trap where the technician tries to force perfection. If you are only interested in future goals you can defeat yourself, because you stifle your perceptive qualities by ordering their attention instead of letting them soak into everything around you, which is what they do best. The rider's practice must develop his or her awareness of movements, not just the incessant execution of movements.

Knowing that technique could always be improved gave me some relief from my image of perfection, which was some static state that you could only reach by obsessive practice of technique. In my vision of perfection everything was perfectly controlled, and yet this image is almost the exact opposite description of art, which is creative, free, open and almost perfectly uncontrolled. I began to see technique as only a tool, a discipline to help you remain stable when facing the unconscious, the creative, the fear of the unknown, and the new. I found some breathing room to allow myself to experiment, to experience without constant stifling comparison and measurement. I was beginning to gain a certain confidence in my work.

Furthermore, knowing that improving the technique will not necessarily improve the art, made technique seem more humble. I could place technique in a more natural and harmonious perspective. The effect was that it relieved an incredible amount of pressure I had built up on and around perfecting technique.

The beautiful and mysterious reward was that as soon as I took the importance off of technique, it automatically improved immeasurably.

Chapter Six

Prize Riding

'A MAN WHO IS completely absorbed in his technical skill degenerates into a "function", a cog in a machine. One who devotes one's life whole-heartedly to the Way of the Samurai does not become the devotee of a particular skill and does not allow oneself to be treated as a simple function. . . . When a Samurai prepares himself mentally to bear single-handedly the burden of the whole (*han*), when he applies himself to his work with great self-confidence, he ceases to be a mere function. He is a *samurai*. He is the Way of the Samurai. There is no fear that such a human being will degenerate into a mere cog in the social machine. However, a man who lives for his technical proficiency cannot fulfil his total human role; all he can do is perform a single function, especially in a technology-oriented society such as ours. If a Samurai who cherishes a total human ideal gives himself over to a particular talent or skill, his whole ideal will be eaten away by his specific function. This is what Jocho (author of *Hagakure*) fears. His image of the ideal human being is not a compromise product: one part function to one part total being. A total person does not need a skill. He represents spirit, he represents action, he represents the ideal principles on which his realm is founded.'

Yukio Mishima[1]

What is Mishima's statement about? What could it possibly have to do with riding? In Jocho Yamamoto's book, *Hagakure*,[2] there is an expressed contempt for technical precision, yet in the techniques of Japanese tea ceremonies, and in Japanese *Haiku* poetry, there seems almost fanatic attention to technique. So how does the total person, the true person, pay attention to technique and not pay attention to technique?

I believe looking at the relationship between classical dressage riding and current prize dressage riding can illuminate this apparent paradox, and show how current the fears of Yamamoto and Mishima still are.

Classical dressage riding is quite old. The writings of Xenophon, a student of Socrates, are still admired today for their humane and gentle approach to horsemanship. Representations of dressage movements practised today

---

[1] MISHIMA, YUKIO, *The Way of the Samurai*, Peregree Books, 1977.
[2] YAMAMOTO, JOCHO AND TASHIRO, TSURAMOTO, *Hagakure*, 1659–1719.

are visible in Greek art that is over two thousand years old. Prize riding, that is the riding of predetermined tests in a competition against other riders and horses, is relatively new.

As an art form, classical dressage riding has a strong similarity to certain kinds of rigidly stylised Japanese arts – *Haiku* (poetry) and painting, for example. In these arts we see that the artist is subject to some relatively strict rules of structure in which he must work. In Japanese *Haiku* poems, the structure is quite defined. The poems are always in three lines and contain seventeen syllables. In classical dressage there are only a relatively small number of movements to be performed at the high school. No matter where you travel – France, England, Germany, Austria, Russia, Denmark, America, Mexico – you will recognise the piaffe, the passage, canter pirouettes, etc., and artists who choose to work in these forms accept the stiff structure and focus their creativity on the execution within these structures.

The *Haiku* poet focuses his attention on new and personal ways to express something within this style. As impossible as it sounds, no two poems are alike, and furthermore, there seems to be no end to the supply of these original works. They are as infinite as creation itself.

In classical dressage the movements performed are representations of natural movements that a horse might do at play or in courtship or territorial displays. This has been *the* central element in describing the classical riding approach – that is, that the movements must complement nature, and what is natural for the horse.

Historically fantastic gaits or gimmicks of movement fall into the category of circus. It is in the circus, after all, where, by its own definition, the unusual and fantastic are displayed. In the circus or in circus riding the emphasis is always on the trick and less on the process. The end result must be obvious, dramatic, thrilling and, above all, entertaining for the large audiences who come to have fun and generally cannot sit too close to the performers. The circus is not the place for subtleties.

Throughout the history of riding there have been bitter and inconclusive arguments as to which movements are really natural to the horse. Alois Podhajsky[3], the late director of the Spanish Riding School, has written that such debates went on inside the citadel of classical equitation, the great Spanish Riding School, itself. Flying changes at every stride, for example, have been such a debatable movement. Flying changes at every stride, in fact even single flying changes, were not practised (as far as I have been able to determine) in the baroque days of la Guerinière. The invention or creation of this movement is generally credited to François Baucher, a controversial, spectacular rider who performed with the circus of Laurent and Adolphe Franconi. Podhajsky once stated that the question of flying changes at every stride had never been resolved in Vienna, yet today they are accepted and are universally performed and exhibited even at that same school.

Much of the time it is not the movement in itself which determines the kind of riding, but the whole approach or philosophy of the training. It is often much easier to see the differences if one looks at the more acceptable, conventional, even simpler exercises, instead of the controversial ones. Holes in the fundamentals will show up readily in the most basic patterns and changes of gait or tempo.

The riders' and trainers' tasks are to execute, within strict structures, something that is unique to the spirit

[3] PODHAJSKY, ALOIS, *The Complete Training of the Horse and Rider in the Principles of Classic Horsemanship*, Wiltshire Book Co., 1967.

of a particular horse. One thousand horses may stand side by side in the piaffe and no two will be the same. The rider and horse's range of expression, like the poems, is also as infinite as creativity itself.

Something very interesting happened in poetry over the years since *Haiku* in Japan and rhyming verse in the West became popular, perhaps because a new generation had a need to experiment, to rebel from the ways of the previous generation. Perhaps it was no more than a very physical and natural cycle, like the rise and fall of a wave, in this case the waves of change. Nevertheless some of the newer poets could not see any reason to have their art and their freedom restricted by these strict structures of form. The newer poetry began to experiment with the structure itself. New poets, like the new painters, focused their creative powers less on the object to be explored within the old strict structure, and more on the structure itself. When ten painters stood side by side and painted a red apple, some apples came out square, some were a different colour, some were unrecognisable as apples. This creation was naturally shocking. The artists seemed to be inventing a new language that only they understood. Were they mad? Was there some conscious attempt to exclude viewers and readers? Was the work too personal, and too far beyond any attempt at communication? Far beyond any art that had preceded it?

The best of this kind of art had just as much integrity as the best rhymed verse, or the best *Haiku*. The artists went deep inside themselves, deep inside the world that was presented to them to find their own world. They tried to feel and see, and go as close to the real source of creativity as possible. Their real struggle was to be free. This could certainly include being free of any precedent around them. If they could be free, they could find originality itself. If it is possible for an artist to push away all contrived goals, pre-suppositions, then they can arrive also at their true selves. Originality, creativity, is also truth. The art becomes very naturally self-enlightening, at the very least. It is self-transforming.

Almost all art forms have followed similar transformations – similar shifts of creative focus, from execution within the bounds of strict structure, to creating with the structure itself. The worst of this art is so disembodied that it is psychotic – by which I mean that no matter how revolutionary one tries to be, there are always some boundaries, some limitations in terms of health or sanity. Suppose a choreographer of ballet had a dream in which dancers standing on two feet rotated their upper bodies through 360° without moving their feet. Well, the human body cannot twist completely around in a circle without breaking. Suppose this choreographer pursued this dream anyway and began forcing his dancers to stretch and stretch – ignoring nature's laws. This work then becomes psychotic. It is damaging, impossible and against life. It is unintelligible and self-defeating. Poetry can be psychotic – and certainly some horse training can definitely be psychotic.

Interestingly enough, many modern poets who are comfortable in a wilder, free-flowing style, have had an interest from time to time in working in *Haiku*. When they do, they accept the structure and create within it. There is nothing impossible about making the shift.

To me this is the site where a lot of the confusion between classical dressage and prize riding starts. Classical dressage riding is a living *art* form, and the practitioner must adhere to its structure. If you want to invent new movements to experiment with the structure, you can, but you move away from the realm of classical dressage. In classical dressage the creative focus is in exploring the personality of a particular horse's movement, within the structure of the art. Whilst all piaffes, for example, are recognisable as piaffes, the true classicist's creative attention will be to find the purest piaffe for that particular horse; a piaffe, recognisable as piaffe, but unlike any other horse's piaffe; this individual horse's ultimate piaffe. The piaffe itself is not as important as *how* the horse piaffes. This horse's best piaffe is a proof of true training. Ultimately there is a similarity of art because the true artist is not burdened by the structure of the piaffe – any more than the true poet is burdened by the structure of *Haiku*. This is precisely how, referring to the beginning of this chapter, a total and true person can pay attention to technique and not pay attention to technique. In the same way, the true artistic rider knows there is a movement called piaffe – but how his horse does it is where art comes in. There is no ultimate piaffe, any more than there is an ultimate poem. There is only the ultimate piaffe for a particular horse, just like there can only be an ultimate poem for a particular poet. The true piaffe, the true work of art, is by definition original.

This is where prize riding comes into some serious problems relating to the art of dressage. Even though prize riding today consists of relatively the same movements as classical dressage, there is a problem.

We know that if we assemble any fifteen horses, we will have fifteen different piaffes. Now, however, for the sake of scoring, a judge must decide which piaffe is best. Subjection enters the picture, and there is quantification and qualification of art. This is impossible. We know from history what a poor record critics, judges, and societies at large have at recognising great art when it is under their nose. The artist whose work was ignored

[95]

until after his death was not the exception. That artist was the rule. Few societies are comfortable with the artist whose chief concern is a freedom from precedents and restraint. Too much freedom can lead to social anarchy. Too much originality makes it difficult to move society *en masse*. So it is logical, if nothing else, that a society moves slowly in recognising its misfits. We also know that art is as personal and individual as each artist's fingerprint, or each horse's whorl patterns. There can be so much difference that there won't even be any points of comparison.

However, if contests are to occur, then subjective idealised movements have to be in the mind's eye of the judge in order to render comparison. One piaffe might be deemed better than another because it is closer to the piaffe which the judge believes to be the correct piaffe. The experienced prize rider is aware of this process. The technician knows this; he knows what forms are most acceptable, or popular. He or she chooses and trains horses that best display these forms. He or she practises these forms. The trouble is that the movements become disembodied from the art. They become an end in themselves. This unconnectedness is the opposite of true dressage. This is also the opposite of true art, for now the movements are no longer original. They are contrived, very conscious, imitative.

Imagine a prize *Haikuist*, who realises that *Haikus* about flowers are winning acclaim, recognition, fame and prizes at *Haiku* competitions. This *Haiku* writer begins writing *Haikus* about flowers. As soon as a conscious decision is made to control the creative process, it automatically loses its originality, its freedom. It is reasoned and trapped. This artist has cut off the path that leads to new territory.

Back to the apparent paradox between Mishima's

words and the Japanese culture. The strict structure of *Haiku* challenges the true artist to go beyond it. Faking an artistic attempt – be it a contrived *Haiku* or a contrived piaffe that the current judges hold in high regard – does not work; not because you can't fool others, but because you can't fool yourself. True art always has this integrity, beyond the technical skill. It has the power to transform the self, to enlighten the self, stemming from control of the self. The true artist, then, is the true man or true woman. Their art is not something high and mighty, esoteric and lofty, with its intention on what people think when looking at it. It is a very practical art. The true art becomes not the art of painting, writing, or riding, but of living, living your own life.

Jocho's disdain for the technician is a disdain for someone who plays a game separate from life; one who consciously aims at targets, one who bases his performance on external messages, or ideas. This is a man or woman who has given up him- or herself, and the very thing that makes him or her unique and original, to an idea of how their life should be or how they wish it to be, or how others think it should be. Such a life becomes a ship without its own integral source of power or guidance. It will move wherever it is pushed, even if it means its own demise. Here is the clue as to how an individual loses his freedom.

When a rider begins to ride for conceptions, ideas of what riding is, and not for the true real action of riding itself, he can enter an imaginary world of intellection which has very little to do with a real world. Invariably the body realises this and the disharmony between mind and body – intellection and action – can be devastating to a personality.

Riding to win, or for high scores, or for the opinion of others, leads one into a strange world of external

[97]

pressures that can destroy riders and horses. When the rider/artist gives up control, he gives up his only real chance to be free. I believe that all these riders are innately aware of their deal with the devil. I also believe that subconsciously they feel imprisoned and this negative feeling eventually swallows up the love and freedom that attracted them to riding in the first place.

I remember a brief conversation I once had with a man who judged riding competitions. In just a few short sentences the man unwittingly revealed much about himself and his life. This judge was noted for being particularly vitriolic in his criticism and scoring of rides. He was middle-aged and at a time in his life when dressage riders are often reaching a peak, but he was not riding. It came out during a serious conversation that he did not ride because he said he could not do it perfectly and therefore he chose not to do it at all. My first instinct was to dismiss this as talk. However, some years went by and I saw he was sticking to his words. He was judging more and more often and still not riding. In this unfolding live theatre, I began to get a sense of the magnitude of the tragedy and especially how serious were Mishima's and Jocho's warnings about losing one's self. Over a period of time, this apparently intelligent man had created a conception about what riding should be. His conception of ideal riding became more and more formidable over the years, until he felt he could not measure up to it. He had created for himself a demon and then he consciously let the demon devour him.

It was apparent that he had a love for riding. What else could have sustained his interest for so long? Even now, defeated by his own creation, he still judged every weekend just to be around riding. No wonder his critiques were vitriolic. Who knows what bitterness he kept within for the thing that tore him away from his beloved riding?

To all outward appearances, this man was highly disciplined but inside he lacked the self-control and strength to resist the challenges of external pressures. To resist the life of the technician as opposed to the life of the artist, or the true man or woman, he sadly let conceptions grow so unchecked by action and reality that his own ideas became too powerful. He intimidated himself, and in the process destroyed his real love in life. The mind can not only freeze the body in terms of immediate reflexes and responses but it also has the power to create permanent paralytic effects as well, as in this case.

It is a hot day. If too many horses are working at once dust drifts upwards like smoke filtering the bright sun. I am judging some dressage classes at a special horse show for handicapped riders. Apart from my secretary, I am alone. We are sited away from the main show traffic, and it is quiet and peaceful. For some years before this, I have been teaching a few instructors of handicapped riders. One year they asked me to judge the dressage at their annual show. I told them that I didn't really judge, but nevertheless they wanted me to do it. I was confronted by blind and deaf riders; children with cerebral palsy, muscular dystrophy, Down's syndrome, brain damage and spina bifida. I felt I needed to be a physician to even begin to give some kind of appraisal of their performances. However, I was so inspired by the courage of these riders that when asked again to judge, I always accepted and even agreed to do other larger shows.

The show that I am at this day is a big show. There are disabled riders from all over. The atmosphere is festive. The range of disabilities is complete. When I first arrive at a show like this I am always a little uneasy. There are so many sad cases – some very severe, and often young children. I don't see many handicapped people from day to day, and the emotional pull can be strong. However, the people are all so friendly and the atmosphere is alive and casual. I get used to it very quickly. I always marvel at the total absence of any kind of prejudice by the horses. They are fine examples. We seem to have lost a lot of natural qualities as we have become so apparently intelligent.

Every time I judge at these shows I experience a familiar feeling. It is the same feeling I get when I am around an outstanding teacher. I see qualities I wish I could develop in myself. I see a certain integrity or a fairness; in other cases a simple fearlessness to try something new; or a ferocity of life, often a plain reluctance to presume something about someone else. Maybe my reasons for coming are selfish, because I always walk away so inspired, flushed with possibilities and charged with energy.

A young girl rides into the arena. The test consists of simple walk and trot manoeuvres. She has very spasmodic hands. It seems difficult for her even to hold the reins. She salutes me before beginning the main body of the test. For me, it is more like the bowing in martial arts, a gesture of mutual respect. She begins the patterns. The horse, like all these horses, is patient and carefully trained. I have seen these horses being groomed in barns by children in wheelchairs. They can be bumped about and vaulted on and off. They seem to revel in the attention. This girl struggles in the first turns. Her hands are almost erupting, but she finishes the circle. She reverses the direction to begin symmetrical patterns. As she turns I notice her eyes. I thought I knew something about

[100]

controlling uncontrollable hands; I thought I knew something about holding down a wild body – certainly I have been struggling with the elusive roundness of a simple circle for a decade. But when I see the mastery in her young eyes, I don't think I have scratched the surface. I am struck with a wave of ambivalence about being anyone's judge.

After her ride in comes a beautiful Asian child with Down's syndrome. His thick-set pony walks in like some great sage returning from his mountainous retreat. He walks humbly but cannot hide the light of all his wisdom. It seems proper that only an innocent child could be a true friend of a creature of such wisdom.

Before a break, a young woman rides in. The tempo is quicker and the test is more difficult. Her face shows strain. I cannot tell if it is the heat or her concentration. I am aware of the difficulty, but she almost has it hidden. I am impressed by her test. It is very well done. At the final salute, she looks tired. Her face has lost colour. I think it is a very good ride. I am mentally scoring it and composing my remarks as she rides towards the exit. Just out of the gate she slumps and begins to fall from her horse. The ever-attentive aides catch her. They attend to her quickly. I stand up. My pulse quickens. I step out into the arena. She regains consciousness whilst being helped off the horse. Her helpers tell me she has fainted from exhaustion, and that she will recover. As I stand there in the empty dressage ring it hits me that what I have just witnessed is what Zen masters have written about for centuries: a way to live your life so completely that in each experience you hold nothing back; you do something fearlessly, live every moment as if it were your last, then life takes on the importance it was meant to have. Just a few moments ago, in front

[101]

of me, I saw this perfection of action, so perfectly timed that for the rider there was nothing left.

Inside I begin to swell. What am I doing here judging? Who do I think I am, assigning my stupid little numbers to a perfect performance – one that embodies all that a person can possibly give. I am inwardly furious with myself. I try to blame the organisers. Why is it that every time four Americans get together and do the same activity, they find a way to make rules so they can rank each other?

I am glad there is a break. I try to calm down, and go off to find something to eat. I walk around the show trying to make some sense of my dilemma. I watch some other classes. I listen to the competitors, and instructors. I wish I could talk to some more experienced teachers. Maybe they could give me some perspective, but they are obviously all busy. I keep walking round, and the spirit of the show begins to seep into me. The more I see, the more a question formulates in my mind: do you really think they are riding for prizes and points? I think it is my problem and I am the one who needs to get a handle on these numbers.

It becomes clear to me that these are not soft, modern, aimless lives that Jocho and Mishima warn about. These riders are internally motivated with many different reasons for being out here.

These teachers are not prize chasers who foster competition and preach winning. They are not externally motivated either. They have inner guiding systems. Above all, I know they are not here for the marks and the prizes.

Being out among these people relieves me of my self-importance, and they teach me by their example. Inside I know that is how I also want to ride, eventually.

[102]

My long abstinences from competitive riding always had their basis in the same particular American dilemma. When I rode in competitions it seemed I should try to win. In America winning is very important. Americans have made folk heroes out of people like Vince Lombardi, a famous professional football coach, whose motto was 'Winning isn't everything, it is the only thing'. On the other hand, I also knew what a bad record the public and critics at large had in recognising good work when it was right in front of them.

When, in my own competitions, I did try to win, and even if I was successful, I had this instinctive suspicion that someone was trying to force some doctrine on me. Winning alone was too simplistic. It didn't take into account any difference that two competitors might have had at the start: how much harder one had to work than the other, how far each had come, or if one just 'bought' the win. The winner's crown was a light hat, often decorated with the loud opinions and ideas of people who usually never played the particular game they professed to know so much about.

One day I saw an interview with a great Zen master, Taisen Deshimaru. He was asked if he thought 'championitis' could become a mental illness. He replied in the affirmative, and went on to say that it was a narrow vision of life. He said that the spirit of competition today was often not good, and that the teachers were partly responsible because they trained the body and technique but did nothing for consciousness. As a result their pupils fought to win like children playing war games. He went on to say that there is no wisdom in this approach and it is of no use at all in managing one's own life.[4]

---

[4] DESHIMARU, TAISEN, *Zen and the Martial Arts.*

[103]

Deshimaru's words solidified many feelings for me. For one, it seemed someone older and wiser, a true master, had voiced a criticism of certain teachers which would have seemed impudent if it had come from a student. There was an element of relief in that alone. It vented some of my frustration and anger at those teachers who I felt deliberately mislead with their own biased certainty.

However, more important was that Deshimaru spoke of the same internal consciousness that Jocho and then Mishima did. I could see connections all around. I saw it as the same thing that every artist tries violently to protect – a free consciousness, a stream of consciousness, a subconsciousness. Here, at the junction, these became the pathway to the truth. They move farther and farther from contrivance and imitation, more and more towards true originality. A free consciousness is housed in a disciplined body like a queen bee in a hive. All the disciplined members nurture the queen, for she alone can create new life. The power to renew one's self, to create out of seemingly nothing, needs help. The true, total, person pays attention to technique and yet does not. There are many parts to the whole.

Finally I seemed to develop a sense of place for competitions. I thought they could be a place of action where good riding could be displayed. After all, if classical theory didn't work, it should be buried. However, I was convinced in the soundness of its elegant simplicity and its benefit to horses and riders. I began to see competitions as more of a display, an exhibition, more like a gallery, less like a contest. When I did resume riding in competitions, I knew I could never ride to win. I would ride instead not to lose. This was no trick of semantics. It was deadly serious. However, I was not talking about losing the competition. What I

[104]

did not want to ever lose was my initial love of horses and riding, the excitement I had as a child. This turned out to be a far greater motivation, and an infinitely more difficult route.

Chapter Seven

Detraining the Mind – The Map is not the Territory

I AM AT A familiar place. I am digesting a lot of theory and literature in an effort to increase my knowledge and skill in riding. Since I have to work alone much of the time this is the only way I know. I often go to my practice with the movements I intend to ride idealised in my mind from the books I am reading. My plans seem good.

I begin riding. I try to train my horses to that pictured movement. I start comparing what is going on underneath me to the finished product in my head. The trouble is, nobody ever prints a photograph of a bad piaffe. All the books show exemplary movements, but none of the horses that I have begun in training re-create the perfect images that I have in my mind. Often my attempts are crude or out of balance. All I seem to see is how far off the mark my work is compared to my examples. After a while, this can get frustrating. I begin to wonder about the seemingly insurmountable gap between my day-to-day practice and these perfect descriptions and photographs.

Everything in my classic western education leads me to believe that, given enough analysis and thought, all apparent mysteries will yield. Nothing can ultimately escape from 'true scientific observation'. Look at western man's accomplishments: space travel, medicine, etc. All one has to do is exercise the mind. Eventually all the mysteries of the world will be explained. Or will they?

If you take up the study of riding through the information from its recorded literature, some certain mysterious holes appear in the fabric of its writings.

For hundreds of years the Spanish Riding School in Vienna has systematically prepared some of the best riders and horses. The web of knowledge that radiates from its disciples is immeasurable in its complexity and vastness. Its teachers have criss-crossed the globe, and these teachers in turn have prepared others who have become coaches, etc. The collective experience of the school, from generation to generation of horses and trainers, is immense. It seems inconceivable that a horse-training problem could exist which has not been corrected ten times over at this great School. It would seem logical that the School, like any other great learning institution, would have libraries full of treatises on every aspect of horsemanship. One would assume that it has produced volumes on the specific steps and correct principles of training the high school dressage horse. However, this is not the case at all. The sum total of the written directives of the Spanish Riding School amounts to literally a few pages. All the amazing consistency and knowledge is transmitted in some other way.

If you continue searching and reading, you cannot fail to notice the constant references to the universally accepted greatness of the French trainer, la Guerinière. However, if you try to find all the answers to specific riding problems in the wisdom of la Guerinière, you may be frustrated. La Guerinière did not leave us volumes and volumes. Furthermore, even though he was noted for the clarity of his work, it has still driven some more analytical modern horsemen to neurosis trying to prove or disprove what he said.

I have in front of me ten different dressage books, each with line drawings and photographs included, and the average number of pages in the books is 140. Ten different masters – and only these few pages. Even today one hears criticisms being made about some great living masters to the effect that they are not really that good because they are unable to express exactly what they do on the back of a horse.

I think this points to a paradox that the western mind does not like to entertain: namely, that observations about riding and riding are two very distinct and separate worlds.

Although we need to use words to learn and to teach, they still are very limited. Breaking up the dynamic movements of riding a horse into 'successive entities' in order to talk about it is very artificial. The flow of riding is too continuous to keep stopping it, chopping it up with analysis of particular movements separated from the whole.

It is no wonder I was so often frustrated with my riding and the horses' performances. My self-imposed projections about what the movements I went to practise should look like were unrealistic. Consequently there was always friction between reality and the mental image. There was no room to grow or to develop. If, for example, I go to practise the piaffe on a young horse and I have this specific idea of the piaffe I would like, a perfect image from some book, this is going to be trouble. For one thing no horse can perform such a finished product at the first attempts and furthermore even the trained horse cannot be expected to perform the same way every time out. As long as I keep this static image, usually a finished example, and try to imitate it, I will be unaware of what is going on in the present. I will be unaware of a particular horse's idiosyncrasies and likes and dislikes. Worse, I will be forgetting that the real essence is the process. The idea behind the piaffe is not to exhibit some kind of specifically calculated movement, for the sake of exhibition or the rider's ego. It is instead to perform a supreme exercise. The piaffe's real value lies in doing it, not in proving anything by exhibiting a trick. The piaffe's value is in the cumulative gymnastic effects it has on the horse. It has little value as something to be observed like a dead piece of art. Riding is a living art. For me this was a thorny issue. If you read books on riding you will often see, for example, separate chapters devoted to piaffe and passage, even entire books analysing specific placement of the legs and angulation. The unintended message, at least to me as an apprentice, is that somehow these movements are different and separate from all the other work. Unfortunately writings are notorious for breaking things up into 'successive entities', with few warnings as to how artificial these statements are.

It is my feeling that the limited amount of writings by the greatest riders and the greatest schools of riding is no accident. I believe the best teachers are much more interested in setting up situations where the student can learn for him/herself since it will be different for each and every one of us.

I think if one does not understand Korzybski's law 'the map is not the territory', or that talking about riding is not riding, one can get into some serious and expanding problems. Instead of your mind helping you ride, it will begin seriously to hinder you. You can suffer from paralysis by analysis. If, on the other hand, a teacher comes along and tells the rider to think of beautiful images, he is no better than the over-analytical non-rider. There is an important use for the mind in riding, but it is not to hold on to immobile projections, fixed images, etc., no matter whether they are under the guise of science, art, or philosophy. If there is an important use for the mind, then what is it?

In order to get some appreciation of the part to be played by the mind, let us take a quick look at the timing involved in certain movements. When performing single-time changes horse and rider can be executing two changes every second. Obviously the rider must have perfect timing and the horse must be responding instantaneously in order to execute new flying changes approximately every six tenths of a second. This gives one an impression of the speeds in the rider's reactions, as well as of the control needed, even at these kinds of speeds. Furthermore, incredible as it may seem, flying changes are not the most difficult movements to be performed. Others will call upon the rider to be reading and reacting so instantaneously that reacting is too slow a word. To execute under these conditions the rider must develop fierce concentration and if he is riding more than one horse per day, he must be able to maintain it for several hours.

What kind of concentration are we talking about? What is the essence of the right kind of concentration? Does this mean when you are riding you should try mentally to lock in on the exercise? If we zero in on an idea, will peripheral distractions lose their impact because we have something called up so solidly front and centre? Aren't the best concentrators the ones who can fix their attention unflinchingly on one particular task or idea or function?

In all the above instances, perceptions will be limited not enhanced, and reactions will be slowed down and not accelerated. Any time there is a strong focussing on one object or one idea, the result is an exclusion of other things in the vicinity. It doesn't matter what the idea is, even if it is the idea not to think about an idea. The more self-conscious, the more limitations. This kind of concentration can deaden the brain. Hypnosis requires this kind of initial focussing to work. Yogi's repetitive recantations of mantras can deaden the mind and body to external stimuli. This kind of concentration is not of much use when one is involved in unfolding, changing action. In fact in any dynamic situation like living or riding, it can be very harmful. In the world of action, one must become aware of everything simultaneously. In the best concentration you stop putting things into your mind. You try to cease the directives and analysis; you let the mind be free to do what it does best – and that is to perceive the entire world around you with all

[111]

your senses at once. Because we are multisensory we can be receiving information etc. on several levels all at the same time. The result of the right concentration can be miraculous. In an open, alert but calm way the body can attain intuitive reactions which are not really reactions because there is no time lag between action and reaction. The horse and rider literally become one, feeling things at the same time. How could I develop this kind of concentration? This is what I was after.

There was a time on this earth when the correct kind of concentration was at a zenith. Several things conspired at once in feudal Japan to effect these incredible advances in concentration. Advances in concentration which demonstrated themselves in the advances of *joba-jutsu*, the major martial art of horsemanship, and in swordfighting, archery, etc. At this time thousands of Samurai fighters were employed by the feudal barons of Japan to protect and embellish their holding of lands and goods. Amazingly enough all Samurai used primarily the same kind of weapons in their battles: two swords. Since fighting was constant, there was obviously intense competition among these swordfighters, horsemen, archers. Weaknesses in technique were quickly and permanently culled in the endless battles. Anyone can imagine the seriousness with which Samurai practised their skills. Schools of technique flourished. In these life-and-death tests the teachings and teachers were also quickly weeded out. The level of skill in horsemanship, swordfighting and archery became very high. Anything that might give a Samurai an edge was intensely studied.

At the same time Zen Buddhism was continuing its development. Zen's firey insistency in being grounded in the real world, on being pragmatic and totally and immediately connected to the world, without cluttering mental philosophies, on being intuitive and natural, free if you will, finally came to the attention of some of the fighters. When these men undertook the study of Zen, a side-effect was an incredible improvement in their particular skill. Without cumbersome analysis of technique and forced manipulation their swordwork, like their lives, became elegantly simple; it became direct as a bolt of lightning. These swordsmen, horsemen and archers became legendary. Some became great teachers. Today *kendo* – swordfighting with bamboo swords – and the other martial arts are the direct descendants of this knowledge concerning the highest development of concentration.

It seemed clear to me that if I were having a problem with concentration and with getting a direct hold on knowledge, I had to pursue these Eastern teachings further. My mind was unsettled. My riding seemed to be pulled in many strange directions at once. It was in this mix, though, that I eventually came to my last lessons as an apprentice.

Chapter Eight

Breathing – A Half-halt for the Rider

AFTER I HAD BEGUN to pursue some of the Eastern teachings, one of my most important riding lessons came in an unusual form. It did not provide a particular answer to a specific problem, but more a way to look for answers. I realised that I would never progress if tension was inhibiting my actions and reactions. In an effort to reduce tension whenever it started to creep in I began using some traditional Japanese breathing exercises. When I started to use deliberate patterns of breathing, it had an almost instantaneous result. Within minutes, sometimes after only a few breaths, I could get myself to relax. Tension would usually build up in a similar fashion: the horse might be disobedient, or an exercise would fall apart – something would cause me to become frustrated. Without knowing it I would start to harden my posture. This muscular tightness would restrict my natural breathing. My form would deteriorate. Obviously as I became less flexible, my dexterity decreased. No matter who started this process, the end results were always the same stiffening effects. In its own right this kind of cycling aggravation is a problem; but when you couple it with the fact that some of the most difficult dressage movements not only require quick fluid executions of complicated combinations of legs, hands, and weight aids, but also a simultaneous wide open monitoring system, it then becomes obvious how even small amounts of tension will hinder the progress of the rider and confuse the horse.

The dressage rider must become more flexible, lighter, quicker and more pliant as the degree of difficulty increases – not harder, stiffer, and heavier.

With the introduction of breathing exercises, I could interrupt this negative chain of events early in the process. If I felt any restriction I began a series of breaths: deep, steady inhalation through the nose, a moment of holding, and then calm, deep exhalation through the mouth. This exhalation should not be forcefully restricted. (It is possible to increase the pressure in the chest

[115]

to the point where it can restrict blood flow back to the heart, and can cause dizziness.)

Koichi Tohei[1] recommends that this is practised sitting, until you can extend the cycle to approximately one breath per minute. He also notes this is only possible with practice and by keeping calm and by 'keeping one point'. Keeping one point can be roughly translated as keeping yourself centered in your abdomen. This happens to be the body's centre of gravity. In martial arts this centre controls and facilitates physical and psychic balance and is the place where all movement originates; it is the real master control centre. To me it is not a coincidence that in the proper dressage seat you are attempting to find this all the time. That is why I think breathing can be so effective to a rider.

Deep, efficient breathing helped my riding physically and psychologically. Physically, as the diaphragm muscle below the lungs contracts and flattens out, pulling fresh air into the lungs, it has the effect of compressing the organs below it. This can have the feeling of sinking the centre of gravity and internally deepening the rider's seat. I remember one time when Nuno Oliviera was making a point to students about the rider's seat. He was talking about each successive vertebra in one's back sinking into the next, and right down into the horse. I am certain that it was this idea of sinking one's centre of gravity, or at least focussing on it, that he was talking about. As the diaphragm contracts the upper rib cage is also expanding to further fill the lungs with the fresh air of every inhalation. In this part of the breath, I could hear Dr Van Schaik's favourite phrase, 'Make yourself tall', being repeated. He often talked about the very natural upward growth from the abdo-

[1] TOHEI, KOICHI, *Book of Ki: Coordinating Mind and Body in Daily Life*, Japan Publishing, Inc. 1976.

[116]

men to the chest which would seat the rider correctly over his seat bones. These pieces of advice were perfectly compatible with the anatomy of breathing. The result of the simple, but life-sustaining process was that in every single cycle of breathing, my posture had the chance of being naturally corrected – pelvis straightened, torso lengthened, shoulders opened. When I practised deeper, steady breathing it actually accentuated my position in the correct form.

Trained breathing helps develop the capacity of the heart and lungs thus increasing muscle fitness and developing a greater anaerobic threshold, so that the rider as an athlete is in better condition. Sheer physical strain is reduced by an increase in fitness. Psychologically, deep, efficient breathing grounded me. The mere fact of paying attention to breathing would adjust my awareness. When a problem loomed up and tried to command all of my mind's attention, it was my regular breathing that would reopen my total perception and unlock any stranglehold one particular dilemma might have had. Only if I were aware would I be able to ride my way to a solution.

To me as a rider, the effects of breathing seemed very analogous to the effect of the half-halt on the horse. Proper breathing alone has the power to rebalance the rider if he is leaning too far forward or back. Through its subtle constant corrections it can make the rider plumb. When breathing re-establishes the rider's psychological rhythm it acts exactly as the half-halt does in calming down a rushing or hurried horse. As the gait takes on its natural swinging pace, the rider's actions relax and smooth out. But breathing's most profound similarity to the half-halt is the way it can prepare the rider for a transition or any change. The attentive and aware rider is not surprised by something new. Sitting there in good balance the rider is expecting it.

Chapter Nine

Retraining the Mind – A Revelation of Centres

I HAD EXPRESSLY begun the study of martial arts to increase my concentration. I was sure I needed stronger powers of attention. I thought I needed more focussing so that I could hold my attention tighter for longer periods of time. I saw this flaw in my concentration as the latest hurdle of my apprenticeship. I was certain that

[119]

this failing was inhibiting my riding and training. The interesting thing was that although I may have pin-pointed the source of trouble, the correction was different to what I expected.

If I were doing a shoulder-in on a fairly green horse, and the horse slipped in and out of balance from three tracks to four then back to straightness, I always felt this was wrong. But how could it be wrong if it was all that the horse could give me at the time? As the horse became stronger and more flexible the movement would change. This business of isolating and then criticising a single movement in one moment of time was a very narrow vision, and pointed out a misunderstanding of the training process. The more I focussed on a concrete image in my mind of what was supposed to happen during my practice, the more disappointed I was when there was deviation from this ideal. Instead of keeping up with my awareness, this is where my concentration faltered. When, for example, I had trouble in movement one, I was carrying the mood into movement two and movement three and so on. In the past I always thought that my aggravation was due to a performance that was off the mark, unlike the photograph in my mind. This was only one part of it. The second part was practically a physical reaction. Getting stuck, agonising over a movement that didn't fit my idea, or someone else's, left me behind the immediate riding I was supposed to be doing. I lost my place in terms of feeling. All my senses became muddled fielding information, perceiving, but my mind stopped processing it as it was. Soon we were all out of synch. I was psychologically dizzy.

I was beginning to see that when you stop your mind to focus intently on something, it doesn't matter if it is in anger over a particular short-coming or if you are blindly pursuing a peaceful image: the result is the same.

[120]

You will be left behind the unfolding action of the here and now. This will make you late, and you will be aware of it. The horse seems to be riding off without you. Whenever I found myself way behind the action, I became confused, and rightly so. A flash of temper seemed to be an acknowledgment of this frustration and loss of control. Even the novice rider will be able to sense this discord and will want the harmony back – that feeling of fitting in with the horse and the world.

There was never anything drastically wrong with my concentration. Certainly there was not a need to be more focussed. In the world of action there just isn't time to be constantly reflecting, theorising, and wondering whilst riding. The more that I segmented the riding, isolating one movement from another, the more unconnected it all became. I had to approach it as a whole.

Throughout my apprenticeship I always was looking for concrete answers to my riding questions. Yet the farther I went, the more I began to get the feeling that the answers are more like questions and, at best, only suggestions. This illusiveness was very confusing to me as an apprentice. I could see that a lot of my impatience and intolerance was with the imprecision of learning and the training process; the illusiveness of things always changing, always in motion. By the time I had arrived at Maruyama's dojo, I began to get the feeling that the right concentration comes from a confidence that you will let yourself do the right thing. The art of riding is an art in motion. I had to become secure to live with the illusiveness of all of this movement. I had to stop limiting my work by seeing it in a preconceived way. Nothing was going to fit the images of my mind's eye. Nor would it fit a picture of another rider on another horse in another moment of time. I had to let myself try. Deep down inside, from very early in my

[121]

apprenticeship, I knew how serious these steps were that I had been taking. There is no turning back when you start to walk into your own circle, and away from the circle of your teachers. You take responsibility for what might happen next. The swift river moves before you; its bottom is full of slippery rocks. You walk along the banks looking for a bridge across, but there is none. If you want to experience the other side, you have to wade in. You know very well that with one slip you will go under, but you decide to try.

It was in Maruyama's dojo that my apprenticeship ended. In Maruyama's dojo, there she was. As I watched this woman's swordwork, and her teaching, I saw grace and beauty, fearlessness, and femininity. So many things about her seemed balanced. I found myself admiring her. As I talked with her, something serious locked into place. I saw that she must have faced tremendous pressure to surrender to a system which seemed to demand that women never assert. As she became more and more adept she must have appeared threatening to many people who had fixed ideas about frail femininity. Who could say how much she had doubted her own femininity as she progressed towards becoming a martial artist? I wondered where she gathered strength to pursue her path when it was dark and she felt alone.

Now anyone could see what a beautiful woman she had become. Her strength did not detract from her femininity. It enhanced it. Her power gave her femininity more drama and depth. She could stand like a lioness. From her long study of fighting she had learned to command respect and exude a comforting peacefulness.

I saw then the mirror struggle within myself against a system suggesting and supporting power, force, domination and aggression in a man. My job, even when I didn't know it, often involved learning not to be afraid

[122]

of softness; being comfortable in allowing softness and intuition a place to thrive in the sphere that was me. I had not only to let it exist, but also, like the great Japanese wrestlers who study gentle painting, I, too, had to cultivate the opposites in order to develop my balance.

My admiration for this woman helped me. As I admired her work and saw the similarities of our struggles, I could admire my own work. I seemed to be able to accept my own work just as it was. In that small understanding I set myself free from my constant goals and expectations. I saw clearly that just as she was the centre of her own struggle, I was the centre of mine. And every other learner had his or her centre. Each was the centre of her/his own universe. There was not just one centre of the universe. There were millions, side by side, coexisting simultaneously. I saw the universality of all apprenticeship struggles, the similarity of all of our roads. We are all alone, and yet there are many of us out there. We could inspire each other with the spirit and integrity of our work, or we could presume, criticise and judge. If a horseman has an abiding respect for his or her own road, then it must show in the respect for others and for the horse. We can never really compete against each other because we are all on different roads. To be a real horseman I knew I would have to keep a careful check on my own ideas and ego and have true respect for the horse's life.

The study of technique and the practice of form gives the body awareness. It cannot be stopped. Whether you are ready or not you will be able to feel things outside your own body. The first cracks in the bubble of yourself will appear. Your awareness grows until you are capable of transcending yourself on horseback. You can move out of your own self centre, out of your ego. It

[123]

will be up to you to take that step and go along. The beauty of the paradox is that as soon as you disconnect from yourself you don't despair but you immediately connect with everything around you. In the right concentration your whole being is listening. You really connect with your horse. Once you can move out of yourself, there is nothing stopping how much you can learn. Without presumption anything is possible. Nothing is strange. Answers, at best, are temporary and questions become more comfortable.

In Maruyama's dojo not only was I making peace with myself but also I was making peace with the learning process. I wouldn't need the constant attention of a teacher any more. I would be able to work alone. Whether you think you know the solution to a problem, or whether you don't, you still must ride the same way. The object is not to get someone to give you the answer, the idea is to figure out your own answers. You cannot think up an answer to every riding problem. You must ride through a riding problem. That is the training process, and the word dressage means training. It is dressage itself which answers its own questions.

As I left I felt very drained, and tired. Something seemed missing. I felt emotionally exhausted. I even felt empty. I also noticed I was very calm. I didn't have any particular answers in mind, but I didn't have any questions either.

I knew that tomorrow I would be riding again. I walked through several blocks of the harsh city. The sun was setting. I got into my car and began the drive home. The sun came in strongly through my windscreen as I travelled west. I thought back to when I was twelve years old. I remembered the first time that the man I worked for in the summers let me go riding by myself. It was in the rolling hills of the New York Finger Lakes country. I rode down an abandoned dirt road out to a section of woods above the long lake. Some of these paths could have been traversed by the members of the great Seneca Indian nation, part of the Iroquois sisterhood that stretched across all of what is now New York State. Small brown puffs of dust rose up behind the footfalls of the horse. Hawks were circling low in the evening sky. How much wiser I seemed then. So excited. So satisfied just to be on the back of a horse, riding towards the light.

Epilogue

I WOULD LIKE TO be able to say that immediately after my experience in Mr Maruyama's training hall, completing what I have called my apprenticeship, I was overcome with joy and celebration.

I guess I always expected it to end like some graduation ceremony – throwing hats into the air in jubilation. Maybe I should have received a piece of paper stating the privileges attached to this culmination. But who would have issued it?

It wasn't like that. And learning the art is not like that. It can never be measured by examinations. The

true feeling was more like a sense of peace. I don't mean
to suggest some overly romantic, calm, god-like trance.
I am talking more about a kind of important relief.
Imagine that for years and years there had been a constant background noise in your ears. You had grown
accustomed to it and could function in spite of it. Yet
you were always aware it was there. Then one day
you found it had gone. Your reaction would not be
jubilation. It would be more one of disbelief, scepticism;
you might sit for a minute and just relish the relief. You
might expect the sound to come back at any moment.
With each new day you would begin to see how much
of a hold it had on you. Your confidence would grow
as you began to really live without it.

What I saw was that knowledge, or wisdom, seemed
to be following exactly the lessons of riding. The idea
of breaking down the process of learning into grades
and degrees, those 'successive entities' again, was just as
artificial as breaking down the piaffe or passage.

I was beginning to see wisdom, knowledge, as a fundamental way of being or looking; a process not an end
result. The best teachers were always above all the best
learners. In fact as far as I could see they were learners
first and always, no matter how old they were or how
much they already knew.

So when I say there was no great joy, elation or
celebration of the completion of a course of training or
learning, it was as much because I finally perceived that
everything was really just beginning. Certainly I wasn't
unhappy.

Why did I think this realisation, this graduation,
should be more dramatic? What could be more dramatic
than to realise that I would never know an ending in
riding, that I would always be beginning? What in the
end could be more profound than to go to my regular

work each day with the excitement and innocence of a beginner?

Book Two

EXPLORING DRESSAGE TECHNIQUE
Journeys into the Art of Classical Riding

Contents

Acknowledgements

I WOULD FIRST LIKE to thank my wife Jeanne, for her countless hours of help in editing and preparing my manuscripts.

I would also like to thank Caroline Burt at J.A. Allen, for literally years of guidance; also Lesley Gowers, who has worked with me over every word of this book and *Riding Towards the Light*. A special thanks to both of them for their initial faith in me when these works surely seemed uncoventional.

I thank Dawn Carrone for her illustrations, which to me are works of art; also Maggie Raynor and Dianne Breeze for their artistic contributions.

To Paul Saunders for his cover designs.

I'd like to thank Lorell Jolliffe, my assistant, for help in the research on lateral work.

Finally, thanks go to the University of Pennsylvania, in particular the library staff at New Bolton Center, for allowing me to read and study from their great collection.

Paul Belasik
January, 1994

Prologue

LET A MAN DECIDE upon his favourite animal and make a study of it – let him learn to understand its sounds and motions. The animals want to communicate with man, but *Wakan Tanka* does not intend they shall do so directly – a man must do the greater part in securing an understanding.

Brave Buffalo, Standing Rock
(Frances Dunsmore, Teton Sioux Music,
Smithsonian Institute, Bureau of
American Ethnology Bulletin,
Washington DC, 1918)

[7]

Introduction

WHEN I HAVE TALKED to musicians and dancers who were in the middle phases of their training and practice, to see if there was one common thread, it was often a conscious and unconscious infatuation with technical bravura. It is as if the growing mastery of the human body and the growing mastery of the body of knowledge that one is immersed in, constantly needed to be tested, stretched, challenged and extended. In any art one is continually faced with historical examples of great artists' past work, as well as the work of one's peers which is in front of you at every performance, exhibition, and/or competition. Comparison is logical. When in dressage competitions several players perform the same work or test, and this piece of work is rated by a panel of judges, comparison becomes further entrenched. The eye and the mind begin to focus on the differences of the performance, but they must focus on the measurable attributes to quantify and verbalise – the height of the piaffe steps, the number of canter pirouettes, the straightness of the changes, the conscious elements. The Journeyman has to be involved in this kind of investigation to develop his riding knowledge. There must be an understanding as complete as possible of all the various exercises, movements, training systems, and there must be an ability as complete as possible to execute all the various exercises, movements and training systems. There has to be complete freedom in and a familiarity with all these techniques.

However, to stop the Journey in the land of technique can be deadly for the growth of the rider. As D.T. Suzuki[1] has suggested, very often people confuse true harmony with tranquillity. You will get all the tranquillity you need in death. To revere tranquillity is to revere death. To revere life is to revere movement, change in all its forms, lovely and frightening. If ever there was a creature of movement it is the horse, whose beauty and grace can be concealed in a stable or at rest, but is revealed in its motion. The art of riding is a celebration of motion, of nature's rhythms. A great ride cannot be preserved and sold for millions of dollars after the artist's death. It always possesses a very fair immediacy. The rider must live and work in the present, always grounded in the here and now.

All of the names of the Japanese martial arts end with the word 'do' meaning 'the way' – *Karatedo*, open hand way; *Kyudo*, the way of the bow. The way, the process, what is important, is that every individual art has a metaphorical property. Each is a reference to something more communal, more universal, namely, the process of life, or as Carl Jung might say, individuation. Master the metaphor and it may tell you about life. Get stuck in the metaphor and you could die. For the rider, getting stuck in the land of technical bravura can be the end of his advance on the journey of horsemastership. In order to get through, though, you must first go in. After the measurable techniques, there are the unconscious elements, the mythic elements, where the art of riding has always come from – where creativity lives.

What follows are some of my trips as a Journeyman in the land of technical bravura. When you travel in that country, and you return to a city where you had once been, it can be completely changed. This need not be fearful because Xenophon, the Duke of Newcastle, Pluvinel, Eisenberg, La Guérinière, Baucher, Steinbrecht and on and on, have all left some beautiful maps. Most important of all, Nature has presented riders with the horse on which to travel.

Chapter One

A Fog of Walks

'THE SCHOOL WALK of the old masters was a diagonalised walk in which the horse lifted his legs and collected himself.'[2]

Nuno Oliveira

A friend of mine who is a trainer and dressage judge had the idea of staging a symposium for upper level dressage riders, trainers and judges. The notion was to allow for some frank, constructive discussion about the current state of dressage in the United States. He had invited the trainer H.L.M. Van Schaik to present a keynote address. For my part, I was to serve in some capacity as a moderator and to interview Van Schaik as I had done many years before in a forum that I had arranged in conjunction with a large horse organisation in Pennsylvania.

We decided to make a fast two-day trip up to Van Schaik's home in Vermont, in order to cement some of the logistics and to meet face to face for discussions. It was in the middle of winter and our destination involved about an eight-hour drive in the heart of the north-east ski country. The forecast was stable, and we decided to take my friend Michael's four-wheel drive truck. With our wives covering for us we took off in the early morning. As we drove through the day we had a chance to talk about many things – our children, our families, but especially horses. Michael and I are the same age and have similar educational backgrounds. We have a mutual love of riding and an admiration for some of the same old masters. (Michael's family has been instrumental in promoting dressage in the US for a long time, and it is only because I have the utmost trust in his integrity that I agree to get involved again in the administration of large groups.)

We drove throughout the day and in the dark we made it into southern Vermont where we stopped to refuel. It was one of my first visits north for a while. To step outside the truck into the northern winter air was refreshing. I walked around the truck and looked out across the street beyond the bright glow of the station lights. It had been a relatively mild winter so far. When I talked to the station attendant he told me that the skiing was off because of insufficient snow. I could only see traces of snow in patches where it had been ploughed into piles. The bare ground was frozen deep and hard. I always feel a similar excitement and apprehension in cold weather –

some psychological hold over from the old days of living a simple life in a northern climate where the temperatures can get seriously low and make little things very difficult.

Soon we were off again for the final leg toward Cavendish where Van Schaik lived, near the top of a high hill just outside the tiny village. Cavendish is a short way from the heart of the ski country in Vermont. The houses usually have steep-pitched roofs and you can smell the wood smoke from early fall until spring. The mountains are old and numerous, and each has its accompanying valley. Many little villages line up in these tiny valleys all through this country. It can give you a remote feeling, and adds to a sense of privacy. When the great Russian author Alexander Solzhenitsyn decided to come to the United States, of all the places, he chose Cavendish. It seems it could fill the requirements for a reclusive life.

If it weren't for the skiers on holiday, on any given winter's night, the roads would be empty and everything closed. Coyotes have returned to the area, and howl in the clear night air.

As we get closer the mountains rise up around us. More and more snow is now visible and the ground is all white. Icy patches glow like phosphorus in the moonlight. Deep in the small valleys clear streams, moving too fast to freeze, spin and steam up the air with larger and larger ice bridges forming over them. Through the winter as the spray condenses and vapour freezes, fine layer upon layer is formed.

When we finally arrive at Van Schaik's, it is cold. Our legs are cramped, and we are tired, but as soon as I see the old man I feel revived. He has cooked dinner for us and greets us with drinks. We have some discussion and fun, and continue more in earnest the next day. We try to prepare the symposium, and several times Van Schaik shifts the conversation to another topic. It is clear to me after

[13]

last night that he is excited about something, the way a scientist can get excited with a new finding. I think he must be preparing to write about it. The subject that seems to have him enthralled is the diagonal walk. I am familiar with this idea through experience with Nuno Oliveira and his writings. However, I also know it can be a confusing topic. It seems that the old masters used to use this diagonal walk, as Oliveira has mentioned, as a preparation for the 'gentle passage'.[2]

When Van Schaik shows us a copy of his address, it begins: 'I have been called the "crazy old man", and some people doubt if I am mentally still all there . . .' Of course, anyone who can write a statement like that and can then deliver a lucid address with some very pointed advice and criticism, must be very sane and very aware. I listen but I have heard it many times before, and in all honesty am thinking of the interview. If this diagonal walk comes up, which is a good possibility since he seems currently enchanted by it, I can just imagine the thoughts of the competitive dressage riders in the room. When we start calling this two-time trot-like gait a walk, they *will* think he is crazy.

I know from past experience that many of these people have no interest in the ancients and only know about gaits asked for in dressage tests. We finish some more work, but before long, we have to leave. As it turned out, that was one of the last times I saw the old man alive.

Van Schaik was not crazy in calling this diagonalised movement a walk. But the diagonal walk which resembles a kind of preliminary passage, a soft passage, is hardly the end of the subject. Let us look for a moment at the idea of a trotting two-time walk.

In the sport of racing harness horses, there are races for trotters and for pacers. Pacers race in a two-beat gait, but unlike the trotter, which propels itself off diagonal (*con-*

tralateral) pairs of legs, the pacer propels itself off its *ipsilateral* pairs of legs – the legs of one side having the same stance phase and the same swing phase. The left front and left hind move as one ipsilateral pair, and then the right front and right hind move in their turn. So we have this two-beat gait which can reach racing speeds. Now, in the walk, the horse can move in a four-beat sequence: right hind, right front, left hind, left front. All dressage riders live in fear of closing up this sequence – some by pushing the walk too hard, some by holding it back too much. In any case the ipsilateral pairs move closer and closer together in timing until they have the same stance phase and the same swing phase, and the horse is pacing at the walk. So we get a gait that, in terms of one description, is the same as the racing pace. In both gaits, the horse is being propelled by its ipsilateral legs, which are paired together with a similar time in the stance phase – i.e. when they are on the ground – and a similar swing phase – i.e. when they both travel through the air. The amazing thing is that if you show even the novice rider a horse that is pacing, he will easily be able to tell when it is pacing at the walk and when it is pacing at the trot. Other factors of speed, suspension, etc., are involved in discriminating the gaits of the horse. So what do we have in the pacing walk, a two-beat gait at the walk? Not many people will disagree with that. Then what about a diagonal walk? Could that be just another two-beat gait at the walk? The diagonal walk is not necessarily as preposterous or illogical as it might first seem. I have already said, though, that the diagonal walk is hardly the end of the story.

There were and are many differentiations in the walk: counted walks, Spanish walks, pacing walks, ambling walks, school walks, collected walks, extended walks, running walks, etc. It is my feeling that the old masters were in no way sloppy horsemen in that their gaits seemed to be so open-ended and apparently impure. I think I can prove the opposite: that they possessed a superior awareness of the many subtleties in any gait, and delighted in the exploration of them. If the modern dressage rider reads the texts of Pluvinel, for example, he will not recognise many of the movements so often practised at that time. How many riders today have any idea of what the *demi-volte*, *passade*, *un pas un sant*, *nez air*, or *terre à terre* are? The easiest thing to do is to claim that today in our competitive tests, we have evolved and our gaits are more pure. Can this evolution be borne out?

Sometime later, after I had returned from our trip, I was driving in my truck. Two days during the week, I leave the farm to give a teaching clinic. On these drives, which often take several hours, I frequently listen to tape recordings. On this day I was relistening to a tape of a lecture by Dr Doug Leach, who was a noted researcher of equine locomotion. Some years before I had arranged a seminar from which this recording was taped. This was the same forum that Van Schaik had spoken at. Dr Leach is an excellent speaker and a careful scientist who is not crazy about the colloquial expressions of gait which many of us horsemen use. He has spent quite some time and effort to get horsemen to begin to use a standard language to describe the biomechanics and locomotion of the equine.

Dr Leach's voice continues. Out of this machine comes a mild Canadian accent talking about locomotion being a reflex action with some conscious motor control. He goes on to talk about the problem of defining and categorising the different types of gait. He talks about rotary gallops, transverse gallops, cross cantering, left leads and right leads, etc. Then he goes on to say, 'but in fact – surprise, surprise! – gaits do not exist.' My attention

[16]

becomes galvanised. I am travelling on a turnpike moving pretty quickly. There is road noise and traffic. I reach for the stop button. I want to be sure I have heard it right. I rewind the tape. I turn up the volume and play it again. Yes. That is exactly what he said. I play it once more. This time I let the machine run. His voice is clear.

'There is such a continuum of changes in the limb coordination patterns seen in horses (that) when you carefully analyse the locomotion of these animals, clearly there is one whole continuum of changes which these animals are capable of. It is us in our simplified way of analysing these animals, that categorise and selectively train for specific gaits. Hildebrand in California has defined over four hundred different strides, and from his work he concluded there is no such thing as stride. I think it is important to recognise this continuum of changes does exist. If you look at the gaits of a foal you will not recognise the gaits that you see because there are so many different types that these young animals can exhibit. They have not been channelled into the gaits that we ourselves rely on. Of course, we need our old terminology, canter etc., but it is important to realise (that) the horse is capable of a whole range of motion.'

My first impression is that Pluvinel and Doug Leach would probably have no trouble talking to each other. However, a lot of people involved in dressage today will be left out of the conversation.

The first chance I get, I begin a systematic review of the relatively current and important works on biomechanics and equine locomotion. I think it is a big mistake to disregard this work because it is too esoteric or impractically scientific. In some cases elaborate force plates and strain gauges have been designed and applied to moving horses to describe accurately what is happening. In others, high-speed films taken as fast as two hundred and forty frames per second, almost three times as fast as the speeds they use in human locomotion research, have been used to describe the horse's motion. Computers have been employed and excellent scientific efforts undertaken and then replicated world-wide to give us a good idea of just how our horses move. So when a statement like 'there is no such thing as stride' surfaces, and when you get a warning from the most current literature to be aware that there is a very real continuum in the changes of horse's limb patterns, and when this also coincides with the old masters' fluid use of different gait patterns, then I think there is an important lesson for the modern dressage trainer.

For the trainer who is completely absorbed in the training of dressage horses for competition with FEI or competitive rules as guidelines, there is a significant danger. These rules are not for training dressage horses. They are guidelines for competing dressage horses. The current competitive standards for the horse at the walk are extremely limited. FEI Rule, Article 403, Sec. 2 states: 'When four beats cease to be distinctly marked, even, and regular, the walk is disunited or broken.' Only the following walks are recognised in dressage competitions: collected walk, medium walk, extended walk, and free walk. The danger is that an implication can be drawn that these are the only walks that should or can exist. This premise cannot be justified or supported by the most current scientific research on gait analysis, nor can it be supported by the historical literature of the old masters.

My point is that even if the trainer is only interested in training the four competitive walks, he must develop an experience with and a knowledge of as much of the continuum of changes of the horse's limb patterns in the walk

[18]

as possible – if for no other reason than to have a way to correct or train out some of the variations of gait patterns that are bound to occur.

Many dressage trainers warn of prematurely trying to collect the walk. Why? When the horse is advancing in a four-beat rhythm at the walk, it is advancing its legs in a pattern like left hind, left front, right hind, right front. The ispilateral pairs of legs (on one side) on the left go, then the ipsilateral pairs of the right, and so on and so on. As soon as the trainer recognises this careful ipsilateral progression it becomes easy to see that if the front foot on one side slows down or the hind foot on the same side speeds up, the horse will close down the interval of time between each foot's time on the ground, or the stance phase. If it gets too close, the result will be that the horse moves from a four-time ipsilateral gait to a two-time ipsilateral gait: two time, because the legs of the right side strike the ground simultaneously as one beat and then the legs of the left side strike the ground simultaneously as the second beat. Simply put, the horse starts pacing.

If the trainer tries to collect the walk by loading the haunches, shifting the centre of gravity backward, he will almost certainly push the walk from a four-time rhythm toward a two-time rhythm. If the ipsilateral legs close up and move as one, then the two-time rhythm will be a pace. If, on the otherhand, the contralateral legs close up and move as one, you have a trot-like gait. Since many of the old masters were more concerned with loading the haunches than they were with keeping a gait rhythmically pure, then they were not bothered it seems by this shift-over. They routinely practised the diagonal walk as an exercise to deepen the haunches. 'A horse that does not go well upon his haunches can never do well in the Manège, so that our whole study is to put him upon them.'[3] (Duke of Newcastle)

[19]

The modern trainer really does the same thing when he actively collects the walk, and deliberately presses it into the two-time rhythms when using half-steps, jog trots, and soft passages all as precursors of the piaffe.

However, if the modern trainer wishes to gather the walk and hold it in a four-beat rhythm, he must be careful to shorten and raise the steps of all four legs uniformly. Any over-zealous attempt to load the haunches and raise the forehand by shifting the centre of gravity of the horse further backward will change the walk rhythm, usually by quickening the hind steps. If the trainer gathers the horse harshly with the hand, he can stiffen the horse's neck and shoulder thus restricting the forelimbs and slowing them down. This, of course, will also shorten the swing time between the front and back limbs.

There is a valid argument concerning whether it is really possible at all to collect the walk, at least the way we usually think of collection in the trot and canter. Yet, as Van Schaik has written, the FEI language describing the collected walk, trot and canter is nearly identical.

At first glance one could think that obviously the lack of a defined suspension phase in the walk clearly shows that there is not enough power or thrust generated to raise the horse's center of gravity very much up and forward. Therefore this is why we can't think of collection in the walk. Without enough thrusting power to generate a suspension phase, it's difficult to think of collection. In order to collect or extend the stride while maintaining the same tempo, one has to change the arc of the horse flight, from a more horizontal trajectory in extension to a more vertically oriented trajectory in collection. Having said this, we will see it is not at all that simple in the next chapter. Suspension alone is not the best indicator of collection or even thrusting power. Suspension can be deceptive.

So if it is not suspension, *per se*, that makes collecting the walk difficult or impossible, what is it? I believe it is the artificial categorisation that the walk remain four-beat. It is very possible to collect the walk, just as the old masters did all the time. What is impossible is to collect the walk and keep it four beat. These are mutually exclusive ideas. This is why, in my opinion, there is so much mystery and confusion. The language of the FEI concerning the collected walk needs to be changed. If one feels that the four beats are the crucial element to the walk, then the notion of collecting it has to be adjusted. If one doesn't care if the beats remain consistent and rhythmical, then the language of collection can remain.

It is my feeling as a trainer of horses that the four-beat imposition in the walk is important. I feel there are other gaits which are better suited to demonstrate collection. I feel that the modern walk, especially the way it punctuates dressage tests, is not there so much to show range of motion within that gait, as much as it is in the test to see if the horse is relaxed. For that purpose it is a good barometer. Horses will not walk in a quiet sustained rhythm if they are too tense or if they move too fast.

> 'The horse cannot maintain this ordinary walk above a maximum speed . . . If the stance time were to decrease to less than the swing time, there would have to be a portion of the stride during which there would be no supporting legs under the hind end, and another where there would be no support for the front. Since the walk has no suspension phase, as do the faster gaits, it would be impossible for the stance time to go below the swing time, i.e. the horse would fall down.'

Strategically placed (and it is very important that it is strategically placed, or like a bad fence on a jumping course it can be a trap instead of a challenge), the walk is a safeguard against wreckless excitement in dressage exhibitions.

I think it is very important when Doug Leach makes the following statement:

'There is such a continuum of changes in limb coordination patterns seen in horses (that) when you carefully analyse the locomotion of these animals clearly there is a whole continuum of changes which these animals are capable of. It is us in our simplified way of analysing these animals that categorise and selectively train for specific gaits.'

A walk, then, is not 'broken' when it moves out of four-beat rhythm any more than it is fixed when it is in that rhythm. When a trainer gets more comfortable in this fog-like continuum of the walk, he need not live with a fear of breaking anything just because it changes. The Journeyman must in fact learn to deliberately evoke change, especially when presented with problematic horses. As a trainer you cannot live your life defending the philosophical territory you may have inherited. These same walls of standardisation which offer you protection can also imprison you. I believe this is a very important perspective, philosophically and pragmatically. In one system you use change – you try to stay open and fluid. In the other system you are always reducing, trying to stop change. This system of training has an inherent flaw built into it because you cannot stop nature. The trainer needs to have the broadest range of experience possible. This will open the rider's feel to more nuance. If you can ride a horse into a pace, you must be able to ride out of it. In many ways, it is a matter of perception.

'We don't teach our students enough of the intellectual content of experiments, their novelty and their capacity for opening new fields . . . My own view is that you take these things personally. You do an experiment because your own philosophy makes you want to know the result. It's too hard, and life is too short, to spend your time doing something because someone else has said it is important. You must feel the thing yourself.'

Isidor I. Rabi
Nobel Prize winner in physics [5]

Chapter Two

The Hovering Trot

'A CONVULSIVELY TIGHTENED, tense back produces artificially exalted and exaggerated steps (also called a floating
trot or the extended passage) whenever the rate is
increased. Similarly a diminution of the rate that is
forcibly achieved by the reins produces hovering . . .
Horses that display a preference for shortened gaits com-
mit this fault very readily, especially when their tight
back facilitates these hovering steps.'

Waldemar Seunig [6]

I did not want Seunig to be wrong. His famous book *Horsemanship* was always a great map to me when I was lost. Everytime I look at it I think how it must have been received when it first came out, before a lot of the new science of biomechanics and equine locomotion. It must have been intimidating. Even today its encyclopaedic scope will humble any equestrian expert.

I have trained quite a few horses over the years, but I have only run into three horses that really exhibited this particular flaw of hovering in the trot, which at first glance resembles the horse in passage. In reality the movement is more like some illegitimate relative of the passage. It is a lofty trot which seems to go up in the air more than it moves forward. Unlike the passage, which is a great display of elastic power, the hover trot seems to dwell aimlessly. Once it is engrained it can be difficult to eradicate.

The first horse wasn't with me long enough to really work on it. The second was never really completely corrected, although he did make good progress. I decided to try to loosen this horse's back with a series of medium-trot-to-collected-trot transitions and trot-walk transitions – basically a steady diet of longitudinal flexing and extending exercises. I thought these accordian-type exercises would help make the horse's back more flexible, and then hopefully the hovering would disappear. It could easily be argued that these are the wrong exercises, nevertheless to a certain extent the hovering did disappear, but I never fully understood why. It was in trying to train the third hovering horse that I learned a lot about the biomechanics of the horse. This eventually led me to some real break-throughs in some problems with the passage, and some finer points of technique.

The third horse had been trained to passage prematurely, obviously because it displayed a tendency towards exaggerated steps. This horse was a disaster when I tried longitudinal transitions. The elevation and stiffening got worse. In downward transitions the horse's hind end bounced up and down like an empty wagon on a rough road. This inability to dampen any concussion behind was a catalyst that sent me back to equine locomotion research.

But before we can talk about corrections it is very important to know just how the horse moves in an efficient forward stride. It has been found that the horse's central nervous system triggers very precise limb movements, and there is considerable similarity in the repeating strides.[7] As the horse's hind limb is protracted (see Fig. 1a), the hoof moves forward toward the horse's centre of gravity, and the croup flexes.[8] As it impacts with the ground (Fig. 1b), there is a vertical force generated, a sort of ricochet which has a braking effect on the horse's smooth forward momentum. The planting of the hoof signals the beginning of the stance phase, which can be divided into two parts: the first, in which there is a braking effect which continues until the horse's hips are more

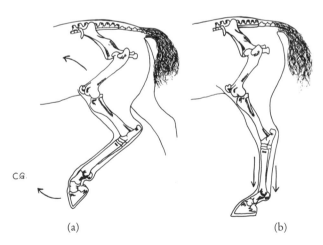

(a)   (b)

Fig. 1 (a) and (b) Hind limb sequence.

or less vertical over the foot; then the second, where propulsion takes over as the horse's centre of gravity is falling or moving forward.[9]

As the hoof impacts, the powerful longissimus dorsi and epaxial muscles of the back contract to resist or to stop the upward push, or one can think of the ground trying to push the horse up into the air.[10] At the same time that the hoof impacts, the stifle and hock are flexing to dampen this shock-wave.

During the stance phase (Fig. 1 c-d), the horse's body is continually moving forward its croup and hips over the hoof planted on the ground, with the fetlock serving as a kind of hub to the spoke-like advance of the leg. Because the stifle is flexing with the croup, sort of pushing down, the femur can come forward, towards vertical, without sending the croup up against the force of gravity. This is a very important phenomenon for the dressage trainer.

Once the horse's hips pass over a vertical line from the planted hoof, the second part of the stance phase, namely the phase of propulsion, begins. The hock will be the

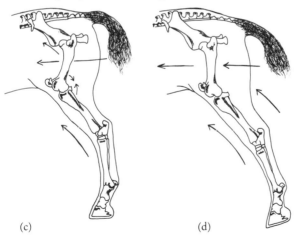

(c)   (d)

Fig. 1 (c) and (d) Hind limb sequence (continued).

[27]

main source of propulsion. Yet even as the hock is extending, the stifle may still be flexing. This insures that the horse's weight will still be falling forward. In this way, the stifle helps the hock minimise the vertical lifting of the hips, and maximises the horizontal push of the hips. The horse cleverly sneaks around the effect of gravity, and provides a stride that is most efficient in forward thrust. As the hock extends, the superficial flexor tendon loosens and this frees the pastern. It strongly rotates forward and now propulsion forces reach maximum.

To a certain extent, although the front limbs are designed more for support than propulsion, a similar action is taking place. As the front hoof impacts with the ground, the joint of the scapula and humerus flexes and the fetlock sinks. This allows the braking forces to be absorbed and the weight of the horse to fall forward. As the front leg approaches vertical, the braking forces subside and the second part of the stance phase, the propulsion, ensues. High-speed films show the entire leg moving steadily forward,

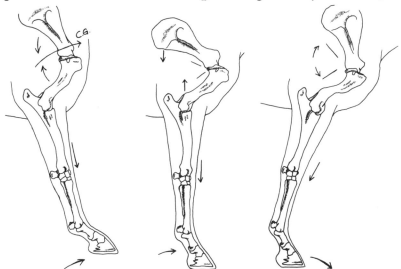

Fig. 2 Front limb sequence.

advancing spokes of an imaginary wheel which has the fetlock as the hub.[11] (See Fig. 2.)

I was continuing my review of some of the equine locomotion and biomechanics literature when one night in the library, I came across a paragraph in a particular study that seized my attention, and in a second crystallised the whole essence of the hover trot. In this study by Kingsbury, Quaddus, Rooney and Geary,[12] they were doing some measuring using live horses and their limbs and cadavered limbs, and some differences were observed. The paragraph that explained these differences reads:

'The major discrepancies between live and severed limbs are to be found in the first segment of the normal, tangential and moment curve. The discrepancies occur as irregular wave forms and are thought to be the result of the absence of the smoothing and pre-stiffening effect of muscle on the stay apparatus . . . the testing system then provides not only positive data in the dynamics of the passive stay apparatus but also on the effects of muscle action on the stay apparatus.'

The paragraph is discussing the muscular effect on the tendo-ligamentus systems. This is what got me. The business of protracting the limbs, and then the rotation around the fetlocks with their sinking and rising, is primarily a reflexive action dependent mostly on tendons and ligaments. The dampening and smoothing of the forward impulse is muscular and largely dependent on flexion in the hip, stifle and hock in the rear, and the shoulder in the front.

My experiences were not jibbing with Seunig's theory. For one thing, none of my hovering horses had a particularly tight back, at least to begin with. In fact, two were long in the back and flexible. The other interesting matter

[29]

was that all three horses were lazy in their way of going and manner. Now things were beginning to fall into place. It was the absence of muscular effort in dampening the stride that let these horses lazily bound along off their tendons and ligaments with little effort toward deepening the step or its complementary powerful propulsion.

Seunig was correct when he said that a tight back facilitates the hovering steps, but was not correct in saying 'a convulsively tightened, tense back produces artificially exalted and exaggerated steps.' My disagreement with the master is not really nit-picking or semantics, because to me there is a serious underlying principle here that is very important in trying to correct trotting flaws in many horses. It has to do with the limbs, not the back. And, later, it is crucial to understanding the passage.

One of the most magical aspects of the biomechanics of a horse in motion is how the stifle can continue to flex in both the braking stage and the propulsion stage of the stance phase – all this in order to keep the horse's hips down and falling forward, away from the force of gravity. When they work together, one extending and one collapsing, the hips stay low and move forward, thus facilitating optimum horizontal thrust. Aside from the rotation of the fetlock, which is primarily a reflexive action and therefore an action which the horseman can only slightly effect, it is really only the stifle, hock and shoulders where conscious muscle manipulation can occur. These are the areas that account for the smooth and impulsive transportation of the horse forward, or, on the other hand, these are the same areas that will collect it.

In that third hovering horse I had in training, it was precisely a lack of muscular effort in flexing the stifle and shoulder that produced the vertical bounding of the hover trot. In the stance phase up front, the knee is locked, so all dampening and changing has to occur in the joint of the scapula and humerus. Likewise, in the stance phase in the rear leg, the hock, until it extends, is fairly locked and braced, so all the dampening and changing has to occur in the stifle and hip. When the horse fails to flex the joints in the stifle, the superficial flexor tendon in the rear leg can't loosen when the hock extends and the fetlock raises against the tightened tendon. The result is that the hips are bounced upward. When this is repeated step after step the horse's centre of gravity bounces up and down with a much diminished forward impulse. What you get is hovering.

My disagreement with Seunig is that the action of the back in a broad way is a reaction to the production of motion by the legs. The action of the back is secondary to the action of the legs. Power must first be generated before the back can react to it. The action of the back cannot produce any steps at all, elastic or 'exalted and exaggerated'. The action of the legs, and more specifically the muscular action of the shoulder, stifle and hock, must produce swift, strong, forward impulsive movement. The inaction of the legs, and again more specifically the muscular inaction of the shoulder, stifle and hock, produces hovering steps. This subject is much more pertinent to the passage, which comes up later, but I don't want to minimise the importance of the back.

Once I understood the mechanics of the hovering flaw, ways to correct it became more apparent and more successful. Longitudinal flexing exercises, such as the series of transitions I practised on the second hovering horse, can work, if the rider can get the horse to work the joints of the hind leg and set the balance more toward the rear. However, if, as in the third hovering horse I tried to train, the movement has become habitual, and the inflexibility of the stifle is really confirmed, then transitions will not be very effective. It will be too easy for the horse to bounce the croup up in the downward transition rather than to flex in the hip, stifle and hock, and 'dampen' the step. The trainer will have a difficult time loading the haunches without great force, which is not the way for an *ecuyer*.

Much more effective is the use of proper lateral exercises, in particular the shoulder-in but also the renvers and half-pass. The shoulder-in has great value as a unilateral exercise. In the left shoulder-in, the rider/trainer can work specifically on the joints of the left hind and this specific loading can make a particularly stiff leg more flexible. Also by working one side at a time in a curve, the rider can arrest the attempt of the horse to stiffen the back, which is certainly what Seunig noticed. The half-pass becomes an enigmatic exercise because it has different effects depending on how shallow the rider traverses sideways. In a fairly straight, shallow half-pass in which the horse is properly bent around the rider's inside leg, the horse's inside leg will work up under the curved body and take up a good deal of loading. As the half-pass moves more radically to the side, and stays parallel to the wall, this demands more cross-over by the hind legs. There is going to be a reverse relationship to loading and the outside leg will have to become more and more prevalent to push the mass of the horse over to the side.

When one sees radical half-passes performed at the Spanish Riding School, one always sees considerable angle in the horses. The shoulders are quite a bit ahead of the hindquarters. The horses are not kept parallel to the wall as one sees in competition horses. The result of more angle is an insurance that the horse will stay classically bent and more loaded on the inside leg and not turn the movement into a flat-out traverse with much cross-over and more push from the outside leg.

By understanding these effects and then using combinations and repetitions of these exercises, I found I could interrupt the habitual pattern of the flawed gait. Secondly because of their ability to work specific sets of muscles unilaterally, I could build strength and flexibility more or less on one side or the other. Thirdly, by frequent changes from left rein to right rein, one has a barometer to compare the sides of the horse, thereby checking development. Finally, by curving the body of the horse, not the neck, repeatedly in rein changes from left to right exercises, the back becomes more flexible laterally and longitudinally along with the joints of the legs.

The hovering trot is a muscular problem. Like most ways of going, predisposition to it is probably genetic. However, the trainer can make headway if he realises the sites at which the work must take place: namely, the stifle, hip, hock and shoulder. Then he needs to apply creatively the traditional exercises to develop flexibility and strength in those areas.

In my impudent challenge of the great horsemaster, I learned something else: that almost all descriptions that become frozen by words are usually on their way toward becoming something else. This is what I alluded to in the introduction. During the Journey the horseman may arrive back at a city where he has already been and find that the city has changed. Beneath one civilisation lies another and another. The Buddhist master used to say that the student must stand on the shoulders of the teacher in order to see farther. Every learning person builds his case as solidly as possible, not to hold it in eternity by its great construction, but to serve as an honourable base well built for something to go on top of it.

In the development of the technical, there are two things going on. One is a pragmatic procedure, brought about by trying to do something quicker, smoother, more efficiently – the world of logical physical development.

[33]

Simultaneously, one's mind is in a floating mode. Even in, and perhaps especially in, ritualised practice, one is aware of another world – the world of the psyche, the creative world, the world of change. Only in this world can new development come out. Only by tapping into this world is any adaptation possible.

Seunig's words are not really wrong any more than mine are right. What they really become are sort of constructs like poems, which encourage by their existence the process of looking. Only by really looking can you really ride.

Chapter Three

Rockin' and Rollin' in the Passage

I ONCE HEARD a painter explain that after he had worked on one painting for a long time, he would find he got a little blind to his work. When this happened he would often look at his painting through a mirror. In this simple inversion the painting would be revitalised for him, and with this fresh vision he would see all kinds of things he wanted to work on. Very often I have learned my greatest lessons about certain movements by dealing with flaws that prevented me or a particular horse I was training from accomplishing them. In trying to correct some of the inversions, or faults, in the training of passage, I began to see more and more what the passage was not. The mysterious, beautiful passage defined itself as I cut through layer after layer of the disguises of evasion.

BALANCÉ

Whenever I go to horse shows I am always drawn to the warm-up areas – even more than to the actual finished performances or exhibitions. On one particular day I was at an international horse show watching several horses warm up. A young man and his horse began to practise passage. As they warmed up the horse was trying harder and harder. The young man was being coached and after a bit the coach kept saying, 'Balancé. It's balancé. You must ride the horse more forward. More forward!' He spoke louder. The more the young man tried, the worse the balancé got. I could not help but empathise with the young rider. I had been in his position, and when the passage gets into stronger and stronger balancé, it can feel like you are riding an octopus with legs reaching out in every direction. It had been at least ten years since I had first ridden the passage on the Lusitano horses of Portugal, who were masters of the air. I know that I did not realise at the time how sublime this experience was. Nor how long it would take to be able to train a horse myself to do a passage even near that expressive. Nor how many ways one could go wrong.

So what is this balancé (bal/un/say) and will riding more forward help? If so, why?

When the trainer at that show implored his student to move the horse more forward to correct the passage, his advice was hardly unique. Yet it was not working. Riding the passage more forward (i.e. getting more engagement behind) is the proposed cure for practically **all** problems of the passage. A review of much of the riding literature

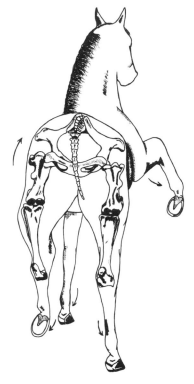

*Fig. 3 The balancé in passage – the front leg action is exaggerated
when compared to the hind leg action.*

will also attest to this. I have found precious little advice
on correcting the problems of balancé, or rolling in of the
front legs, or swinging hind legs, etc. When I have asked
many trainers to tell me why they think riding the horse
forward works, it is usually a similar answer that the hind
end is not carrying enough load, or it is being too inac-
tive. Yet why do so many problems of passage manifest
themselves in the odd action of the front limbs. To sum-
marily dismiss the balancé as a problem of the hind legs
was just too easy. So I went back to the scientists to study
movement again and again, and little by little the motion
revealed itself.

The balancé has been described as a circus passage. In general, when a horse passages in balancé, the front leg action is exaggerated as compared to the hind leg action. Furthermore the traditional description is also that as each front leg lifts into and through its exaggerated position it does not move straight but moves over to the side. The result is that the horse seems to sway from left to right and vice versa. For me the key descriptive identifier of balancé is that in the stance phase of each front leg, the hoof will be placed away from the horse's body (see Fig. 3), stretched out over its respective side. The left foot will reach out over to the left and the right over to the right. Whenever a horse starts to widen its stance, it usually is trying to widen its base of support. There is a physical rule which states that for an object to remain upright, a line drawn down from its centre of gravity must fall within its base of support. If the horse starts widening its stance on either front leg or hind, that can be the tip-off to where the horse is trying to carry the load.

The first matter to consider is how is this possible, since this kind of movement is unique to the front limbs. The front limbs have this greater facility for sideways motion because in the front legs there are no bony attachments to the trunk of the horse.[13] This allows for a lot of room for muscular adjustment, and therefore, muscular effect.

Even though the front limbs are primarily constructed for receiving force, as we have already noted, it is often forgotten that they can also generate considerable force. In the balancé the horse is deliberately using the forelimbs to help propel itself upward into a passage. In their effort to extend and propel forward they also generate sideways force. In a passage where the horizontal forward force is restrained and the upward vertical force is accented, the sideways force can be substantial. When the

[38]

left front pushes off, extending through the second half of the stance phase, it forces the shoulder and trunk sideways, at which point the right front limb reaches out and plants itself to block sideways push, and returns it over to the left with its own extension. The front legs then are bouncing the horse's centre of gravity from side to side, as well as vertically up for passage. Forward riding at that point can eliminate the balancé because it re-establishes the horizontal forces of the trot and takes the emphasis off the vertical forces which define the passage. However, although forward riding may eliminate balancé, it might not necessarily help the horse's passage. He must learn to handle these vertical forces.

Although it is true that the hind end needs to carry more weight, that the centre of balance must be shifted more onto the hind legs with better engagement and better flexion, I think it is a real mistake to assume that the horse is not working in balancé and therefore needs to be pushed more. When the rider at the show in the beginning of this chapter tried to drive the passage more forward the horse only exaggerated the balancé. In my experience I have found that in balancé the horse may be working very hard, but he is working the wrong end, if you will. The horse can be confused and needs to be calmed down. The balancé showed me how a horse can try to balance its weight, to try to show a passage, but it is a passage that keeps the stifle and hock from doing the greater work. This does not mean that the horse is categorically lazy. It is my feeling now that, again, more forward riding can eliminate the balancé because it re-establishes the horizontal forces, but we need the vertical element in order to display real passage. In my opinion the cure lies in more fundamental collection. If the rear end and abdomen of the horse is systematically prepared and gets stronger and more flexible, it will be

[39]

able to carry more weight. The attempt can go too far, though, if the trainer crouches the horse too far down and forward with the hind legs. They can be cramped and will actually lose carrying power. Once the collection is cleaned, then and only then, will the horse be able to attempt passage without the over-zealous help from the front limbs.

There are, of course, many ways to develop and improve collection with more flexion and extension in the hock, stifle and hip. Some of these exercises are three hundred years old and still relevant. 'Trotting and stopping a horse is the foundation of all airs. They settle his head and croup and put him well up in his haunches and make him light before.' – Duke of Newcastle.[3] Progressive transitions develop flexibility and carrying power. Short-trot-to-walk transitions and vice versa, walk-to-soft-piaffe steps, longer-trot-to-collected-trot – all of these have a similar effect, of which Newcastle knew so much.

I think work in hand is also very useful in developing the action and strength of the stifle and hock. This is especially true in the early stages because, being an unmounted exercise, it is easier for the horse to find its own newer balance over the rear.

Perhaps the most important thing to remember in all these exercises, is that in order for them to have the desired gymnastic effect, the rider must use as little hand as possible. This not being the case, the horse will be blocked from using its neck properly, and also the horse may tip onto the forehand due to the hand's braking effect. The transition, especially downward, needs to be controlled by the rider's back, seat and leg. At the moment of the downward transition, the hands become passive but the rider almost holds the horse forward with his back and abdomen pressed toward the pommel. The upper body stretches tall so that the rider does not lean back. The thighs close to give strength to the back and to help absorb some of the roughness that is bound to occur when young horses are learning transitions. The experienced rider of young horses will dissipate some of the shock of the transition throughout the upper leg. This does not mean so much grip that it holds the rider up off the horse. No. It is a commonsense adjustment to keep the young horse from hollowing through the downward transitions, which would have an opposite effect of building a round horse. The rider keeps the driving aids on to teach the horse to go through the transitions, to carry itself behind and not throw itself on the forehand. This is done with constant repetitions. The joints of the rear will then develop more flexibility and strength until it is capable of sinking under and holding itself in balance in soft but powerfully flexible transitions. Finally, the horse develops such strength and flexibility that it will be able to propel the centre of gravity more upward as in the passage without needing the assistance of the front legs. Without the force of the front legs, the balancé will disappear. This I know from experience.

ROLLING IN AT THE PASSAGE

Another deviant relative of the passage is one that is again most noticeable in the action of the front legs. It can be seen in the passage when the front legs roll toward each other with the hooves being placed on the ground closer and closer to each other. In some of the worse cases the hooves will land during the stance phases under the chest in the same single track or even criss-cross to leave two tracks on the ground, but of the opposite legs! At first glance this seems to be the flip side of balancé. However, rolling in embodies the complexity of certain evasions and exposes the necessity of having to look at evasions holistically. The rider needs to keep an open mind lest he forces the horse into what he thinks is proper movement.

Between the shoulders and the hips of the horse, the individual vertebrae of the spinal column form a linked bridge. The bottom of those vertebrae make an upward curve, and in a very real way, the trunk hangs off this great arch. It is important to remember that it is the bottom of the vertebrae that form the upward curve because a look at the top-line of the horse can be deceiving. Since the vertebrae of the withers and then again at the hips are higher, it gives the appearance of the back sinking down when in fact it is actually curved upward, forming a strong arch. The muscles of the back can stiffen this arch so that propulsion generated by the rear legs will drive straight up through the shoulders and forward with the most efficient horizontal force. The opposite effect is like that found in the sophisticated bumpers of modern cars. Upon impact or force, the bumper is designed to continuously collapse, absorbing the impact force and dissipating it to deaden the rigid shock and absorb the energy. For the maximum horizontal movement the horse's back does not want to absorb and deaden the propulsion of the rear. It wants to relay it forward through its strength and firmness.

We know already from our look at the hover trot, that the passage will require some transfer of the efficient horizontal push into the more dramatic, albeit less efficient, vertical push. Imagine, then, as the left hind pushes off powerfully for passage, sending the horse less forward but more upward in great suspension, there will be a forward or horizontal force and an upward or vertical force. If the back of the horse is too weak and disconnected the upward force of the left hind pushing off the ground will throw the left hip upward and set off an axial

[42]

twist* (see Fig. 4). Since its force is greater than its diagonal partner, the right front, the body of the horse will turn during suspension, forcing the right shoulder to dip down and the right legs to swing under the chest. In this kind of rolling there is good impulsion and engagement but the back of the horse needs strengthening so it will act more normally as in standard forward trotting. There the epaxial muscles etc. resist the torque and keep the horse level. Round transitions and shoulder-ins can help to stretch and strengthen such backs.

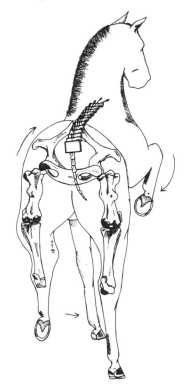

Fig. 4 The effect of a weak or disconnected back in passage (see text).

*For more information on axial rotation, see Leach paper, 'Kinematics of the equine thoracolumbar spine', Townsend, H.G.G., Leach, D.H., and Fretz, P.B., *Equine Veterinary Journal*, 1983, 15(2), 117-122.

Fig. 5 Front view of rolling in passage.

There can be another kind of rolling in: where there is little engagement from behind. The horse is not carrying the movement more on the hind legs and the centre of gravity is too far forward towards the shoulders. In an effort to help support the passage, the front limbs swing under the torso toward the centre of gravity in the middle of the body to support the overburdened forehand in their stance phase (see Fig. 5). This rolling in is a sort of flip side of balancé. Obviously exercises to correct this kind of defect will differ from the first rolling in. Here the horse needs more collecting and engagement to achieve more carrying power. More carrying power in the hind legs will free up the front limbs from their support work so they can travel out straight again.

Rolling in can be further complicated by actions of the head and neck of the horse, which can account for five per cent of the horse's bodyweight. Even slight deviations in the carrying or movement of the head and neck can have a drastic effect on the limb travel of the horse.

Stiff shoulders which restrict forward reach of the front limbs can encourage inward movement which will have the same stance and swing time as a full passage – except that now the front leg does not swing out and forward, but it swings stiffly in towards the body. Here the shoulder-in can be very useful in developing more flexibility in the shoulder, and freedom in the torso.

Obviously there are also deviations in travel and use of the hind legs. For example, if the horse is in balancé with the front legs generating more vertical force than the hind legs, and if the back is twisting, one sees a reverse of the rolling passage (see Fig. 6). Namely, the front legs are standing wide and the shoulders bind up and twist the

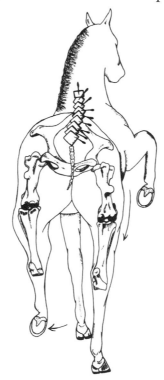

Fig. 6 Rear view of horse in balancé, but with an additional problem –
he is exhibiting an action that is the reverse of the rolling passage (see text).

[45]

opposite hip down causing that hind leg to roll under. The problem is dual: firstly, the centre of gravity is too far forward on the front legs; and secondly, the back is not solid and is lacking in resilient strength. When a passage has this much wrong with it, the horse needs fundamental work, and I think is categorically in over its head. The efforts to passage have to stop until better collection can be maintained together with flexibility. Flexibility in collection demands great strength from the horse and this kind of muscular development takes time. Fortunately there are many riding books, old and new, which carefully list and describe the whole transition of these traditional exercises and in the proper order of training.

In general, exercises which combine deep work and collection will develop strength and flexibility longitudinally. I think one always needs to keep in mind longitudinal exercises, be they collecting or stretching. These need to be done with the spine and top-line in extension. If the neck gets above the bit and shortens, or it gets below the bit and shortens, the effect can be the same: the back vertebrae fully flex or become hollow the moment this occurs. Roundness is lost. The hind legs get locked out behind because of the pressure on the top-line. Without good roundness and reach under by the hind legs, all transitions will fail. This is why one can see horses who passage hollowly, stop and make themselves round before they can go into piaffe. You might get away with a hollow passage and a hyperflexed back, and you might even get away with a hollow piaffe, but you will not get through the transitions of passage into piaffe. If the hind legs are camped out behind, they cannot come smoothly up a little more for the piaffe. If the horse is already round in the passage, then to become a little rounder for the piaffe is not deadly.

There are certainly many more deviations of the hind limbs but some of them I feel are better exposed in the piaffe. However, I think it is very important for the rider/trainer to have a system for investigating these deviations and then developing a knowledge of the traditional exercises which can be applied to specific weaknesses or flaws. As I have tried to show, blanket corrections such as riding forward can be too general to eradicate some of the idiosyncratic evasions that will develop if one trains more than one horse. As I alluded earlier it was in the struggle with these evasions, the feints of the false passages, that the real passage began to solidify before me.

MORE THOUGHTS ON PASSAGE

In the hover trot, the horse bounces its centre of gravity up and down. Its lazy forward motion is propelled seemingly only by tendo-ligamentous action. Muscle flexion and extensions of the stifle, hock and shoulder seem to be minimal.

In the balancé the horse is energised by the rider, but the centre of gravity is towards the shoulders and as the horse throws its weight vertically up with its front legs in an attempt to passage, it also pushes its torso to the side. The horse's centre of gravity is bouncing up and down, but it is also bouncing in the third dimension – sideways, left and right. The stifle and hock are carrying less weight than the shoulders.

In the rolling passage, the horse can be often well energised. The stifle and hock are extending and flexing exuberantly. There is good forward and vertical force, but the back and shoulders break apart. The horse begins to twist through the bridge of its back so that when the left hind pushes up, it forces its diagonal partner, the right front, down and under, and vice versa.

There is often much talk about propulsion in the passage – all this great thrust. My feeling is that this kind of language is better suited to describe the extended trot. The passage reveals its trademark in its conscious adjustment of the muscles which flex the hips, stifle, hock and shoulder, and pull this trot up in the air with an equally great horizontal and vertical extension. It is not the stiff recoil off the pasterns like the tendo-ligamentous hover trot which is simply reflexive. No. It is a conscious interruption of the simple reflex, a controlled exhibition of the greatest and smoothest joint flexion and extension. It is a display of trained flexibility and strength. The spine of the horse is supported at two places: one, at the forelegs and shoulder; and the other at the sacroilliac joint in the hind legs. Any area in between these two connections can twist, especially when moving.[13] In the passage the back muscles do two things simultaneously: they must be strong enough to transmit the considerable forward force of the passage, and absorb the twisting effects due to the vertical forces generated by the hind legs. The back must be flexible enough to swing and even bend as in ultimate passage on two tracks. Since the passage is principally a two-time gait with the same stance and swing time, the shoulder then, although not necessarily matching in propulsion, must match the rear in flexibility.

What makes the passage so difficult is its requirement for great flexibility in the joint of the limbs, and great strength to deliberately interrupt the reflexive trotting stride, which has a more horizontal force, and consciously extend the stifle early so that it sends the horse more upward with less horizontal force and more vertical force. All this must occur without any major lateral deviation of the limbs' travel direction. Finally, it must be symmetrical and even, regardless of which diagonal pair is doing it. To accomplish this, the horse must be gymnastically prepared over a relatively long period of time, and tested slowly. The trainer has to be careful to avoid

[48]

over-working the movement. As soon as the horse stops carrying the load behind, or loses its balance, evasions will appear. This is especially true in a game horse or an ambitious trainer. Even though a horse may be mentally ready, the work has to go slowly because it takes much longer for the musculature to develop over the comprehension. It is my feeling now that the great majority of evasions are the result of muscular inadequacies with the game horse. Unable to execute the strenuous passage, this horse tries to compensate and the dull trainer forgets to interrupt.

In general the passage is trained in one of two broad systems. The first and most traditional and popular is to train the passage out of the piaffe. In this system, the passage will be developed by lengthening the great collection of the piaffe. The centre of gravity is already well set back toward the rear. If the trainer advances this piaffe rhythm judiciously forward, he can keep the balance more toward the rear because careful acceleration will keep the weight back. This will avoid falling into many of the balancing problems that occur when the balance gets too far out over the front legs.

There is a funny thing about the piaffe-to-passage transition. If the trainer allows the horse to jump into the passage and change the shape of its back, i.e. become too flat, he may get away with it on the transition upward. But he will pay for it when he tries to make the transition from passage back to piaffe. The horse, as I have said, will not be able to round the back without first stopping the passage and then regenerating the piaffe which always seems faulty.

The second broad system is to train the passage by restraining the extension forces. By holding in a medium trot, compressing the horse at the urge to extend, when the horizontal forces are dammed up, the force gets transferred up and vertically into the suspension of passage. This system, which works through restraining forces, has built into it a serious pitfall. Namely, the braking forces inherent in any restraint can tip the balance forward onto the shoulders and off the haunches. Knowing what we do about balancé it takes a little imagination to see that it is easy to develop front-end deviations if too much weight is being carried by the forehand. Furthermore if the horse gets used to the suspension of passage with its balance more in the middle, it can be very difficult to get the horse to settle back on its haunches in piaffe out of passage, and learn the passage-piaffe transitions.

If the horse is already in a proper passage, the balance will be on four legs, but a little more toward the rear. The transition from passage into piaffe will require the moving horse to shift the balance even farther toward the rear. This is especially difficult while moving forward with some horizontal force. It takes great strength and even more flexion and extension in the hock than that already being shown by the horse. There is also a risk when shortening the passage to use the reins and to stiffen the back, which, as we already have seen, can lead to rolling. It is a transition of great demands. This is the reason why, in general, trainers have preferred to train the passage out of the collection of the piaffe.

There are always exceptions with horses, and flexibility in training regimens is the hallmark of a good trainer/rider. In any case I think General Decarpentry's advice is worth nothing:

'In whichever order the passage and the piaffe are obtained, the trainer's big difficulty will always be the transition from one to the other, the perfect 'blending' of the two which is the major part of the artistic value of these movements as a whole . . .'[14]

He goes on to say that this is a good reason to start 'conventionalising' the trot at both ends simultaneously, i.e. start passage and piaffe at the same time. I think this is good advice.

Some years ago a controversial project to restore Michaelangelo's painting in the Sistine Chapel was undertaken. In great privacy, using space-age techniques, the most careful process of washing began. When it was finished, by all accounts there was a spectacular difference. Flesh tones that had faded to grey were now restored as if to life. The paintings' original colours were astonishing. Then the most amazing thing happened. Many great authorities of art hated it. There was a barrage of criticism – some of it highly intellectual, some instinctive. Obviously many 'experts' had come to like the artwork dirty and dull. Maybe in its darkened amorphous state they had more room for their own interpretations, more room to make it their own. Over a period of time, even the most sophisticated opinions had trouble holding their voices – because it was clear above everything else that Michaelangelo did not paint it overcast in grey and brown. In the end, every arguer, no matter how powerful, political, dogmatic, erudite or clever, had to stand in front of Michaelangelo himself and tell him why his own creation was somehow lacking in its original colours.

Every horse has a passage in its own original colour. The way I see it, the best trainers 'wash' the movements of the developing horse over and over to take off filtering affectations, to find the original, the natural, the real. But there has always been a class of trainers who set themselves apart because of their erudition, charm, sophistication or power. They are like the art critics. They need to make the horse's movements their own.

[51]

They seem always to want to do better than the natural and original. If you train a horse this way, always trying to add something, instead of washing something off, you can lose the dignity of the original horse, whichever one you are working with.

You have forgotten why you are riding, and someday when you are telling the horse how he must move, you will have to stand in front of him and convince him that Michaelangelo could not really paint either.

Chapter Four

The Piaffe

ONE SUMMER, through a twist of fate, the dressage rider and trainer John Winnett came to the area where I live. Eventually, and for a time toward that winter, he kept his horses at our stable. John was one of the most experienced international competitive dressage riders in the United States. At the time we each had a chestnut coloured Grand Prix horse and we were asked to try to prepare a Pas de Deux. John was always helpful to me and I enjoyed his company.

John was raised in France and by his own admission began riding in a Baucherist tradition. Later he knew and worked with many of the top German riders and trainers, having spent years living and competing in Germany. This fascinated me and I always wanted him to pursue these differences and similarities in his writings and conversations – especially from a historical sense. I thought his situation was unique and his perceptions valuable. I was curious as to his ideas and how he synthesised these apparently different approaches into his own dressage. Having sat through several meetings that concerned American dressage, engaged in lengthy discussions with him, I think John got bored with those endless historical arguments and I remember he almost chided me that we had come a long way from Baucher and Guérinière.

It was that statement that came to my mind when I was walking into the library at New Bolton Center, the famous large animal hospital and equine research facility of the University of Pennsylvania. New Bolton is only three miles from our farm. It is set right in the middle of some old horse country. This evening it was snowing as I drove by the post and railed pastures on either side of the road. There were no other cars as I passed the old brick and stone farmhouses and the horses. The Jean Austin Dupont Library is housed in a research unit at New Bolton. I walked into the warm building. It was quiet inside. During part of the winter when students come out from the city campus, the library is open at night. There are rarely more than a few people there and the research folk are usually gone.

As I walked down the hall it was shadowy, lacking the brightness of the daytime lighting. State-of-the-art machines hummed. I passed by rooms for 'Microbiology Research'; heavy doors warning: 'BIOHAZARD – Extremely Infectious Agents Inside'; locked doors with elaborate time-clocks; autoclaves; sterilising rooms; rooms for medical research. The office for 'Cytogenetics' had a board outside naming some of the breakthroughs in identifying chromosome abnormalities. I felt I was in some space-age cell which had entered a quieter pause for the evening. This is a place where searches take off into the unknown; where excitement emanates from even the most obscure discoveries – even the potential for discovery. Always there is the sound of beautifully wierd and specific machines of high science.

I had come to read from two old volumes of the Duke of Newcastle's (William Cavendish) *A General System of Horsemanship in all Its Branches.* It is over three hundred and fifty years old. At New Bolton, The Fairman Rogers Collection contains a magnificent assemblage of historical equestrian masterpieces. These are kept under lock and key and I have been given permission to study them in the library.

When I walked into the small modern library, the irony of this place and John's words came poignantly to life. On the left side of a small aisle are the wood and glass cases which house the works of Guérinière, the Duke of Newcastle, Pluvinel, Baucher, Seeger, and hundreds of leather-bound treatises. On the right are stacks of the most current research articles published in veterinary journals, and magazines, books and records of conferences. In some ways a step across that three-foot aisle could traverse hundreds of years of horsemanship.

At times it is difficult to place this distance in perspective. For many people that aisle of just three feet can represent an impassable chasm. To some modern horsemen the literature on the left is archaic, antique and useless. To some other old-fashioned horsemen, horsemanship has not advanced since these writings. For these horsemen the equitation of today is a pure regression from those earlier times.

Tonight the library is practically deserted, and there is

[55]

something in this chilly winter evening that plays on my mind in a melancholy way. As I stare at the physically small space of the aisle, I realise that all the writer-riders to the left are dead. Whereas, to the right most of the writers are alive. It isn't a morbid feeling that I have, just weighty, sombre. I am thinking about all the great thoughts there, the lessons, the calibre of these horsemen. I dwell on the idea of the words on the pages – as each one was written it became fixed in time and space; it has no chance to grow anymore. New explanations, even by the same writer, will need new words. So the written word cannot grow as can the man or woman who wrote it, but neither can it grow old, as can its author. It is a strange deal: the immortal but fixed word, and the mortal but moveable man. When I look at all the books and words of Guérinière, Pluvinel, Newcastle, Steinbrecht, Baucher, Grisone, all right there, it is like seeing a great equestrian graveyard. And yet, from any study of these words, one sees how one horseman picked up the dead words of another and moved them in some way. So the seemingly stiff and unchangeable words may become enhanced or they may be abused – but they are moved.

Ideas have moved on and fanned out like a river at a delta. Rivulets wind and dry up, or wind and rewind, or wind and rejoin. Wherever you stand in your time, if you turn around and look back at the delta, you know that back there through the thousands of twists and dead-ends is the same source. The journey back on this river of words sometimes dries up in the archaic – like an unadaptable species, it becomes extinct. But then in others the source is vibrant and pulsing. At these moments Guéninière can come alive for you. Pluvinel can point to something just for you. You feel the attitude of the Duke of Newcastle as if you, yourself, were being rebuked.

The Piaffe

No matter what some people would have you believe, that river of words has never stopped and it does not stop at that aisle in this library. It isn't easy to follow it sometimes. Like desert streams which can go underground to surface surprisingly in another part of the country, these rivers of words can go underground, disappearing seemingly without trace, only to surface again, sometimes in an archaic form and sometimes amazingly current. It is worth the trouble to try to follow these courses. It is in these always-moving rivers of information, these lineages of knowledge, that many of the answers to the problems of training horses lie. Great riders have told you something. They thought it was important.

Sometimes the movements that we train reflect the forces of vibrancy, and sometimes the forces of extinction. A movement like *'aubin'** is not seen any more. Even *'terre à terre'*†, although it is still performed in France, is almost extinct. If the modern horseman were to read Pluvinel without help, he might not know what kinds of movements the master is talking about. But the piaffe! There is vibrancy. The piaffe travels right across that aisle easily. Everybody knows about the piaffe, don't they?

Before we look at the mechanics of this movement, there is an important introductory perspective that has to be mentioned. It later explained to me how it is possible for there to be so much confusion about what constitutes a good quality piaffe among some apparently knowledgeable modern horsemen.

It has to do with the use of the piaffe, if you will, because there is a considerable difference between its past use and its common use today. I call these differences

---

* *aubin* = canter in front, trot behind.

† *terre à terre* = a kind of rocking back and forth from both front legs to both hind legs.

[57]

Piaffe as Preparation, and *Piaffe as Culmination*. In the past, even though the piaffe was practised as an 'air' in itself, as was *terre à terre*, it was also the critical springboard for all the jumps or 'airs above the ground'. The piaffe, because of its collecting abilities, prepared the horse just before the moment of take-off, by getting the haunches to begin to pull the weight back and carry it on the hindquarters, thereby freeing the forelegs to come off the ground entirely. If you watch practice sessions at Saumur or the Spanish Riding School, you will see the exuberant horses often piaffing vigorously just before the set-up for a capriole or courbette. Sometimes *terre à terre* is also seen. In my opinion this is why one can still observe excellent piaffe at those places. It is not only because of the conformation and breeding of the horse, it is also because the jumps keep the piaffe honest. The forehand must be light and free because in a second it is going to come up entirely off the ground in a very specific and controlled jump executed entirely on the hind legs.

Today we mostly see *piaffe as culmination*. Very few people in the world still practise the airs above the ground. In competitions they are not allowed, and the piaffe is the summit of the FEI's requirements. The result is that today you can see complex evasions occuring in the piaffe, primarily because they are misbalanced in one way or another. Sometimes these piaffes are executed by clever horses, sometimes they are trained by clever riders. Nevertheless, they are the piaffes that score well in competitions and fulfil the requirements of the rules of competition. But they are piaffes that no horse could ever jump out of in a controlled way because they are not being carried by the hind legs and are balanced more towards the reins.

When you analyse the piaffe from its classical descriptions, you see a two-beat gait, a kind of trot in place or what has sometimes been called passage on the spot. Neither of these phrases is adequate. The harmony of the piaffe comes from the diagonal pairs of legs having approximately the same stance and swing time. The piaffe gets its rhythm from the left hind and right front staying on the ground for the same amount of time, then smoothly transferring to the other diagonal pair. What happens in the swing time is a very different story.

The traditional description, in general, is that piaffe allows for the hind foot of the horse to raise off the ground to the coronet band, or so. The exact place is not that important providing both hind feet raise to the same height along with the requirements of engagement. The front feet should raise up halfway up the cannon – sometimes more, sometimes less. What is important here is that the front feet have been traditionally asked to come off the ground approximately twice as high as the hinds. Now, if the stance time is the same for front and rear legs, it goes without saying that the swing time, the time in the air, must also be the same. Yet we have this requirement that during the same swing time, or same amount of time off ground, the front feet must travel twice as far (twice as high). It doesn't take a genius to realise that the front feet must therefore travel twice as fast as the hind ones. Then something important happens because one of the first requirements of the classic piaffe, contrary to a lot of opinion, is that it not be symmetrical front to back in spite of its sublime appearance. If you ask how this is possible, the first thing that comes up is that the haunches are carrying more load so the front legs will be more unencumbered. Relieving them of some of the weight-bearing duties, they will be able to travel faster. In this respect a classic piaffe should prove that the horse is carrying his weight with the hind legs and that the rider has mastered collection. It seems logical then to say that if a horse displays a piaffe with the front feet moving up to mid-cannon and the hind feet moving up to the coronet, and the diagonal pairs have the same stance and swing times, it must be a classical piaffe.

The answer is no. The reason is that some horses can stay in this rhythm, meeting these requirements, but they can hold the bulk of the balance on their front legs and even one front leg. Such a horse can show a deceptively low hind end and raise its front feet high, and yet hide from the first and most important requirement, namely that the piaffe show ultimate collection, i.e. that it is being balanced more on the rear legs. How can a horse or rider do this? One way is for the horse to 'triangulate'.

TRIANGULATION IN THE PIAFFE

One year I was given a gift of a clock for the stable, and on its face is a graphic silhouette of a horse in a piaffe. I have seen this particular shape of piaffe in countless advertisements and horse magazines. No doubt it seems like a great piaffe to the artist, to the many illustrators who draw it over and over again, and to many advertising people who use pictures of horses piaffing in this form. The hind legs are always well engaged under the horse. The croup seems deep set, with one hind foot in elevation, at least to the coronet band but usually higher. The front leg that is raised is high and proud. But the stance-phase leg is always pointed or slanted back toward the hind feet. In all its different versions the common denominator is that the front feet creep back toward the centre of gravity, and the hind feet creep forward, moving towards one another and forming the point of a triangle. The front legs form one side of the triangle, the hind legs form another, while the body of the horse forms the third

Fig. 7 Triangulation in the piaffe.

(see Fig. 7). When the horse begins to bring its front legs back from the vertical, it ceases to matter what is happening behind because even if it looks deeply engaged, it is false. The front legs are shifting back to get under the centre of gravity and to relieve the hind legs. This is the opposite of the classical piaffe, which demands that the hind legs carry the load.

The curious thing I have learned about this triangulation is that it is often caused by the over-zealous trainer, who in an effort to really load the haunches, pushes them *too* far under the horse so they become very cramped. When they become this stretched they have no room to flex, and, more importantly, the stance leg cannot extend properly because the centre of gravity always seems behind the hind legs. Remember that in the trotting stride there are two phases: the braking phase, where the hips flex upon the foot hitting the ground; then as the hips move over the foot, the propulsion phase takes over and propels the centre of gravity which is falling downward, forward. If the hind legs are always too far forward of the hips, and the horse is held on the spot, the propulsion phase can't happen. The centre of gravity of the hind end must move forward over the leg, where extension can propel the weight vertically and horizontally. The horse, realising that it can't propel, shifts its front legs back to relieve the cramped hindquarters and, as in the balancé at passage, it uses its shoulders to help carry more weight. This is why the best riding masters always insist in training that the piaffe move forward a little. In triangulated piaffes, the haunches can be very deep set and the hocks very well flexed and yet be carrying almost no weight. Lowering the haunches does not necessarily mean that one has loaded them. This apparently deep-set piaffe is exactly the opposite of the classical piaffe in that it is actually carrying more weight on the shoulders and on the front legs. This is a classic example of *piaffe as culmination* – the piaffe looks all right, but a horse could never jump out of it without changing the balance.

Although clarification of this mechanism has come about through analysis of some very high-speed films and in through reviewing some current research in biomechanics, it is very clear that among knowledgeable trainers of *haute école* this problem of falsely deep-set haunches was known. The Duke of Newcastle[3] says that the whole study is to put the manège horse on the haunches, but that it is important to understand when the horse is really on his haunches and when not. He clearly explains that a horse can be almost sitting on his croup but will not be on his haunches if his hind legs are too distant from their normal and natural lines 'which is to have them (too) much asunder'. He then describes how the horse should have as much flexion, bending in the

[62]

hock, as possible but the legs should not deviate from their normal position.

(Sometimes a horse that does a piaffe which, as French writers often say, resembles a passage on the spot – meaning the front and hind legs move closer in symmetry and the haunches don't sink excessively – can actually be more classical. This shows better collection even if the croup is a little higher than in a horse which shows a piaffe with a deeply set hind end but is holding it up with the front legs.)

There is a very good analogy for triangulation in human locomotion: when a person who has an injured hip walks and leans the upper body over the injured hip when that leg is in its stance phase – on the ground. By moving the centre of gravity toward the injured hip, the person reduces the moment (a product of quantity [as force] and the distance to axis) in the stance phase. Perhaps more simple put, he reduces the force on that hip in the stance phase. The triangulating horse moves the front leg back. Thus both human and horses are leaning or balancing toward their respective centre of gravity in order to reduce the stress or work of moving correctly in balance over all limbs. The curious thing is that in correcting the human's way of going, the physiotherapist will give the patient a cane for support – but in the oppsite hand! The therapist wants to establish the correct balance over two limbs. If one uses the cane on the same side as the injured hip it will allow the patient to put even more unbalanced weight over that side.

In this therapy lies the clue for correcting triangulation in the horse as well. Namely the trainer must allow and encourage the hind legs to back away from the front feet. Then, uncramped, they will be able to carry their share of the weight and relieve the front legs, which will also return more towards the perpendicular.

PIAFFE WITH HIND FEET TOO HIGH

When a horse piaffes with the hind feet high and loose, sometimes even raising them up higher than the front feet, we have a kind of mirror problem of cramped hindquarters which are 'too much asunder'. Here the hindquarters are not loaded either, but in a very different manner; and the front legs are still carrying the bulk of the piaffe. This flaw is easier to see because the hip of the horse bounces freely and stiffly up and down. There is an anecdote that when one of the riders at the Spanish Riding School wanted to demonstrate what real flexibility and elasticity in the piaffe meant, he had a glass of water placed on his horse's croup in the piaffe. The elasticity and flexion was so clean and smooth that there was not enough shock to spill the water. In the horse who piaffes with his hind feet too high the glass would be sent flying. This kind of action in the piaffe can be caused by inflexible joints in the hind legs. Sometimes it is conformational, as in horses who have a high croup and find it difficult to sink behind or to come under with their legs. This conformation is not necessarily the kiss of death. Even though these horses may be limited as to how much they can come under, if they are developed muscularly, the muscles of the abdomen, neck and back can compensate and still produce loading behind, even if the sinking is less noticeable. As I have said, these piaffes will look more like a passage on the spot, but they cannot be considered bad piaffes as long as they show real collection and good rhythm, especially in and out of piaffe-passage transitions.

If the horse that piaffes too high behind can be brought to do better piaffe, it will be done by increasing overall strength in the abdomen, neck and rump, but particularly the strength and flexibility in the hind legs. I think work in hand is excellent to show these horses how to engage more, initially without the weight of the rider. Once the behaviour, in a sense, is trained into the horse, and the horse understands, the new neuro-muscular pattern of loading the haunches then becomes a matter of repetition and progressive training exercises by the rider.

PIAFFE WITH THE HIND LEGS TOO CLOSE TOGETHER AND THE HIND LEGS TO FAR APART (THE LESSON OF LEVADE)

In order for an object to remain upright a vertical line projected downward from its centre of gravity must fall within the area of support. If the line falls outside this area, the object will topple over.

If you look at any picture of a horse in levade, its hind feet will be well placed under its body and they will be placed well apart from each other. The great muscle and ligament systems of the rump, abdomen and neck will be bristling as they pull the horse back and up over the legs. In the levade all weight is carried on the two legs of the hindquarters. The front end is suspended off the ground and held in balance. So if you reverse the above physical rule, and draw a line on the ground from hind foot to hind foot, and then draw another imaginary line up into the horse from the groundline between the horse's hind feet, it will go up through the horse's centre of gravity. The wider the feet, and thus the wider base of support, the more room for the centre of gravity to balance inside this area of support. The closer the horse's hind feet are together in the levade, the less the area or base of support and the more difficult it is to balance or stay upright. For the sake of argument if the hind feet were to move practically right on top of one another, it would be like

[65]

trying to do a levade on a fence post; the base of support has dwindled down almost to a point. So when the line from the horse's centre of gravity moves even a little outside this point of support, the horse topples over or back down.

When the hind legs of the horse start coming very close together in the piaffe, you can assume that they are carrying less and less weight. Their area of support is very narrow and small because it is unnecessary. Most likely, this piaffe is balanced too far out on the forehand and needs more collection. Traditional collecting exercises are needed. Also in-hand work with a stiff, long whip, which can point to the legs and push them to indicate more engagement, is excellent to show the horse what we want.

When the hind legs of the horse are widening like in a levade stance it can signal that they are beginning to carry too much weight. I know some trainers who would say it is impossible to carry too much weight behind. These trainers love to see a piaffe that lives in the moment before levade. To me, this kind of piaffe is overdone and ostentatious. It is not a traditional or natural piaffe, because when the forehand is carrying almost no weight the piaffe can disassociate too much.

The difference in the speed that the front foot is travelling while in the swing phase and the speed that the rear diagonal partner is travelling can be so disparate that the piaffe moves farther and farther from the trot-like gait. So instead of the piaffe representing the ultimate culmination of collecting a trot, it becomes a gait of its own with the front feet travelling two or three times faster than the hind ones. To me, the piaffe has a certain responsibility to remain a trot-like gait. Furthermore, if the piaffe is set too deeply, teetering on the point of levade, it becomes difficult to make transitions from piaffe to passage and vice versa.

When the rider/trainer notices in training that the horse is getting too wide behind in the piaffe, he should encourage or allow the piaffe to go more forward. Then the hind legs will exhibit more extension and the front legs will resume a proper supporting role, but **only** the supporting role of purifying the diagonals – not of holding the horse up.

LATERAL DEVIATIONS IN THE PIAFFE

I am convinced from my experience that balancé in the piaffe is similar to balancé in the passage. It is a result of inferior collection and engagement behind. Nevertheless the spirited horse tries for the movement, helping with the front legs. Thrust from either front leg can have considerable sideways force, especially in the piaffe where almost all the energy is being sent vertically instead of forward (horizontally). The front end gets pushed from side to side as each front leg reaches out to block the lateral forces and sends the torso back up and over in a vicious cycle. I think the horse has to relax a little and go back to a highly collected trot or some less-pressured half-steps. When collection over the rear legs is perfected one can try for a more accented piaffe. Once the balance is back in order and the horse accepts the rein going through the body, the forehand will be lighter. Now, without the need to be doing what the hind legs were supposed to be doing, the front limbs stop driving so hard and raise up and down like yo-yo's, falling and rising straight from the trunk of the horse.

I believe that the flaw of rolling the front legs in towards a centre line, and even criss-crossing, in the piaffe is again similar to the same flaw in the passage – with the exception, as Podhajsky[15] has noted, that it can be even worse. As in the passage, if a very stiff back is not

[67]

absorbing the axial roll and a stiff shoulder is not allowing the front leg to flex and extend properly, the horse has to move the front limbs when they are in the swing phase (when they are airborne). If the shoulder is exceedingly stiff it will not allow the leg to flex and extend nor the foot to raise up and come back down in as straight a vertical path as conformation will allow. Instead it will swing the whole stiff limb sideways – similar to a person with a stiff knee who swings the leg in or out to move the leg forward because the knee won't flex.

In the two worst cases of crossing over in front that I have seen, both horses were standing wide behind. This was perplexing to me at first but the more I understood this flaw, the more logical this stance became.

We have already mentioned that a widened stance is a tip-off in general that the horse is trying to carry more load over those legs. Why are those horses that cross over in front standing wide behind? Because unlike the balancé where the front legs are doing too much to help balance the piaffe, the stiff front legs are just swinging from side to side – almost painfully avoiding flexion. If they are not flexing up, they cannot possibly extend with any force either. Therefore the hind legs are carrying the greater proportion of the load. In rolling under, the front legs are doing nothing to help balance and maintain the diagonals. In balancé they are doing too much.

FEATURES OF THE TRADITIONAL PIAFFE

The piaffe is a movement in which the horse is moving its diagonal limb pairs in the same stance and swing time with very little forward advancement. In this trot-on-the-spot of sorts, the front feet are required to travel higher than the hind feet in the swing phase and therefore must travel faster, which is what makes it different from the trot. This is biomechanically possible because in the piaffe the horse has always been asked to move its centre of balance more toward the rear, deliberately disproportionately loading the hind legs and lightening the front. As well as a development exercise in itself, traditionally the piaffe was often used to coil the horse over its hind legs to prepare it to jump off the hind legs in one of the airs above the ground, as already described.

While the horse is in the piaffe it should exhibit little or no lateral deviation. We now know that many of these lateral deviations in limb travel expose weaknesses in the horse's ability to collect itself and to hold itself in balance. These weaknesses, when they can be fixed, need to be corrected at the most fundamental levels. Odd placements of legs need to be analysed to determine if more collection is needed, or more flexibility in the back, etc. Of course, it is always easier if these faults are noticed early and are not allowed to become engrained. Many good trainers have often suggested it is all right to let the horse carry its head a little lower in the beginning of piaffe training to allow the horse to use its neck in the initial difficult attempts to move into piaffe, and to ensure that the horse stays round and does not lock up in the back. I think this is also good advice.

Although the horse in piaffe should be fairly static laterally, that is, not swaying, the most experienced trainers have always suggested and insisted that it not be static longitudinally: that the horse be allowed to move forward. Again, from the mechanical point of view this makes absolute sense. Allowing the horse to move will ensure that there is flexion and extension of the hind limbs. It is this extension that moves the horse forward. It is also this extension which insures the complementary flexion thereby gymnasticising the hind legs. Only in a circuit of flexion and extension of the hind limbs will the trainer avoid cramping the hind limbs – as Newcastle would say, 'too much asunder' – with a falsely lowered croup and a horse falsely on its haunches.

It should be remembered that when the piaffe is held on the spot, in order to polish it, this is done as a finishing touch at the end of piaffe training. Very often this polishing has been done in hand or between the pillars. In the latter case it is almost always done unmounted. The inference seems clear. A piaffe performed without any forward movement is the most vulnerable to evasions, chiefly because it lacks the purifying factor of a complete cycle of flexion and extension, and is the most difficult to keep in balance. It can be polished and it can be destroyed when worked on the spot. In the end, the piaffe is an exercise. As a particular exercise it has the great abilities to strengthen the hind legs' carrying power as it calls into play the complete 'ring of muscle' – abdomen, neck, back and rump – and systematically develops them.

In the beginning of this chapter I was talking about fixations in time and space and about the progression of techniques and the sources of such progressions. If you read Guérinière you can see he credits La Broue and Newcastle as great influences. If you read Newcastle you can see the progression in technique in a movement like a shoulder-in, which is generally credited entirely to Guérinière. This goes on and on. One sees technique as a state of time, yet it does not describe the whole state of horsemanship. It can be argued, for example, that Leonardo Da Vinci's technology is inferior to that of today's average television repair man. Yet Da Vinci's artistry is timeless. It is so timeless, unfixed in space, that people still swear his paintings move. Newcastle's technology in his veterinary work, Volume 2, is inferior to the technology of today. His horsemanship is timeless. Inside a place in space and time one develops a quality unaffected by space-time. There are many serious scientists, and serious spiritual people, who say things like 'many realities lie side by side'.[5] If you can think only linearly, as in following the progression of technique, this concept is impossible to consider. Guérinière is dead and cannot speak to me now. However, if instead of thinking of the separate techniques of Xenophon, Newcastle, Pluvinel, Guérinière, you think of the artistry of each, a funny thing happens. You cannot place them in a neat and tidy progression. Instead, they stand side by side with their work, their art, in the same time – art time. In a very real sense, each one of us has to re-invent the wheel in our own time. What we must try to do is not necessarily re-invent the technological wheel with every generation, but we must re-invent the pyschological wheel, the artistic wheel, the psychic wheel. When one can find the wheel of the unconscious, Pluvinel comes back alive, and Guérinière has never died. You yourself come alive. By using the technological wheel correctly, you can move beyond it. You can see the source. You see your part as part of the source. You can see past the field of inferiority and superiority. You can be right there with Pluvinel now. The restraints of space and time are in your mind.

In the library, among the ghosts and words of all these great *ecuyers*, I see that this is no ordinary graveyard. Two things emanate from these ancient texts. One is technological and one is spiritual. They are equally real. One is sentence and structure requirements, description – the bone you might find in a grave. The other is the energy or spirit of a man. It hovers around the place where a person was, or the things a person made. Even when unrecorded consciously, it etches into and through the collective unconscious and it is very much present, real and available. The restraints are in one's own psyche.

[71]

I was beginning to see some of the limits of technological bravura, some of the traps on its measurements. In that same view I was beginning to get the signals of a way out.

Chapter Five

Deep Work

'... THE FIRST PART [of practice] is loosening up and suppling the horse; second is work; third is riding dry. In the loosening-up phase, I try to set my horse long and low, meaning that the neck shall stretch forward and downward, so the horse loosens his back. During this phase, I don't watch so much the expression of the movements, but I do try to get rid of the stable exuberance and the superfluous drive to move, and to loosen up stiffness caused by standing in the stable, For me that is the loosening work – to ride my horse long and low during this phase.'[16]

Reiner Klimke
From an interview with Christian Thiess, *Dressage & CT Magazine*
Feburary, 1994

There are many trainers who do not use or believe in long and low or deep work. This seems more than anything to reflect a general past bias in the west towards muscular developments over tendo-ligamentus exercises. In many sports and some arts we have sought to develop more powerful and acrobatic athletes and the gains in muscle mass and strength have often been at the expense of flexibility. I say 'past bias' because I think most open-minded trainers have realised that a lot of current injuries are attributable to this system of training. Most athletes today are well aware of the importance of stretching in general and put important emphasis on it in training routines, especially in warm-ups. This is no different for the equine performer.

I have personally heard the rationale from dressage trainers that they can better raise the back of the horse through collection. Of course, one of the most basic requirements of collection is that the horse be round. The horse's head and neck must not be forcefully elevated so that the raised neck flattens the back down and forces the horse to go hollow. Instead, the horse is systematically prepared to engage behind and develop more carrying power on the hind legs through deeper flexion and extension. The abdominal muscles will gain strength and will add upward support for the back; as the belly contracts, the top-line extends. The neck will extend and raise, adding a kind of fulcrum torque over the withers, enhancing the back's lifting. Through a complex coordination the horse will become round, using his 'ring of muscle'. I would like to say one thing about the ring theory. As a pedagogical tool the 'ring' may have merit. However, in reality it is describing nothing less than how the whole body moves the horse. The complexity of this muscular activity cannot be underestimated. In 1978, Wentick, in looking just at the flexion and extension of

[74]

the hind leg, analysed some thirteen active muscles, which clearly showed how complicated the muscle physiology can be.

Think for a second about opening and closing your hand. It is one thing to identify the components of the process, but then you have to apply them to actual situations of motion. For example, you can open your hand quickly and close it slowly, or open it slowly and close it quickly. The variations are infinite. All one has to do is look at the current technology involved in the design of human prostheses to get an idea of the mind-numbing complexities involved in the practical applications of the nuances of motion. It is my feeling that because of this complexity of muscle physiology one can sometimes get a better description of equine locomotion from a mechanical physicist's approach than from a biologically mechanical one. I think this is why you see such varying opinions when you talk to different biomechanical people. To this end I know there are some fascinating force-field instruments being built which are able to measure precisely the force exerted by certain limbs of the horse. It doesn't take much imagination to realise that this kind of work can actually prove or disprove some of the ideologies of dressage. At the least it will be able to show subtle differences in certain movements, i.e. whether a piaffe is on the forehand or not.

In general, the back of the horse is lifted, rounded, basculed in collection by complementary abdominal support, and by stretching over two fulcrums – one being the withers and the other being the lumbo-sacral joint. When the hind legs reach under, the great muscle-tendon ligament systems pull around the lumbo-sacral joint and lift the back like a see-saw. When the neck is stretched the dorsal and nuchal ligament system pulls on the spinal processes of the withers and the scaleni muscles at the base of the neck stabilise and push the lower neck up, the withers become another fulcrum so that the back lifts from the front also as the neck is stretched.[17]

Collection and deep work require vigorous activity behind. In collection, the abdominal muscles are used more and weight is being pulled onto the hind legs, so the forward motion or energy gets transported more vertically and less horizontally. The forehand is less encumbered because it carries less weight. Simultaneously the neck is carried higher but is still stretched forward in an uncramped arch. This retains an effective pull on the withers fulcrum, enhancing the round shape of the back even more. If the neck is cramped in an artificial arch or an arch that is too high and tight, the top-side of the neck will actually shorten, nullifying the fulcrum effect. Furthermore the underside of the neck will develop great muscles like goitres. Then the two ends of the horse begin working at cross-purposes. The first thing that suffers is the horse's back, which gets hyperflexed in its hollow form. There is then great stress on the stifle and hocks which are cramped out behind. This is what happens when you try to collect your horse with your hands. The horse becomes stiff with its back hollowed from restraining the neck.

So, in this complicated regard the back is of course lifted in collection. However, this requires a horse that is capable of collection. Therefore, the young horse is left out. Furthermore the warm-up becomes problematic because in order to have the back up you must start right away with collection. If not, your warm-up is hollow, and can be counter-productive.

The beauty of deep work is that it can be started with the horse whose back needs it the most, the young horse. Secondly, it serves as the ideal warm-up for the trained horse, because it is primarily a stretching exercise and helps keep the older horse flexible and free in its big gaits.

In deep work there are two principal schools of thought. Both require active forward movement behind, thereby fulfilling the fulcrum requirement over the lumbo-sacral joint and getting lift in the back in front of that joint. Differences lie in the position of the head and neck. In one school it is sufficient to have the horse's head low with the neck stretched. The nose of the horse may be pointing out. The fundamental requirement is that the neck be lower than the withers so that it satisfies the see-saw effect – when the neck goes down, the back behind the fulcrum of the withers goes up. The problem with deep work in this system is that it is possible for the horse to stretch but not along the crest; the nuchal system can be slack and the horse may be ewe-necked in spite of being low.

In the second school the horse needn't be as low in the neck but it can be. However, the horse should have more flexion – the nose must be in and the horse's head can even be slightly behind the vertical (see Fig. 8). If you

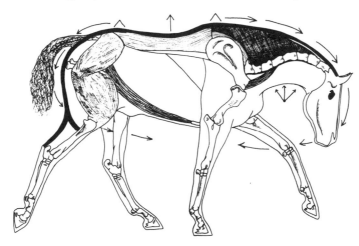

Fig. 8 Deep work. When correctly performed,
the back of the horse is lifted, rounded and stretched.

want to get a little feel for the difference, sit in a chair at your desk or table and lean forward slowly. Touch the flat surface in front of you with your chin. Next lean forward slowly again, and touch the table with your forehead. In touching with your chin, you can feel how straight your neck can be, even hollow, down to your own back. When you touch with your forehead, you can feel the stretch, the pull or curl all through the neck into the back.

When we work the horse in this second deep-work system, the crested neck ensures the stretching of the great nuchal ligament system along the top-line. When the horse is flexed slightly at the poll, this lever action adds a little more pull to this ligament system. It also helps to ensure that the horse, even when in a low-neck position, starts the cresting, or as Deb Bennett has said, the 'telescoping neck gesture' at the base of the neck where the scaleni muscles stabilise the underside of the neck and push up on the spine just above the chest. The lower neck, then, comes back and up and the crest seems to grow forward out of this base, and the spine extends.

This is fundamentally the same position the neck has in proper collection, as I have said, not elevated too high and tight, but reaching from the withers on top and from the base of the neck underneath toward the poll, which is at the highest point. Thus deep work in this shape has a very smooth and logical progression into the shapes of collection. What, in effect, changes between deep work and collection is not really the shape of the neck but the lowering or engaging of the hindquarters. In a real sense, the forehand does not levitate higher in collection; it is the hind end that sinks down. Of course, in collection the poll is up higher, but both exercises require an expansive extending spine and top-line. Only in that shape will the horse stay round in the back. Whereas when a horse is in

[78]

flat, long and low, it will need to be 'put on the bit' and made round before it can move into collection. Dorso-ventral flexion must change into dorso-ventral extension.

The important thing is that the horse stretches out into an arch. Then even when the neck is low, it still maintains an arch. It is this arch which stretches the top-line of the neck into the withers and pulls the back up behind them. When this nuchal system is stretched, it acts like a spring[18] and with each step an elastic ripple can be felt. It is my opinion that the horse needs to be only slightly curved in order to be flexed at the poll to effect the elastic stretching. But it does need to be flexed. Sometimes the horse may be behind the vertical in the deep work. Yet when the haunches engage for collection, the forehand raises the same arched neck which will now assume the correct position of poll high and nose not behind the vertical. When correctly done, arched deep work can enhance the horse's natural movement and keep the horse flexible in the back and body so its stretching complements the later flexions of collection.

I also think it is very important that the deep work be done on as light a rein as possible for two reasons. One is that with the lightest of reins, the horse cannot seek support from the rider's hands. This will build big elastic gaits into the horse while emphasising self-carriage, even in a long and low position. This is very possible and in fact is easy to do. After a while the horse also develops psychologically and will stay responsible with complete freedom of the reins. The self-carriage and balance improves as well as the self-confidence.

The second and perhaps most important reason for riding this exercise with the lightest of reins is that the rider **will not force the horse into overbending or over-flexing,** which can tear physical tissue and eventually have the exact opposite effect of stiffening a horse instead of freeing it. With light reins the rider can only suggest stretching and arching. The horse will seek a level of stretching it is capable of, which, over time, of course, should improve. The depth of the deep work should be determined by the horse and not the rider/trainer.

The deep work then is primarily a careful stretching regimen which stresses the long movement. It can develop self-confidence and self-carriage because it should be done with vigorous movement behind but with a very free rein. It is the antidote to bunchy or short-ened gaits which can occur if the horse stays in collection all the time. It offers healthy counter-play to the physical demands of collection and makes sure that the rider keeps his horse elastic. When correctly used, the dorso-ventral extension of the spine in the deep work will be similar to the dorso-ventrally extended spine in collection. In the end, all this dorso-ventral extension or roundness is the only way to help the horse carry weight in the middle of its back, which is not something it comes by naturally. The millions of years of genetics in the horse's body type have not yet adjusted to being ridden. When weight is dropped on the horse's back without preparation, the horse's back will certainly flex and even hyper-flex to become hollow. To wander around without making an effort to round the horse's back is not kind. It borders on a kind of presumption that the animal will somehow adjust. The trouble is, of course, that most of the adjust-ments – high head, hind end out behind, short steps – are all detrimental to the horse's well-being. Deep work can help a horse not only to accommodate the rider but also actually enhance the natural movement of any riding horse.

Chapter Six

Lateral Work – In Search of the

Mother Load

MUCH OF RIDING knowledge is passed from teacher to pupil orally. Alois Podhajsky states in his book *The Riding Teacher* that 'the riding teacher should expect his pupil to follow his orders without qualification and to be willing to work hard in order to reach the goal set.'[19]

This statement goes beyond the obvious requirement of plain discipline needed in any learning situation. Since so much of teaching riding is the passing along of feelings and not just intellectual formulas, and since the novice rider has to learn to recognise the feelings with and without intellectual understanding, there is often a great deal of blind faith on the part of the student.

On the part of the instructor, it requires the carrying of a heavy ethical load. He/she must be responsible and thoroughly prepared in the lessons on any given day. He/she must continually upgrade his/her own knowledge with studently pursuit and an open mind. Where the student stops and the teacher begins is difficult to answer. Where faith must yield to the open mind and vice versa is impossible to answer.

When this process is at its best it can maintain its balance. However, because of strong loyalties and the transmission of feelings over facts, an unfortunate repercussion of this faith and trust can be a continued passing of incorrect information from generation to generation. Science can have a difficult road when trying to break into the tight traditions of horsemen. I think this explains why, in spite of conventional wisdom in the hundreds of systems for training the four classical lateral exercises – shoulder-in, travers, renvers, half-pass – the explanations, even from some outstanding expert sources, are contradictory and inaccurate. In some cases their use can produce the opposite effect of the one intended. However, there are some fairly simple biomechanical rules which I believe can clarify the forces involved in these exercises and thus advise the rider/trainer in their proper use.

Since the primary use of the bending exercises has to do with the asymmetrical loading of the hind legs for the purpose of conquering the natural asymmetry in all horses, it is imperative that the rider/trainer knows which hind leg exerts more force and is therefore doing more work or carrying more load, in which exercise. He/she can then try to develop more engagement of a deficient

[82]

hind leg. When the hind legs have more equal engagement this will enhance collection and straightness.

In order to understand the mechanics of the lateral exercises, the first thing to realise is that if both hind legs propel the horse equally, the horse will move straight. In order for the horse to move off a straight line, one leg will have to exert more force than the other to lift the horse's mass and project it sideways, obliquely forward or on a bias, over the less loaded leg.

We have developed a simple rule-of-thumb to determine which leg is dominant. Whichever hind leg is crossing over, or in front of, the other, will be the limb that is exerting more force, doing more work, and carrying a greater load. The reasons for this is that it will always be that limb which will be directing the horse's line of travel. That limb will be the primary source of propulsion for the horse's mass in the line of travel. In spite of many assumptive explanations and theories, this rule holds true, regardless of the bend in any of these exercises.

For the sake of simplification, I will use the left bend in describing all these exercises and will consider all movement to be on three tracks. Riders and trainers can extrapolate from there.

In the **shoulder-in**, bent to the left, the horse is curved around the rider's left leg. The horse's line of travel, although relatively straight, will be on a bias left to right. The horse will leave three imaginary lines of tracks on the ground. (See Fig. 9.) The right hind travels forward by itself. The left hind travels forward on the same line as the right fore. The left fore travels forward on its own line. In the shoulder-in, bent left, the left hind steps over in front of the right hind. Its line of flight travels up under the belly of the horse. Of the two hind legs, it is the left which moves closer to the centre of mass and centre of gravity. Of the two hind legs it is the left hind which will

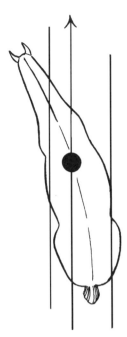

Fig. 9 Left shoulder-in. The left hind crosses in front of the right hind,
closer to the centre of gravity. It is therefore the load leg.

exert more force, do more work and therefore harness more forces of load. The key to understanding the effect of these exercises is the line of travel. If the line of travel is left to right, obliquely left to right or even on a bias left to right, the left hind crosses in front of the right hind to step under the centre of gravity. This leg will be dominant in lifting the horse's mass and propelling it in the line of travel sideways. Remember, if both hind legs propel equally, the horse cannot move sideways.

In **travers**, bent to the left, the mechanics are identical to renvers. The difference between the two is only one of references to the wall and not in biomechanics.

In **renvers**, bent to the left, the horse will be bent around the rider's left leg. The horse will be travelling on a bias this time from right to left. The rider's outside leg will be slightly behind the girth encouraging the horse to move forward and towards the left. (See Fig. 10.) If we use the three imaginary tracks again, the left hind travels forward in the same line; the right hind travels forward in the same line as the left fore for the second line; and the right fore travels forward alone for the third track. In the renvers, bent to the left, the right hind steps up in front of the left hind. The right hind moves closer to the centre of mass and centre of gravity than the left hind which moves more off into space. The right hind lifts and propels the horse's mass from right to left. The right hind exerts more force, does more work and is the primary (i.e. load bearing) limb as it directs the line of travel off straightness and over to the left.

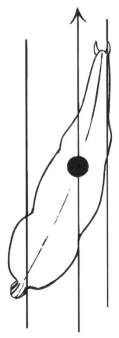

Fig. 10 In renvers bent to the left, the right hind steps over in front of the left hind,
closer to the centre of gravity. It lifts and propels the horse's mass.
It is therefore the load leg.

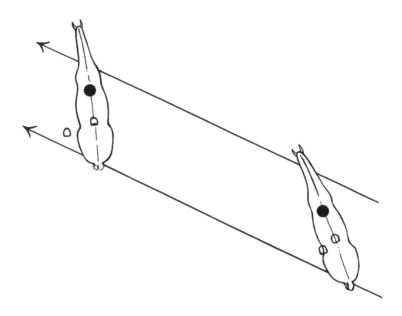

Fig. 11 Half-pass bent to the left. Depending on the angle the horse's body the exercise can be made more gymnastic (see text).

In Podhajsky's book, *The Complete Training of the Horse and Rider*,[15] he mentions that a popular gymnastic exercise at the Spanish Riding School is to move from the shoulder-in into renvers. Going from right shoulder-in, where the right hind is the inside leg but is the leg crossing up in front of the left, the rider changes the bend of the horse's body, but in fact the right hind still remains the leg that crosses over in front of the left hind. That this exercise is possible is due to that fact that, irrespective of bend, the right hind in this case continues from shoulder-in into renvers to remain directing the line of travel from right to left. It remains the leg that continues to exert more force and does more work.

The last of the four lateral exercises is the **half-pass**. It is one of the most interesting and points out the genius of some of the classical masters. In the half-pass, bent to the left, the horse will be bent around the rider's left leg and the rider's right leg will coax the horse forward and over to the left. The horse's line of travel will be on a bias from right to left. The right hind leg will step over in front of the left hind. It will be the primary load leg because it is directing the horse's mass over to the left. (See Fig. 11.) If the half-pass is ridden on an angle with the shoulders well ahead of the haunches, as many of the old masters demanded, something interesting happens. The body of the horse will be in the way, if you will, of the forward advance of the left hind. Unlike in the renvers where the left inside moves out into space, the left inside leg in the angled half-pass moves more under the body. The result of the half-pass ridden on a bias, well angled into the direction of travel and with good bend in the body, is that both hind limbs can be stressed, albeit in different ways. Nevertheless it makes it unique as a developing exercise.

The modern competitive half-pass is often ridden almost straight – parallel to the wall. This kind of half-pass makes counter changes of hand easier. However, the rider/trainer must always keep in mind that there is an inverse relationship between impulsion – engagement of the hind limbs – and the amount of lateral movement. The more the hind limbs criss-cross sideways, the less power they will have to step under the centre of gravity and propel the horse forward, or upward as in the case of collection. A straight half-pass parallel to the wall can often show more scissoring (crossing over) of the legs, but it will have less engagement and transmit less power. Therefore as a gymnastic exercise which is meant to foster collection, it is inferior.

To summarise – to find the primary load leg in the lateral exercises the rider needs only to determine which hind leg is crossing over in front of the other. That is the leg which is moving closer toward the centre of mass and centre of gravity in order to lift and propel the horse's mass in that line of travel, irrespective of the bend.

If the rider/trainer juxtaposes these exercises in a proper way they can serve as a great tool for suppling with different bends in the body. They also can develop collection by fostering extra work on a particular limb. Perhaps most importantly they can help straighten a horse by developing a more symmetrical loading in both hind legs.

In an issue of the magazine *Parabola* devoted to tradition and transmission, there was a passage quoted from Ibn Khaldun, a fourteenth-century North African historian:

'Since it is the nature of tradition to incorporate false statements, we must examine the causes which produce them. They are:

(a) attachments to certain opinions and schools of thought. Now if a man's mind is impartial in receiving tradition, he examines it with all due care so that he can distinguish between true and false; but if he is pervaded by attachment to any particular opinion or sect he immediately accepts any tradition which supports it; and this tendency and attachment clouds his judgment so that he is unable to criticise and scrutinise what he hears, and straightaway accepts [that] which is false and hands it on to others.

(b) over-confidence in the probity of those who hand on the tradition;

(c) ignorance of the real significance of events; for many traditionists, not knowing the significance of what they saw and heard, record events together with their own interpretations or conjectures and so give false information.

(d) belief that one has the truth. This is widespread and comes generally from over-confidence in the narrators of the past;

(e) ignorance of the circumstances surrounding an event induced by ambiguity or embellishment. The narrator hands on the story as he understands it with these misleading and false elements.'[20]

As I have said, in the study of the art of horsemanship we are often bound by a strong oral tradition, and, as Ibn Khaldun has stated, with it by definition there will also be false and misleading messages. In one sense with the continued advance of technology and technique, it is often easier to fix the inaccuracies of science. For the inaccuracies of science, an inquisitive mind will notice, search and find. It is harder to fix the inaccuracies of feeling. Here a rider must close the mind and open the body. So much of riding is the personal way one asks and answers without words. An inaccurate feeling is not one where the student feels something different to that felt by the teacher. All of us are different. So, by definition, we will feel things differently. Inaccuracies come about in how the rider goes about getting his/her feelings. The teacher cultivates the integrity of how you ask and answer. The feeling is between you and your horse.

In that same issue of *Parabola* magazine in the editorial introducing the article, D.M. Dooling says,

'Distortions are in us and all around us and can be as obvious as the folksy tone of modern books on "how to achieve peace of mind" . . . none of us is immune from this kind of distortion; but if we were as honest as we dare and as alert as we might be – as attentive as St Simeon urges – we could save ourselves, and the message, at least from the worst of our own betrayal.'[21]

[89]

If the student and the teacher pursue the art of riding with a flexible mind and with integrity, then, as Dooling suggests, just maybe the message will get through. The interesting part of riding is how you receive and/or deliver the message is one of its biggest messages.

Chapter Seven

Confucius and the Canter Pirouette

'AT WHATEVER PACE [walk, canter, piaffe] the pirouette is executed, the horse slightly bent in the direction in which he is turning, should, remaining on the bit with light contact, turn smoothly round maintaining the exact cadence and sequence of footfalls of that pace. The poll stays the highest point during the entire movement.'

Article 412, Paragraph 4
FEI Rules for Dressage

'The canter is a pace of three-time, where at the canter to

the right for instance the footfalls follow one another as follows: left hind, left diagonal (simultaneously left fore and right hind), right fore, followed by a moment of suspension with all four feet in the air before the next stride begins.'

Article 405, Paragraph 2
FEI Rules for Dressage

'In the canter pirouette the quarters should describe the smallest possible circle, but the horse should not lose the clear three-beat[s] of the canter . . .'

Das Dressur Pferd
Harry Boldt[22]

'In the beginning [of teaching collected canter] many faults may appear: the horse will slacken the movement and drag his hind legs without force; he will become longer in his whole body and his movements will be slovenly; the canter will become four-time instead of three.'

The Complete Training of the Horse and Rider
Alois Podhajsky[15]

'The canter pirouette is developed from the "school canter", which is in fact a four-time canter, though the unassisted human eye is too slow to recognise it as such . . . Nevertheless the pirouette shows more impulsion if the illusion of the three-time canter is preserved.'

A Dressage Judge's Handbook
Brig. Gen. Kurt Albrecht[23]

Confucius and the Canter Pirouette

'In order that the pirouette be judged correct, the horse must go into it in the rhythm of his canter, carrying out the entire pirouette in the same canter, and leaving it also in the same rhythm, which is the great difficulty of this exercise. It loses all its value when it is done with variations of cadence and rhythm by a horse who is unable to do a collected canter in four-time.'

Reflections on Equestrian Art
Nuno Oliveira[2]

The pirouette is to the canter what the piaffe is to the trot. Namely, the ultimate expression of collection in this particular pace. In the same way that I have already stated that I think the piaffe has an obligation to try to remain a two-time movement because its foundation is the trot, I am also from the school that believes the pirouette has an obligation to try to remain a three-time movement because of its foundation in the canter.

Having said that I also know that Brigadier General Albrecht and the late Nuno Oliveira are correct. A pirouette which is executed close to being 'on the spot' or 'the size of a plate behind', will be four-time.

The pirouette has been described as a turn around the inside hind leg, which although acting as the hub must not stick to the ground and pivot. It must be raised up and down on the same spot or move slightly forward in its normal sequence of action. It has also been described as a circle on two tracks in which the radius of the circle is the length of the horse. The pirouette requires the hind legs to scribe a small circle on the ground, often described as the size of a plate. Giving the plate generous dimensions this could be a circle with a circumference of three feet. The front legs stepping sideways scribe another circle, whose circumference is approximately twenty-five feet.

[93]

While the horse is scribing these two concentric circles the next requirement of the pirouette is that it maintain the rhythm of canter. So if you enter into the pirouette on a three-beat canter you are supposed to stay in three-beat during the pirouette and as you leave it. In general, a canter will remain three-beat as long as the diagonal pair of legs, which are the second beat, strike the ground simultaneously. If this diagonal pair of legs disassociates, the canter will become four-beat with each leg striking the ground individually in a rotary action – the same way a galloping racehorse moves in a four-beat gait with each leg acting like a spoke of a wheel, transmitting the impulsion forward in even, efficient increments.

In the pirouette, what would make the diagonal pair of legs in the three-beat canter disassociate and create a four-beat canter? One is a clear loss of impulsion and a reduction in the moment of suspension. If the rider enters the pirouette and pulls on the reins he may slow the canter tempo down, which coupled with the difficult turn of the pirouette, will dwindle the suspension phase to almost nothing. This is easy to do if the rider is concentrating too hard on keeping the hind legs 'on the spot', or on a very small circle. In a normal, or even collected, canter the horse floats over considerable ground in the suspension phase. The three beats all help each other to develop the thrust that sends the horse through the air in the moment of suspension. When you ride into the pirouette and practically stop all the forward impetus and limit it to only a few inches of lateral movement, yet you are to keep the same rhythm, the horse would have to literally jump straight up into the air during the moment of suspension. If he didn't, he would not keep the same time in the air as he did in the canter coming up to the pirouette. If the horse changes the time of suspension, he changes the rhythm.

It may be useful to think in musical terms here. Imagine three notes and a pause – corresponding to the three beats and a moment of suspension of the canter. In music the space will be defined and timed. Very often the space becomes as important, or even more important, than the notes. In any case the whole phrase is composed of the four parts. If you play the notes twice in exactly the same way and you shorten the pause once, but not the second time, you have created a slightly different musical phrase. The notes will run together without the space and the overall phrase is shorter, but it will still be recognisable.

This happens in the pirouette all the time because of its great physical demands on the hind legs. It is one thing to shorten the space in the phrase, if you will. However, if in an effort to relieve some of this work, the horse opens up the canter to a rotary form, and gives itself more support by spreading out the limb placement in order to have one leg on the ground at almost all times, then this is tantamount to placing a fourth note in the space. This becomes a very different phrase. When the canter breaks apart in a weak way, avoiding work, it is analogous in its relationship to a true collected canter in the way that the hover trot is related to the passage. Both the broken canter and the hover trot are gaits executed with minimum flexion of the hind legs and therefore with minimum complementary extension.

The second critical matter in what breaks up the three-beat canter during a pirouette will be the number of strides it takes to complete a 360° or full circle revolution. Let's say, for example, a horse takes eight strides to complete the pirouette, making two concentric circles of three feet for the rear legs and twenty-five feet for the front. If the horse is relatively straight in each stride, when the hind legs are moving approximately four and a half inches sideways, the front legs are moving three feet.

If, for the sake of our argument, a horse cuts the number of strides in half, then when the hind legs move approximately nine inches sideways, the front legs will have to move six feet.

There comes a point when the disparity of these distances puts too much torque on the body. The horse cannot remain relatively straight with the diagonal pair in tact. In an effort to make up the long distance, the front legs will need to help throw the shoulders over. The gait breaks up as each leg leads into the next in a fan-like advance. In the left pirouette, for instance, the right hind starts, and the left hind takes over placed more to the left. The right front is next, even more towards the left, and finally the left front is placed way over to the left. Advancing the canter pirouette in this fan-like four-time rotary manner is much easier on the horse, and can cover much more lateral ground in a single stride. In fact it is the only way a horse can do a pirouette if the rider leaves out too many strides. Instead of pure canter strides with a distinct moment of suspension (enough of a moment of suspension to do a flying change, for example) and great carrying power from the abdominal, hind-end muscles, and the horse's ring of muscle, the horse starts using the shoulders to push the pirouette over and around. This is not collection.

If you agree philosophically that the canter pirouette is a culmination of the canter work, then it seems to me that the emphasis in training has to be more on the canter purity than on the size of the pirouette. This is precisely the essence of of Podhajsky's warning: '. . . a pirouette in which the hind legs turn on the spot, but lose the rhythm of the canter, is a worse fault than one in which the hind legs describe a larger circle but maintain the regular rhythm.'[15]

When Albrecht and Oliveira talk about a four-beat

canter they are not referring to a sluggish, disunited four-beat canter but a school canter which is slightly four beat and has great carrying power behind.

I know it seems like rationalising – one should get off the fence and pick one or the other, three beat or four. Even with great horsemen lining up on either side, it doesn't make it any easier. The study of horsemanship does this to you all the time: presents you with questions that have several answers.

Listen how carefully Seunig writes about the three-beat/four-beat dilemma, how he addresses its existence and then practically apologises for it.

> 'In the highly developed manège [school] gallop the three-beat gait becomes a four-beat gait because the load rests for an instant only upon the hindquarters, even after the grounding of the inside hind leg. The outside foreleg alights only an instant after the inside hind leg. [The forehand is carried higher.] The difference being hardly perceptible to the observer's senses as in the pirouette. This statement, however, is merely theoretical. In practice, whenever we clearly hear and see the four-beat gait, we also observe that the gallop loses it distinguishing characteristic – the powerful and lively forward engagement of the hindquarters. Its movements lose their fluidity and roundness and become dragging dull, stiff and choppy. . .'[6]

After watching hours of films in slow motion, I agree with Brigadier General Albrecht and Oliveira that it must happen in four time; but, as Oliveira has said, it has to be the right kind of four beat. And when in Albrecht's book it says to try to keep the illusion of three beats, the emphasis shouldn't be on illusion. I don't think he is encouraging any subterfuge. The emphasis is on staying

[97]

close to three-beat. His words are advising us to keep the canter moving!

By now one can see that the canter pirouette is a technical quagmire. If you ride in competitions it becomes practically a moral dilemma. There is only one way you can follow Article 412's requirement of 'maintaining the exact cadence and sequence of footfalls of that pace'. That is, to keep all the canter work in the four-beat school canter so that when you perform the four-beat pirouette you haven't changed the pace. If you do this you violate Article 405 which says 'the canter is a pace of three-time'. If you ride the canter in clear three-time to accommodate Article 405, you will not be able to accommodate Article 412, which insists that you maintain the three-beat rhythm.

It is possible to solve this dilemma?

'The wave-particle duality was (is) one of the thorniest problems in quantum mechanics. Physicists like to have tidy theories which explain everything, and if they are not able to do that they like to have tidy theories about why they can't. The wave-particle duality is not a tidy situation. In fact, its untidiness has forced physicists into a radical new way to perceiving physical reality. . . For most of us life is seldom black and white. The wave-particle duality marked an end to the 'either-or' way of looking at the world. Physicists no longer could accept the proposition that light is either a particle or a wave because they had 'proved' to themselves that it was both – depending on how they looked at it.'[5]

I think a great deal of confusion comes from the limitations of human vision. At regular speed it can be difficult to determine the breakdown of rhythm. In slow-motion films it is easy to see. Very often people who are scoring

[98]

the pirouette have little experience of feeling and training them. Most experienced trainers and riders would not and have not been fooled by the differences of the three-beat canter, the four-beat school or manège canter, and the four-beat broken-down canter. They feel the rhythms and don't really see them. In fact when you ride the pirouette you can never see it. Films are always after the fact, and even if you watch in a mirror part will be blocked from view as you turn. You must learn to feel it.

To this day I still have found no philosophical compromise to the dilemma presented in the literature, the bodies of rules, and the biomechanics of the horse. I have made peace with it in the world of action. To me, the pirouette is not a trick. It is an exercise. Being an exercise it has built into it a relativity, a certain amount of freedom in its form, because the form will be changing as it develops.

The pirouette can be a proof that your horse has mastered bending properly. In order to negotiate those disparate concentric circles the horse's torso has to be flexible. It must be able to move into the tightest of circles without the back stiffening and the horse leaning over on the inside shoulder. The trainer has to remember that the pirouette is still in the family of circles. In that circle the horse, being a quadraped, will leave two lines of tracks – one from the inside front and hind leg, and the other from the outside front and hind leg. Of these two concentric circles the outside one will be larger. One of the earliest requirements of dressage is that the horse's hind feet track along into the same line as the front feet. Although in dressage we say that the horse is then straight, we mean it is bent evenly through the body and it is this bend which allows the horse to stay more perpendicular to the ground, even in tight circles.

A critical fact is that the outside has to be allowed to

[99]

stretch a little in order to cover the longer distance. If the outside rein goes beyond a support or guiding influence to a blocking one (or worse an inversion), the effect is to shorten the outside and either tip the horse onto its inside shoulder, or to force its hindquarters off straightness to the outside. Either of these flaws will be amplified in the pirouette. Once the pirouette is started, the rider should be riding it round with the back, seat and legs which will insure impulsive bounding strides into and through it. He should not be pulling it round with the reins, which will either shift the balance to the forehand or onto a single shoulder.

I have found in training that it is important not to hurry the closing in of the pirouette, but to ride it large in exercises such as renvers to a large passade, or travers to passade to half-pass to counter-canter. After the horse masters steady and equal individual canter strides on two tracks, it will not be difficult to reduce the circles and half circles into rhythmic pirouettes without the danger of spinning or losing the haunches to the outside. I have always preferred these kind of preparatory exercises to spiralling down for that very reason. If the rider is not very experienced it is easy to let the horse fall a little forward so that it starts turning around the shoulder with the hind end escaping to the outside.

When the pirouette is executed in good rhythm it can demonstrate the highest collection in the canter the way the piaffe can demonstrate high collection in the trot. This is a classic principle: that the exercise's real value lies in the gymnasticising or 'dressing' of the horse and not in the display.

Finally I have never given up trying to ride the pirouette in three-beat. To me, it is a reverence for the unattainable goal of pure paces. It is my homage to collection and its gymnastic values and to vigorous impulsion, which must be at the heart of all collection.

Good teachers have always sought to prevent us from having to reinvent the wheel with every new generation. Yet it is this wheel – circle – pirouette – circle metaphor – which is particularly rich and quizzical. We do not have to invent a new movement. We have to execute the one that is here. How we try to do it will reveal everything about our riding. In another sense we do need to reinvent the wheel with every generation. In each relearning more of us get trained, so we learn for ourselves all about the wheel and the circle.

Even if the FEI changed its rules it would not solve the duality presented by the circling pirouette. Certainly it would not stop new dualities from occurring. If the rider/trainer invests all his allegiance to one side when dual things present themselves in riding, which they do all the time, then each negates the other. This kind of causal thinking or mentality can be very limiting in riding as well as in life. Our physicists have already proved that light can be a wave or a particle depending on how you look at it. This is not supposed to be possible. Let me quote from Thomas Cleary:

'In later Chan [Chinese for Zen] schools, it was openly stated that classic texts were meant to be read by putting yourself in everyone's place to get a comprehensive view of subjective and objective relationships . . . In a classical aphorism on education frequently encountered in Chan literature, Confucius said, "If I bring up one corner, and those to whom I am speaking cannot come back with the other three, I don't talk to them any more'.[24]

When Albrecht brings up one corner, the Journeyman rider must bring up the other three. When Oliveira brings up one corner, the Journeyman must bring up the

[101]

other three. When Podhajsky brings up a different corner, the Journeyman trainer must bring up the other
three. When the FEI brings up a corner, the Journeyman
must bring up the other three.

If our comprehension of technique approaches that,
and if we do not get stuck on one corner, then maybe
Confucius will still talk to us.

Chapter Eight

Resistance and Ethics

'WHAT WE DO to animals troubles us – the horror of laboratory experiments, trophy shooting, factory farming – and our loss of contact with them leaves us mysteriously bereaved. If we could re-establish an atmosphere of respect in our relationships simple awe for the complexities of animals' lives, I think we would feel revivified as a species. And we would know more, deeply more, about what we are fighting for when we raise our voices against tyranny of any sort.'

Barry Lopez[25]

[103]

I had volunteered myself and one of my horses to be part of some research work being done by a veterinarian from Canada specialising in equine locomotion. This doctor was at the University of Pennsylvania's New Bolton Centre for a short time. A small team was to come over to our farm to film the Grand Prix test and to record heart-rate changes and other data. On the day we chose it was raining very hard but since there were many schedules to consider we decided to stick to the plan and try it in the indoor arena. My horse was fitted with an electrode that could relay heart rates to an expensive monitor set up in the corner. The camera was prepared. The three doctors arranged the equipment with lighted screens. The bright sodium lights of the arena reflected silver off the metal machines. It seemed ironic to be riding some of these ancient exercises under the scrutiny of these high-tech instruments. The horse I was riding was pretty green at this, the most difficult, FEI test, but for the sake of science, we tried. There were some problems with the camera, so the first and second tests weren't recorded. Finally, the machines were all in sync. While I was riding the tests, one of the doctors was monitoring the horse's heart rate. The machine would make a beep that I could hear, and it was in time with my horse's heart beat. Every few seconds, she would announce the computed rate for the film to record. The effect of this was surreal: there, over in the corner, was the electronically beating heart from the horse that was directly under me in all the movements. To hear this beat accelerating and decelerating through the different movements was in itself a revelation. At first I was too engrossed in the novelty to attach much to it. All the doctors were surprised at the horse's fitness from just dressage work. At the end of each test as I halted, the rate was in the lower 100s; by the time I took a couple of steps, and then when I patted the

[104]

horse the rate would drop into the 60s.

As I finished riding the third test, I made a startling discovery. I had been having difficulty with this horse in the passage. In our practices the resistance in the passage had been increasing. When I pushed the horse on more, the resistance increased. The horse was losing all the suppleness he had in the piaffe, and seemed to be getting increasingly rigid. It was getting to the point where I was re-examining how I was going to proceed. I was feeling that I had to take a new tact in developing this movement. The horse just seemed to be getting too upset and nervous about the whole issue.

As I rode the second test I could hear the heart-rate pulse go up as we did, say, the extended trot, then settle and climb again with the difficult canter work. When I got to the passage, and after repeated attempts, the horse was fuming around in a extravagant effort. I was trying to produce at least some semblance of passage when I heard the heart rate dropping down. I couldn't believe it. I was sure I heard wrong. In the next pieces of passage and in the next test, every time the passage came up, no matter what effort I thought we were putting in, the heart rate went down. I was amazed. This horse was not getting upset from the strenuous passage. He was holding back. Up until that point I was about to back down in the training, or at least try something different. However, it was obvious that I was misreading the horse. At first this bothered me, and on two counts. One, because I felt my judgment was pretty good. My interpretation of the horse's problem was becoming more instinctive and more exact. I seemed to be getting better at isolating the difficulties and selecting exercises which could correct them. However, here I seemed to have really missed.

Second, it bothered me because I felt my partner was somehow disloyal. I was giving my best effort but the

[105]

horse wasn't. And I didn't even know it. I began seriously thinking about resistances. Is it possible to know all the time what is the real level of resistance? If I can't know, how am I going to proceed? I know very well how some trainers handle problems of resistance. . .

A rider I know was competing at a famous international dressage show in Europe, and was being coached by a well-known dressage trainer. In the test the horse he rode played up. It didn't really bother that person I know, but it highly embarrassed his well-known trainer in front of his peers. After the show, the horse was taken back to be 'straightened out'. My friend told me that his horse was taken into the woods and beaten with chains.

The rider then had to continue on the competition circuit and in due course the next show came up. I know that every person who ever loved a horse could write a scenario as to how this story should end. However, the reality was different. My friend told me that the horse performed the best test of his life in terms of his score.

There is a nagging fact that in the training of some animals to do certain things brutality will work. Because so many people are riding, and a lot of them are riding in competitions under pressure, you see this kind of training more and more. If you are a trainer of horses you have to address the fact that all over the world horses trained in this manner are receiving praise and recognition in the form of prizes and accolades at riding competitions, and at the highest levels. This is certainly something I have become aware of, and I also realise that it is not new. Historically there are many examples of severe brutality and torture in training horses.

The more I went over the realisation of the heart rate experiment, the more I began to wonder about its significance? What if I was fooled by the horse? What if the horse was cheating? What if I unnecessarily changed the course of training when it really didn't need it? Do you need this kind of absolute mind control in order to proceed? It was not as if I was going to quit training the passage entirely – I was just going to change tracks.

Suppose you have an appointment with someone who is notoriously late. You know almost certainly that if you arrive on time you will waste a half an hour waiting. There is something you could do during that time. Do you still arrive on time? Of course, you must. This imbues your action with an integrity. This integrity is mutually exclusive of any other event. It is not dependent on any other act. It isn't dependent on the outcome.

As a trainer of horses you cannot make a dishonest horse honest. You can make yourself more honest. You can be less deceitful and more open. You become easier to read by virtue of your greater skill. Your actions may become more economical and certainly they become more effective, if for no other reason than because the quality of your communication with the horse is cleaner and less confusing.

You are the one who initiates the training of the horse. You lead, you assume authority. Where does the right to assume authority come from? I would like to quote Vicki Hearne from her book *Adam's Task: Calling Animals by Name*[26] in which she explores, among other training subjects, this one. 'You must realize the ability to exact obedience doesn't give you the right to do so – it is the willingness to obey that confers the right to command.'

The assumption of authority, as Vicki Hearne so ably explains, is nothing unusual. Suppose you see a stranger in danger's way. You shout to him to move; he moves. You have commanded; he has yielded. In the reverse, we yield all the time when it is in our own self-interest. To yield to commands of natural integrity, of course, presupposes the commands have integrity. You take care of your own integrity. You try to arrive on time, all the time. Your intentions are clear. Your commands have integrity. They come out of the same kinds of natural energies that support all of us on the earth – all the other commands.

Who or what does the trainer obey? He or she obeys the code, the way, the life of a trainer. Most of all, the horse. You do not obey the judge, the prize, the trophy. You obey your own integrity. You obey yourself. You have self-respect, and mutual respect. Once you act with integrity, in the issuance of commands, it is almost not your business what the horse does in response. If you are doing your work well, the horse will probably train well. However, if after a long while of your best work, the horse does not respond, there is no more you can do. The horse has decided not to be trained and you may have to let go. If you approach training this way, you will give the horse that ultimate respect. You give it a choice.

If you are a sadistic trainer, who will you obey? Are you going to demand authority over the horse's action? Are you going to demand that you never be fooled? Will you be humiliated if you arrive on time but your appointment doesn't? Are you going to chain the horse into answering your commands?

If you can never be fooled, neither can you be surprised by the mysteries and gifts that animals can bestow upon you.

Too many people assume that they have the right to ride the horse without respect for some proper communication. They have the right to this authority without granting any authority to the horse; without any reverence for the process; without any willingness to be ordered or changed by the horse. If you acknowledge the idea that you go into training the horse with the possibility that you can be changed and ordered by the horse, you have built in a flexibility in your style, a movability

[108]

in your system, a freedom in your reactions. To further this, you have no choice but to explore and develop your technique in riding. Horses do not speak to people with words. Yet man has been communicating with horses for some six thousand years.[27] The lexicon of his communication with horses is no less than the story of riding. How the trainer handles resistance is directly related to how well he knows the story of riding. If you handle resistance with force, you don't need technique. You need bigger muscles. If you want to handle resistance in other ways, it is going to be directly related to: the level of your skill; the quality of your horsemanship; your knowledge of different options.

In Thomas Cleary's[24] beautiful translation of the two-thousand-year-old Chinese masterpiece of strategy by Sun Tzu, *The Art of War*, he says, 'the master warrior is likewise the one who knows the psychology and mechanics of conflict so intimately that every move of an opponent is seen through at once, and one who is able to act in precise accord with situations, riding on their natural patterns with a minimum of effort.'

Of course, I am not suggesting the trainer is at war with the horse. I am saying that the greater the psychic and physical knowledge of the horse and riding, the better the handling of potential trouble. One has to keep in mind that 'Sun Tzu showed how understanding conflict can lead not only to its resolution, but even to its avoidance altogether.'[24]

This, then, predetermines the masterful rider/trainer to a long and detailed study of technique. In order to advance, (s)he must arrive at the same place that *The Book of Balance and Harmony*, a medieval Taoist text, refers to as: 'A state of deep knowledge'.[24]

'Deep knowledge is to be aware of disturbance before disturbance, to be aware of danger before danger, to be aware of destruction before destruction, to be aware of calamity before calamity. Strong action is training the body without being burdened by the body, exercising the mind without being used by the mind, working in the world without being affected by the world, carrying out tasks without being obstructed by tasks.

'By deep knowledge of principle, one can change disturbance into order, change danger into safety, change destruction into survival, change calamity into fortune. By strong action on the Way, one can bring the body to the realm of longevity, bring the mind to the sphere of mystery, bring the world to great peace, and bring tasks to great fulfilment.'

Hasn't that always been the aim of dressage – to bring the horse's body to the realm of longevity, to bring the rider's mind to the sphere of mystery?

I would like to make a strong point that deep knowledge is not easily attainable. Nor should it be taken lightly as some kind of poetic gesture. It is very real and extremely practical. Deep knowledge is not intellectual philosophising. It takes a mastery of a high level of practical psychology and physical development. The modern rider who hires a masseur to prepare the back of his horse may be shirking some of the duties of a rider. This is one of those fundamental tasks that the rider/trainer must know about. Today, people do these kinds of things all the time. This short-circuits the rider's own development, and steps out from under the weight of integrity. It avoids the responsibility to master the lessons, the theory and the material. The Journeyman rider has to try to know these things.

Yet six thousand years of horsemanship can be an imposing study – if not paralysing. By now I have spent thirty years reading and riding. I find myself going back further in time in reading the literature, and I find myself consulting with state of the art scientists on analysis of movement and anatomy. Often the work is redundant. However, every once in a while a sentence will lift me high with some enlightenment. Maybe a riding experience will crystallise a point of technique. To me, this is still exciting. The feeling is revitalising. I love the technical pursuit. Yet I started to realise that the body of knowledge is unknowable. It is too vast and our time on the earth too short. It was hard for me not to be saddened by this realisation. I wasn't going to make it. I saw every day how much I improved from the technical lessons. I wanted to obtain all the information. I wanted to acquire the perfect form. It took a long time before I began to see that wisdom is the knowledge that there is no knowledge. You cannot know a thing completely because it changes all the time. However, you can try to know a thing. The way you try to know something is what life is about. Two thousand years later businessmen read *The Art of War*.[24] Two thousand years later horsemen read Xenophon.[28] Too many of us read them in order to find a way to know or gain something, when really you study something, anything, in order to experience the Way. The relativity of our different skills does not limit any one of us from personal development or enlightenment. When the goal is irrelevant to the glory of the process, the saddness of things unattained is lifted by the rapture of every revelation you do have, every experience you live out.

In the handling of resistance, you don't beat a horse for the things you don't see – the height of the passage that isn't there, which is your own momentary subjective appraisal anyway. The horse may have no idea what it is you are after besides domination. You polish and develop the things that are there. In the case of the horse at the beginning of the chapter, I made headway with the passage when I returned to the piaffe, which was solid. I practised advancing and then collecting the piaffe almost on the spot. The horse learned to stay round with the rein going through the body, instead of hurling himself forward in a hollow passage. He began to extend his piaffe. Riding that develops presupposes that the trainer has a good technical knowledge of how the movements work and which exercises affect which muscles, tendons and ligament groups. The trainer must develop the ability to perceive things other than his own feelings. It is this cultivation of perception that the trainer must seek. An answer to a problem will reveal itself if you know how to look. I mean *how* to look, not where. Even though a book may point you in a direction, eventually the problems are so specific to horse and rider that you fix them while you are riding. What are we talking about is, of course, 'deep knowledge'.

You need to develop 'deep knowledge'. There is a wonderful anecdote illuminating the spirit of this kind of development. It seems the great swordsman Bokuden had three sons all trained in swordsmanship and he wanted to test them.

'He placed a little pillow over the curtain at the entrance to his room, and it was so arranged that a slight touch on the curtain, when it was raised upon entering, would make the pillow fall right on one's head. Bokuden called in the eldest son first. When he approached he noticed the pillow on the curtain, so he took it down, and after entering, he placed it back in the original position. The second son was now called in. He touched the curtain to raise it, and as soon as he saw the pillow coming down, he caught it with his hands and then carefully put it back where it had been. It was the third son's turn to touch the curtain. He came in brusquely, and the pillow fell right

[112]

on his neck. But he cut it in two with his sword even before it came down on the floor.

'Bokuden passed his judgment: "Eldest son, you are well qualified for swordsmanship." So saying, he gave him a sword. To the second son, he said, "Train yourself yet assiduously." But the youngest son, Bokuden most severely reproved, for he was pronounced to be a disgrace to his family.'[1]

It is a similar disgrace for the horseman to routinely use force to overcome resistance and faulty perceptions. The true Journeyman/horseman must also assiduously seek deep knowledge, to avoid battles or force. To understand the Way is more important than the result. When you handle resistance, you handle the tyranny Barry Lopez was talking about in the quote at the beginning of this chapter. If you as a rider/trainer can avoid being an oppressive force from the outside, then you may have a chance to become one with the horse, which may be an overworked phrase, but an underworked reality.

Chapter Nine

The Myths of the Outside Rein

'THE RIDER should not try to support the movement by the aid of the rein; this never leads to true success. Leg and back aids must always be predominant. The horse must learn to move in self-carriage and must only be *guided* and not pulled by the rider.'

Richard L. Watjen[29]

I once witnessed a clinic given by a famous competitive dressage rider, and in the course of three days there were non-stop references to the use of the outside rein. Not one time in three days did I hear any reference to the rider's seat or legs. I was beginning to see that this experience was not unique. Even when a lot of instructors were trying to get their pupils to be lighter with their hands, the instructors' focus of attention never seemed to leave the reins, and so neither did their pupils'.

What this outside rein is all about of course is the turn. If you are riding in a straight line in an open field with no reference to a wall, then theoretically there is no outside rein. To understand the correct and most classical use of the outside rein one must understand the way a dressage horse moves around a circle. This concept is one of the most fundamental and also one of the most pervasive in the whole training of the dressage horse. Before I start analysing the theory of the horse in the turn, and this talk about the outside rein, I would like to make the most important point of this whole topic: **Any and every rein effect must be preceded by a leg or seat effect.** If one imagines a sail boat in a dead calm, you can pull on the sail until you drop but you will not be able to have any steering or guiding effect until some wind force comes from behind to fill the sail with air. This is an obvious and absolute prerequisite. The outside rein functions very much like the sail. It catches power coming from behind, and usually from behind and from the inside. As the wind blows up from behind across the boat. Remember, the wind moves the boat. The sail only helps to guide it. The legs and seat move the horse. The rein only guides it.

All these mechanical analogies have drawbacks. In this one, the hull of the boat is rigid and the horse's body is not. Although some trainers have constantly proposed, and still do, that the horse's body should be as straight as the hull of the ship, this has never been the classical approach. The classical approach has always recognised the bendability of the horse and trained for it in a very

[115]

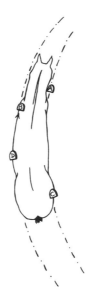

Fig. 12 When travelling on a circle, the horse follows the arc of circle with an arc through its body. It should then leave only two imaginary lines of tracks.

careful way. The trouble with the classical view, though, is one of very confusing language. One of the most fundamental requirements and descriptions of the dressage horse is that it is straight when it is evenly bent around a circle. Yes, it is straight when it is bent. No wonder people get confused about the outside rein! What this means of course is that when training on a circle the horse follows the approximate arc of the circle with an arc through its body. It should then leave only two imaginary lines of tracks. The left hind should track on the same line as the left front, and the right hind tracking behind the right front (see Fig. 12). The horse then, in moving around a circle, will leave two lines of tracks or two concentric circles separated by the distance between the horse's left and right feet. This leads to some very interesting developments. The classical horse trainers are all aware of these.

[116]

The only possible way the horse can track up with both right feet and both left feet in their respective lines is to bend through its body. Now if a horse is travelling on a 10 metre circle and its feet are about 6 inches (or 15 cms) apart, the outside circle scribed on the ground will be approximately 3-6 feet (or 1-2 metres) longer than the inside circle. It is precisely these physical facts which determine the classicists' aids and requirements for negotiating a circle.

One can clearly see that if the outside rein has a retropulsive – or braking – effect, it will restrict the outside stretch and the rider can literally pull the bend out of the horse. There are at least two objective proofs that any horseman can use to see if in fact the horse is too straight on the circle and has lost all bend. One is that the haunches will slip to the outside, so that the tracks of the horse do not line up; the tracks of the hind feet are both outside the tracks of the front feet. Remember, it has always been a key element of dressage training that when the haunches deviate too much laterally, the loading and carrying power are diminished.

The second is that the horse will lean over, to counteract centrifugal force, in the same way that a rigid-framed bicycle has to lean inwards to negotiate a circle and account for centrifugal force. The horse's centre of gravity tips onto the shoulders and the hind legs push instead of carry.

The proper use of the outside rein is to guide the power generated from behind, just as the trimmed sail helps guide the boat. Never does it take an active role and actually bend the neck. This will only succeed in eventually disconnecting the neck from the horse's body and lead to a rubbery neck in front of the withers and a stiff body behind the withers – instead of a flexible body and solidly connected neck, i.e. the horse moving in one piece. The classicist, as Watjen says, can never be a hand rider but must ride the horse predominantly with leg and back aids.

If the rider/trainer always keeps in mind the elementary principles that we train the dressage horse to circle with bend in the body and standing up perpendicular to the ground, and that there must be room for the outside to stretch, then the proper leg aids for circling will also reveal themselves.

So where is the rider's wind power coming from to fill up the outside rein? Obviously, the rider's seat and legs. However, it is easy to see that traditionally the inside leg is stressed. The rider's inside leg can dually act on the horse, not only to move the horse forward by signalling the hind leg on that side to step up more, but also to encourage bend around that leg. So the inside leg generates power into the horse toward the outside rein, which encourages or guides the horse around the curve. Although the rider's outside leg cannot be asleep, it cannot be overactive near the girth or it will push the bend out of the horse and have a discouraging effect on the impulsive travel around the circle. The outside leg needs to be slightly back to catch the haunches if they deviate too much to the outside and to help encourage expanding impulsive steps on the outside of the horse's body. Too much strength and the rider will squash the horse into rigidity between both legs. It is not the easiest thing in the world to have independent leg aids but they are critical to good, free, forward movement. I have seen this many, many times in teaching novice riders. In leg yield, for example, they cannot get the horse to move sideways in spite of what they feel is enormous pressure from their inside leg. When you stand in front of them as they approach you, you can see that every time they use their left leg, for the sake of an argument, to try to move the horse over to the right, their right leg pulses right along with the left. The result is that one signal nullifies the other and the horse continues to go straight in spite of the greatest leg effort from the rider. This is very typical. Even much later in the rider's training, you can see riders playing a kind of ping-pong, chasing the horse's body from one leg to the other, bouncing back and forth without a clear transmission of forward power. To me, it stems from a lack of proper execution of the simplest of figures – the circle.

I have been taught by teachers who were traditional, and those who had Baucherist influences. I was always taught that hand riding was the crudest of riding. It had no place in classical equitation. Even if I did not agree with these teachers philosophically, I would have come to the same conclusion that hand riding was not real equitation, just through the study of technique. One can see in the analysis of the turn alone, how destructive the hands can be. Rough hands will effect every physical and psychological aspect of riding.

Even when pulling on the reins is done under the guise of increasing flexibility, the real effect can be the opposite. While pulling the horse's head from side to side may make the horse respond quicker to the bit and reins, it can disconnect the neck from the body of the horse with the result that the neck is rubbery and the torso is stiff. The horse has been 'broken into two pieces' and it is impossible for the rein then 'to go through the body'. Classical riders have always sought to make the horse flexible in the body.

As I studied some of the old texts and in particular the engravings in the books of Newcastle, Pluvinel, Eisenberg and Guérinière, in spite of many differences and much egotistical posturing, I could not find one illustration with the horse's head and neck bent to the outside.

[119]

Not one. (I found this astounding and yet logical.) Even when the '*pli*', or neck bend, is quite exaggerated, it is still very clear that these riders were all aware of the importance of bend inside. The arc in the horse's body conformed to the arc of the circle they were moving on. This is a passage from one of the Duke of Newcastle's books published in 1667. Preceding this passage he is talking about using his cavesson with a rein tied to it, but listen to the description of how he considers the dressed horse of over three hundred years ago should go around a turn:

'For without it [the cavesson rein] no horse can be perfectly dressed, in any kind, to have ply of his neck, and to supple his shoulders, to look into the turn, to have the legs go right, as they ought to in all actions, his body rightly bent to be part of the circle he goes in.'

Duke of Newcastle[30]

One sees a logical progression to Guérinière's invention of the shoulder-in, one of the most masterful inside-bending exercises of all. Guérinière himself pays frequent homage to the preparatory work of the Duke of Newcastle.

'We can only seek after the truth in the principle of those who have left us written record of the fruits of their labours and inspirations. Among many authors we have according to the unanimous sentiment of all connoisseurs only two whose works are esteemed, these being M. de la Broue, and the Duke of Newcastle.'

François de la Guérinière[31]

Although Newcastle does not use the term 'shoulder-in', read the following passage and see what exercise comes to mind.

'Thus the Horse being bias [diagonal] in the inward rein pulled thus [inward] inlarges the horse before, in pulling his inward Foreleg from the outward Foreleg; which puts his inward Hinder-Leg to his outward Hinder-Leg which narrows him behind, makes him bow in the Gambrels [hocks] especially on his outward Hinder-Leg which he rests on and thrusts his inward Hinder-Leg under his belly; which all these things makes him very much upon the Haunches.'

Duke of Newcastle[30]

This is a man who understands collection. So there is this progression to Guérinière and beyond, continuing toward Seeger, Steinbrecht and L'Hotte, up to the modern writer-riders like Watjen and Decarpentry. Make your horse straight. Ride him evenly bent on the circle. The great *pli*, or neck bend inside, was gradually reduced as the riders became more masterful at bending the body vis à vis the shoulder-in, renvers. All this continuing work being based on the inside bend, around a pillar, around the leg. Eventually this bending developed connectedness and straightness.

Today, just as our deep work aims at connecting the horse longitudinally, making the neck and body connected, so proper lateral work has always aimed at this connection of neck, back, and hindquarters. This keeps the integrity of the spine, by enhancing the bend inside and making the outside stretch. Thereby the horse is made supple throughout its length.

So, then, where did so much harsh handwork come from, especially the swinging of the horse's head and neck from side to side that we see everywhere today? I think the greatest single influence was from François Baucher and his disciples, including James Fillis, com-

[121]

pounded by a lot of misinterpretation of his work. When Baucher*, a controversial albeit brilliant rider who performed in circuses in France in the 1800s, came along, he developed a method of training horses. To rid the horse of resistances, he opened the horse's jaws, and bent the horse's jaws and neck, and he bent them a lot – inside and out, up and down, standing still and moving. His work caused a maelstrom of rage, dividing French riders and promoting some Germans to dub Baucher the 'gravedigger of French equitation'. This scenario has many political and social elements in it besides the riding and riding theory. Professor Hilda Nelson has written a wonderful book which illuminates many of these issues, including Baucher's own words. It is critical to understanding the roots of modern riding. James Fillis, who learned from a student of Baucher, went on to develop his own style of neck flexions, specialising in flexions in movement. For me, a lot of Fillis' work can be described by his own words: 'Finally, as the hands are much more effective for guiding than the legs, they should be used in a very light manner.[32] The photographs that accompany Fillis' book of himself show a rider quite focused on the hands and reins.

Before Baucher you simply do not see neck bending to the outside nor a whole system of bending the neck with the bit and reins. What all this debate turned into was, for one thing, a referendum on hand riding. Although Baucher's work involved many aspects of riding practice and theory, including such things as inventing one-time flying changes, a great portion of his legacy is these neck flexions. It was when these rein pullings and neck bendings occurred in motion, that the real potential for destruction and disconnection came to be. For the horse

---

* For outstanding background information, see Nelson, H., *Baucher, A Man and His Method*, J.A. Allen, London, 1992

to transmit efficient power from the hind legs, a certain amount of rigidity is necessary in the whole torso. If a trainer has a notion to get some false flexibility in the body of a moving horse, it can be at cross-purposes to the biomechanics and cause severe damage to the neck, back and/or rump. It certainly is born out of a misinterpretation of the anatomy of the horse's motion. In all fairness to Baucher, one can't say he advocated what we see today. When one watched someone like Nuno Oliveira ride, who was strongly influenced by Baucher, you never saw pulling on the reins. Whereas if you watch competitive riders trained from the school of Steinbrecht, who warned riders to beware of Baucher and his methods over and over, you can see ferocious rein pulling from side to side.

In terms of this Steinbrecht warning, I once had a conversation with Dr Van Schaik. I made the comment that the current FEI Grand Prix test had some thirty-seven flying changes, not one single complete circular figure except for two canter pirouettes, and was basically connecting all movements by straight lines. I told him I thought Baucher would have loved the test and probably could have designed one very like it. We both agreed that Steinbrecht would probably roll over in his grave at the sight of some the new German riders riding their horses with straight bodies, flexed in the middle of their necks not at the poll, and constantly pulling them from side to side. We both concluded some of these new German riders were perhaps the most Baucherist in the world.[33]

The fact is that bad riding can occur in any school. There is a difficulty today because with fewer and fewer examples of classically dressed horses, plus a general unwillingness to study riding instead of just imitating, many young riders are being inculcated into an acceptance of hand manipulation as a method toward collection and lightness, when it is in fact a physical and biological impossibility.

I believe that a lot of trainers who promote neck bending are misapplying Baucher's system. I think they fail to remember that Baucher was often interested in getting his horses off the haunches with the distribution of weight more over all four legs. His system of neck bending with this goal in mind may be argued. However, to claim that rein manipulation can put a horse further on its haunches or collect it, would be quite another matter. Since every rein aid when in motion has the mechanical effect of a hand brake, to a greater or lesser degree, then when a brake is applied to any object in motion, the weight will shift forward. For the horse, the balance goes onto the forehand by definition.

What often happens in excessive neck bending is that the horse comes lighter in the rider's hands but the neck is bent in the middle and the poll is not the highest point. This horse will not be light in the bridle as a result of engagement of the hind legs and a cresting neck promoting bascule and therefore entire lighter forehand. No. The horse will be light in the bridle only by virtue of spitting out the bit and being behind. An objective proof of this kind of riding is that almost invariably these horses will execute poor transitions, and will ride from trick to trick. Horses that are ridden strongly, athletically, without the neck cresting up and out, lose their overall bascule. When the bascule suffers, so does the horse – usually first in the back, and therefore in the transmission of power.

Every way you come to analyse hand riding in daily training and practice, you find trouble. Furthermore it leads riders even further away from the importance of a good seat and dexterity in the legs.

I am certain this is one of the reasons why lungeing the

novice rider has always been a cornerstone of classical equitation. Lungeing forces the rider to make his/her first communications to the horse, and vice versa, through the seat and legs. Since riders are not allowed to hold the reins, they can't rely on the dexterity of their hands. The language becomes clear. It is up to the teachers of riding to insist on the acceptance of the common language of classical riding: the seat, and not the hands. This is not for sentimental nostalgia, but because if one doesn't understand all the reasons why hand riding is crude, including the biomechanical and spiritual, one cannot understand the finer forms of classical equitation.

All the best riders have tried to exalt the horse, to ride it carefully, as a reverent thank you for the gift of travel – real travel towards enlightenment.

However, if you use the horse for travel toward some destination of your ego, you are no better than a bad farmer who has no love for the land, and your horse is nothing but a misused beast of burden. One of those fundamental tasks of the Journeyman is to learn to carry your own burden, and not project it onto other living things.

Chapter Ten

Riding as a Meditation

'"VERY INTERESTING, Dr Jung, very interesting indeed. Now another concept related to motivational development is the process of individuation, which you frequently refer to in your writings. Would you care to comment on this process of psychic development towards a whole, a totality?"

"Well, you know that is something quite simple. Take an acorn, put it in the ground, it grows and becomes an oak. That is man. Man develops from an egg, and grows into the whole man, and that is the law that is in him. . . As each plant, each tree grows from a seed and becomes in the end, say, an oak tree, so man becomes what he is meant to be. At least, he ought to get there. But most get stuck by unfavourable external conditions, by all sorts of hindrances or pathological distortions, wrong education – no end of reasons why one shouldn't get there where one belongs.'"

C.G. Jung in an interview with Stephen Blake[34]

In the review of riding literature, the words of the great trainers of the past are heard. Many researchers have claimed to notice a thread among the myriad of inconsistencies and extinct movements, etc. Namely that there are two philosophies in training horses. One philosophy of training bases much of its advice on 'gentleness', 'judicious treatment', and 'naturalness'. This thread is clear in its lineage from the Greek general Xenophon, 400 BC, to Pluvinel, 1555-1620, the Ecuyer to the French King Louis XIII, to Guérinière, 1730, a professional whose reputation is still without match. The second group of trainers of horses had never limited themselves with this attitude. The likes of Grisone, Pignatelli and the Duke of Newcastle never shied away from being extremely rough and severe in the training of their horses. Whether you like it or not both these groups produced highly trained horses. If you read the Duke of Newcastle's work you cannot help but be impressed by his technical prowess. Guérinière himself refers to the Duke of Newcastle's great work many times. If you can get past his ego, his work on freeing the shoulders of the horses, and the correct way to get the horse on its haunches, is amazingly pertinent.

Podhajsky, the late Director of the Spanish Riding School, in his treatise *The Complete Training of Horse and Rider*,[15] states in his own review of the literature and

[127]

history of the branches of riding that 'as a result of the development of humaneness, the doctrines of the Duke of Newcastle . . . failed to create a durable basis for the art of riding in England . . . The influence built up by Grisone, Pignatelli and their pupils was lost.'

I would love to believe this, but it is impossible. If you go anywhere near a modern dressage show today, right through to the highest levels, you will see and hear many trainers who will not limit themselves to the humane approach. They train and admit that they train in order to win. They demand absolute obedience from the horse and claim they get it or else.

Having studied different writers and trainers for a long time, I now have a different opinion. It is my feeling that is not humaneness versus brutality that divides the two great philosophical schools of riding: it is whether the riding is used for mundane purposes or whether it is realised for its metaphorical meditative properties. This is what separates the lineage of Xenophon, Pluvinel, Guérinière, and those types, from Grisone, Pignatelli, the Duke of Newcastle and their types.

Xenophon was not an animal trainer. Not that there is anything wrong with being an animal trainer. But Xenophon was a philosopher, political man and teacher. He was interested in raising consciousness. It is clear in his writings that he sees horsemanship as another way to do this.

'Anything that is forced can never be beautiful.'[28] This is his language, which is about equestrian art. Webster's Dictionary defines meditation as 'a discourse intended to express its author's reflections or to guide others in contemplation'. Xenophon's book, *The Art of Horsemanship*, is a classical meditation.

Morris Morgan, the English translator of *The Art of Horsemanship*, noted when talking about Xenophon's equestrian writings: 'One likes to believe the both (books) were designed by the old soldier to serve for the guidance of his sons.' Xenophon was well aware that work with horses has metaphorical properties, and meditative value. His writings clearly reflect this as opposed to being only a treatise on animal behaviour or horse training.

If you read Pluvinel's writings you will see he is partially obsessed with the consciousness-raising of France's youth at a time when they were killing each other in senseless duels.[35]

His love of and skill in riding was a way to pursue personal development. There is no question as to riding's use as a meditative and physical exercise. 'Thus your majesty can see quite clearly how useful this beautiful exercise is to the mind, since it instructs and accustoms it to perform with clarity and order all these functions amid noise, worry, agitation, and . . . fear. . .'[35]

In the beginning of the first chapter of the second section of Guérinière's book, *Ecole de Cavalerie,*[31] he talks about the qualities necessary to become a horseman and why there are so few real horsemen.

'Practice without true principles is nothing other than routine, the fruit of which is an execution strained and unsure, a false diamond which dazzles semi-connoisseurs often more impressed by the fineness of the horse than by the merit of horseman . . . This scarcity of principles renders pupils unable to distinguish short-comings from perfection. They have no other recourse but to imitation.'

Now the eminent psychologist C.G. Jung:

'Human beings have one faculty which, though it is of

[129]

the greatest utility for collective purposes, is most perni-
cious for individuation, and that is the faculty of imitation . . . as a rule these specious attempts at individual dif-
ferentiation stiffen into a pose, and the imitator remains
at the same level as he always was, only several degrees
more sterile than before. To find out what is truly individual to ourselves, profound reflection in needed, and
suddenly we realise how uncommonly difficult the discovery of individuality is . . . You cannot imagine how
one-sided people are nowadays. And so it needs no end
of work to get people rounded out, or mentally more
developed, more conscious.'[34]

This psychological meditational approach is not specific
to equestrian art at all. In the Orient (even during this
same time) practitioners of the martial arts were understanding and espousing the mental – psychical – aspect of
their art. They were exploring the metaphorical qualities
of their disciplines and their value as meditations capable
of developing self-awareness, self-enlightenment and
natural understanding.

In Hans Joachin Stein's book about Kyudo, the *Art of
Zen Archery*, he (a German studying in the Orient) talks
about meditation:

'Meditation, in whatever form, with or without a bow, *as
contemplation it has always been known to us.* If such
meditation is practised for its own sake without any
intentionally determined aim, our belief in the existence
of an individual (I) confronted by the universe will gradually fall away as we return to our Self. That will happen
as gently and unresistingly as a leaf detaches itself from a
branch in autumn. We shake off the chains of our I with
its desires and cravings. The opposites return to the unity
of the whole. The meditator experiences a deep inner

[130]

calm which makes him immune to the externalities of his every day life – and yet he will not resist them.'³⁶

Pluvinel again: 'Riding instructs and accustoms the mind to perform with clarity and order all these functions amid noise, worry, agitation and . . . fear. . .'

Modern Kendo is the way of the sword or swordmanship. A dull bamboo sword is conventionally used in practice. This sword is a vehicle but it is not capable of cutting through an opponent. Its real use is to cut through one's own ego. The study of sword fighting is metaphorical, meditative, a physical and mental developing exercise to get at life itself. In horsemanship the vehicle of enlightenment is the horse, and the horse is nature itself. This is one of the reasons for the rich mythology involving horses and men. Since the horse is nature itself, the lessons are incredibly profound. The moment the horseman/rider succumbs to the lessons of the horse, they have transcended the duality of man and nature, man against nature. For modern western philosophy, this can be a great jump. However, if it happens, the I-ego dissolves, and the rider sees right into nature, his own and the horse's which are, of course, from the same source.

Anila Jaffe wrote a book on the life and work of C.G. Jung. She told how the great psychologist Jung came upon the ancient Chinese meditational text, *The Secret of the Golden Flower*, how profoundly it pressed him into some of his greatest insights:

'Above all there was an affinity between the goals to be reached: the production of the diamond body through meditation was a symbol for the shifting of the psychic centre from the ego to a transpersonal, spiritual authority. The meditative process thus involved a psychic trans-

[131]

formation which Jung had recognised and experienced as the goal of individuation, the recession of the ego in favour of the totality of the self.'[37]

There is another famous quote of Jung's which goes, 'the man who must win at something has not yet arrived'. Arrived where? Arrived at the totality of the self, the development of the self. The Journeyman rider knows this place well. To get stuck in this world of winning at something means the totality of the self cannot be reached because the ego won't recede. The ego stops the rider's development on all levels and leaves him an imitator, not just on a personal level but on a technical level also. So Jung's oak tree is stunted.

Returning to riding's two great philosophies, we have on one hand an animal behaviour training system. Reward the horse for the desired response, punish him for the undesired response. Give the horse a carrot. Reward the rider for the desired response with a prize. These are externally applied systems of gratification. For the rider it only works for a rider 'who has not yet arrived', who has stopped on the road to his own enlightenment, his own individuation. The ego reigns in these places. It will not recede. The rider can't further develop and must be vulnerable to manipulation from the outside. The whole process gets arrested on a certain plane.

Riding's second philosophy is that the act and art of riding is in itself the reward, the path to enlightenment, education, self-development. The gratification is determined internally, as each individual reaches his or her own very unique potential. As long as the process is in motion, it has to be right.

I don't think that experienced horsemen practising the humane school of riding necessarily believe that this is a superior animal-training system. In some cases brutality is an easier route when you are trying to eliminate or develop certain behaviour – manipulate horses, or people for that matter. However, if you are using riding as a meditation, a way to explore yourself and nature, a way to get through, as Jung says, the 'pathological distortions, wrong education – no end of reasons why one shouldn't get there where one belongs'.[34]

Expedience, then, is not the only criteria. There are some obvious observations. The horse is nature. You are Nature. Horse and man are in the same world, with a commonality. Brutality to nature is brutality to yourself. Brutality toward the horse is doubly destructive; destructive to the horse, as well as destructive to the person riding the horse. The doctrine of humaneness comes from this meditation and not from a search for the most cost-effective way to get the horse to do what the trainer/rider wants. (It is almost as though one says it is not really that I care how the horse feels after I brutalise it, it is how I will feel after I brutalise it.)

All along in my Journeyman stage I thought a technical thread would appear if I studied the lineages and exercises hard enough. In my search for the purest line of riding technique, the best exercises, the only airs, I talked to and read classical trainers and circus trainers and competitive trainers, past and present. I couldn't find clear threads. When I studied movements like ballotade, capriole, courbette, croupade, demi-volte, volte, falcade, ferme à ferme, mesair, pessade, passage, passade, levade, pirouette, shoulder-in, terre à terre, un pas un saut, Spanish walk, Spanish trot, and so on and on, I couldn't find real reasons for certain ones' extinctions and others' popularity. It became apparent that a lot of technique was accepted or rejected not as much on physical anatomical, or scientific horse-related reasons as much as it was accepted because of the virtuosity and charisma of certain

[133]

trainers. The more I studied the movements through history, the more I saw how they have changed. It is impossible to base the idea of riding classically on the performance of certain movements alone. Saying this or that exercise is classical can become increasingly cloudy the deeper you research them. My continuous study of technique kept showing me that the movements themselves were not the glue of classical riding.

In all my searchings I did not find the thread of Xenophon, Pluvinel on Guérinière to be a technical one. I did find a thread, though, and it was a metaphysical one. It was aesthetic. It was artistic. I was beginning to see that even if and when riding was dazzling in technical bravura, unless it made the step from mundane to meditation, it could not be art. No matter how great the technique, the rider could get arrested from arriving. I think it can be said that both philosophies of training produced well-trained horses, but only one also produced well-trained men.

Being arrested in the technical plane in the Journeyman phase can be described as being stuck in a certain plane of psychological development. Namely, stuck in the world of the ego. Both technical and psychological growth can falter as the human organism searches for a totality that it knows deep inside is out there. Since each of our potentials is unique, they really can't be compared. Each must follow the plan mapped out for that person in a sense at birth. The oak must become the oak, the spruce, the spruce, etc.

The glue of classical riding is the aesthetic, with its strong and profound mythological connections, which are vast. There is Pegasus, and Quixote's horse. When the knights Gawain and Galahad search for the Holy Grail it is on the backs of horses. When Mohammed was flown to heaven it was on the back of a horse. At the end of time

[134]

the Messiah and Vishnu are supposed to descend from
the clouds on horses. It was a dragon horse from heaven
that revealed the forces of the Universe, the Yin and the
Yang, to the Yellow Emperor of China.'³⁸ It goes on and
on. The Horse, the superior mover, carries man.

Towards the end of my time as a Journeyman, I had a
strong and vivid dream-like image appear. I was riding
fast across a wide, big, arid plane. The ground was dusty
and dry, the vegetation browned and tanned from a long
season of heat. Waves radiated off the hot earth. I could
see all the way to the blue sky horizon. Far in the distance
in the direction I was going I could see another/rider
standing still on a small rise. His image shimmered in the
heat waves but I could see he was on a white Spanish
horse. The only movement I could detect was the occasionally swish of the horse's wide tail. As I approached
closer, my own horse leaving a trail of powdery dust, I
could see that the rider was an old man. He seemed thin,
almost frail, on top of the beautiful horse, but he looked
comfortable, the way old horsemen sit on horses – better
than they do on chairs. I kept approaching. He seemed to
be waiting. I was too far away to make out any of his fea-
tures but I was aware of his eyes. Somehow I could sense
his light-coloured, squinting eyes set in his wrinkled face.
I knew they were staring at me. They were not menacing
eyes. They were kind eyes, and somehow I felt they were
approving, patient eyes, accepting eyes. I kept up the
pace. The waves seemed to settle his image, which
became clearer. But he remained motionless. The closer I
got, the older he seemed to look, and yet there was something familiar in his form. I got even closer, my horse still
in strong motion. Then, with enough shock to stop my
horse in full arrest, I recognised the old man.

It was me.

I was looking at myself in both directions of time. Seeing myself as an old man. In the same moment I could feel one part of myself flying toward the end of my own life, and the other part quietly waiting for the younger part. The young man rides to the old man. The old man waits to accept the young man. I saw the struggle of the Journeyman in this image: the movement toward the final stages, and the acceptance of growth; the inevitability of movement in time and the advance of age; the necessity to address it, to believe it, and to allow maturation and growth toward it. I saw the horse, the great carrier, the mythological horse that carried men through the dark forests of complacency, across the desert of conformity and imitation. The horse, always man's fearless companion, his most trusting ally, could carry him through any danger, through all those distortions that keep a man from being where he should be. I saw that the beautiful horse was, in the end, always ready to carry me toward my own real self. Somehow the horse knows that you are out there waiting for yourself. The horse will help the man. I began to feel that in the end this is the only job worthy of the horse's effort: not to serve a man's childish egocentric impulses and insecure desires – these jobs demean the horse and the lessons of the mythology. The horse, it seems, has always been there to help carry the man to his own real self, if the rider wants that challenge.

> 'There is a wonderful image in King Arthur where the knights of the Round Table are about to enter the search for the Grail in the Dark Forest, and the narrator says, "They thought it would be a disgrace to go forth in a group. So each entered the forest at a separate point of his choice." You've interpreted that to express the Western emphasis upon the unique phenomenon of a single human life – the individual confronting darkness.'
>
> Bill Moyers[39]

Joseph Campbell, the great teacher and mythologist, answers the journalist Moyers:

'What struck me when I read that in the thirteenth century Queste del Saint Graal, was that it epitomizes an especially Western spiritual aim and ideal, which is, of living the life that is potential in you, and was never in anyone else as a possibility.

'This, I believe, is the great Western truth: That each of us is a completely unique creature, and that, if we are ever to give any gift to the world, it will have to come out of our own experience and fulfillment of our own potentialities, not someone else's.'

Joseph Campbell[39]

Epilogue

THE SCIENTIST HILDEBRAND defines four hundred different strides and concludes that there is no such thing as stride. The scientist Wentick studies the physiology of muscle movement only partially in a single leg and its complexity can bring smoke out of a computer. Dr Leach tell us there is a whole continuum of limb patterns. When you study the historical literature, it is filled with riding movements and gaits that are extinct. The most prestigious classical riding school in the world practises some movements that are younger than some chairs in the building.

Once you begin to study the movement of the horse, and once you begin to study the historical literature, you learn to be careful about what or whom you call 'classical'.

My own study of riding forced me over and over out of my presumptions, biases and prejudices. One must learn to handle these inevitable dualisms in riding. As they say in Zen, you learn to take the middle path. In spite of the paradoxes and apparent confusion about classical riding, it actually has become more solid to me over the years of training horses. For the horse and its dressage movements, I have come, like others before me, to put the emphasis on what comes naturally to the horse. In some thirty years of observing horses, I have never seen an untrained horse canter backwards or on three legs. I have seen untrained horses do flying changes and even multiple flying changes. So I consider flying changes to be a natural movement for the horse and therefore suitable for enhancement through (dressage) training. I have never seen an untrained horse do Spanish walk. I have seen countless untrained horses passage in excitement when a new horse enters a pasture. So, to me, the passage is natural for the horse and can be classically adapted. I have a three-year-old horse in my barn at the moment, that is barely broken. She will break into an expressive piaffe in her stall if a lawn-mower comes too close to her window. I have seen horses extend and collect all their paces. I have seen pirouettes and plenty of leaps and levades as young horses play.

This naturalness then has become my criteria for which movements are classical. Even though classical has come to mean many things to many people, I have come to agree with those writers and riders who insist on keeping the integrity of what is natural for the horse. Classical riding is an artistic homage to nature

What about for the human? What is the quintessence of the classical rider? Certainly the Journeyman phase is

[139]

one thick with technique, and yet, I myself hit a certain wall, focusing only on the technical plane. I knew any real advancement was going to have to come on a different plane, a metaphysical, spiritual, psychological plane. The study of technique is arduous. It is painful. You will need discipline. Here, many riders go astray. They use the discipline as punishment for their apparent failures in achievement the same way they use a prize for reward. 'I only got the second prize. I have to work harder, drive myself and my horse harder,'; 'My practice isn't good enough yet.' Pain becomes the big feeling as the work crackles with ambition. Ironically this is the way of the loser. Failure is built in when everything must be measured by those riders. Everyone must be compared and ranked. Their minds are engrossed in calibration. It becomes the way of the unbalanced mind. This trouble is very serious because it is the way of death. Horses today are dying and people are dying inside and out as a result of unbridled ambition and relentless egos. All this pain and anger. All this mentality. What does this mind fear? Rejection? What does this mind want? Acceptance, recognition, respect? All this misused discipline and torture to get something from the mind. What this mind really wants is something the mind can't give. This mind really wants something from the heart. Something like love. But the heart can't be tricked out of it. The heart can only give to another heart.

So every rider will come to a fork in his or her path. Choosing the path of the winner, will make you the loser. Yet there is another way. Not the Way of Death, but the Way of Life. If you choose this path, then you will need all the discipline you can possibly come by. Childish tantrums won't help here at all. It is the most difficult path. All the work of the Journeyman will be necessary if you want to come out alive, and this is no metaphor. I mean literally alive. Many people never find themselves. They become a construct of other people's opinions and ideas about them. This becomes their guiding light. What was unique in them has disappeared. They become imposters. 'I am what my father always wanted me to be/what my mother expected,'etc. 'There was not time to find the original me, and that is OK because maybe I wouldn't like me.'

No one will really be able to help you on your Journey. Sometimes because they don't want to. Even the people closest to you may try to talk you out of it; maybe even impede you because of their own fears of change, theirs or yours. Yet the Way of Life is the Way of Changes. Sometime even people who love you still can't help just because they are in a different place. We are all so different that it would be presumptions to try to stand in the way of someone's destiny for good or bad reasons.

One has to prove oneself in the technical and theoretical areas. Learning to ride is not learning to compete. If you think this is so, you may have to go to a big show, ride and then leave before the prizes are given out or before the assessments of others are voiced. Especially if you've never done it. Go home. Alone. See what you feel like. See if you know what happened. See if you know if it was good enough. See if you can sustain yourself. If you go to watch the show, you should do the same. Leave early and see if you know for yourself what happened. The Journeyman cannot project his own missing face onto the spirit of the horse. That was something certainly I was unwilling to do any more. The horse could carry me but as my respect for the horse grew and grew, I knew it was not put on the earth to carry my goals and ambitions, all the weaknesses, as Jung might say, that keep one from becoming a complete man or woman. No one has the right to project one's imperfect view or analysis of what life should be onto another living thing in the world.

It is in the proving of oneself that this second path comes about. So you learn all you can. All the technique to keep you calm and strong. All the discipline will be necessary now so you won't fall apart when you let yourself get out of control. When you begin the hardest phase of riding. When you run with the highest technique. When you fall in love with riding.

References

1. SUZUKI, DAISETZ, T. *Zen and Japanese Culture*, Princeton University Press, Princeton, New Jersey, 1970.
2. OLIVEIRA, NUNO, *Reflections on Equestrian Art*, J.A. Allen, London, 1976.
3. NEWCASTLE, DUKE OF, *A General System of Horsemanship*, 1627.
4. PRATT, G.W. JNR, Remarks on Gait Analysis, Dept of Electrical Engineering and Computer Science, MIT, Cambridge, Mass. and Tufts University School of Veterinary Medicine, Boston. Mass.
5. ZUKAV, G., *The Dancing Wu Li Masters*, Bantam Book, New York, 1980.
6. SEUNIG, WALDEMAR, *Horsemanship*, Doubleday and Company Inc., New York, 1956.
7. DREVEMO, S., FREDRICKSON, I., DALIN, G., and HJERTEN, G. (1980b), Equine Locomotion. 1. 'The analysis of coordination between limbs of trotting Standardbreds,' *Equine Vet. Jnl*, 12, 66-70.
8. ROONEY, J.R., *Biomechanics of Lameness in Horses*, William and Wilkens, Baltimore, 1969.
9. PRATT, G.W. JNR, and O'CONNOR, J.T. JNR, (1976), 'Force plate studies of equine biomechanics,' *Am Jnl Vet. Res.*, 37, 1251-1255.
10. DREVEMO, S., FREDRICKSON, I., DALIN, G., and HJERTEN, G. (1980a), Equine Locomotion. 1. 'The analysis of linear and temporal stride characteristics of trotting Standardbreds', *Equine Vet. Jnl*, 12, 60-65.
11. SCHRYVER, H.F., BARTEL, D.L, LANGRANA, N., and LOWE, J.E. (1978), 'Locomo

[143]

tion in the horse: kinematics and external and internal forces in the normal equine digit in the walk and trot,' *Am. Jnl Vet. Res.*, 38, 1728-1733.

12. KINGSBURY, H.B., QUADDUS, M.A., ROONEY, J.R., and GEARY, H.E. (1978), 'A laboratory system for production of flexion rates and forces in the forelimb of the horse', *Am. Jnl. Vet. Res.*, 39, 365-369.
13. GOODY, PETER, *Horse Anatomy, A Pictorial Approach to Equine Structure*, J.A. Allen, London, 1976.
14. DECARPENTRY, GENERAL, *Academic Equitation*, translated by N. Bartle, J.A. Allen, London, 1971.
15. PODHAJSKY, ALOIS, *The Complete Training of Horse and Rider*, Doubleday and Company Inc., New York, and Harrap, London, 1967.
16. Interview with Reiner Klimke by Christian Thiess, *Dressage & CT Magazine*, February, 1994.
17. BENNET, DEB. PhD, *Principles of Conformation Analysis*, Vol 1, Fleet Street Publishing Corporation, Gaithersburg, MD, 1990.
18. TOWNSEND, H.G.G., LEACH, D.H., FRETZ. P.B., 'Kinematics of the equine thoracolumbar spine', *Equine Vet. Jnl*, (1983), 15, (2), 117-122.
19. PODHAJSKY, ALOIS, *The Riding Teacher*, Doubleday and Company Inc., New York, and Harrap, London, 1973.
20. IBN KHALDUN, *Parabola*, Vol. XIV, No. 2, May, 1969.
21. DOOLING, D.M., *Parabola*, Vol. XIV, No. 2, May, 1989.
22. BOLDT, H., *Das Dressur Pferd*, Edition Haberbeck, Germany, 1978.
23. ALBRECHT, K., *A Dressage Judge's Handbook*, J.A. Allen, London, 1978.
24. TZU, SUN, *The Art of War*, translated by Thomas Cleary, Shambhala, Boston and London, 1988.
25. LOPEZ, B., 'Renegotiating contracts', *Parabola*, Vol. VIII, No. 2, May, 1983.
26. HEARNE, V., *Adam's Task: Calling the Animals by Name*, Vintage Books, Random House, New York, 1986.
27. ANTHONY, D., TELEGIN, D., BROWN, D., 'The origin of horseback riding', *Scientific American*, December, 1991, pp 94-98.
28. XENOPHON, *The Art of Horsemanship*, J.A. Allen, London, 1962.
29. WATJEN, R., *Dressage Riding*, J.A. Allen, London, 1958.
30. NEWCASTLE, DUKE OF, *A new method and extraordinary invention to Dress Horses and work them according to Nature: as also to perfect Nature by the Subtilty of Art which was never found out, by the Thrice Noble High and puissant Prince, William Cavendish, 1667*.
31. GUÉRINIERE, F., *Ecole de Cavalerie, 1751*.
32. FILLIS, J., *Breaking and Riding*, J.A. Allen, London, 1986.
33. Video tape: 'Warming up in Aachen', Dressage at Aachen, 1991, Cloverlea Dressage Videotapes, Columbia, Connecticut, 16237.
34. MCGUIRE, W. and HULL, R.F.C. (editors), *C.G. Jung Speaking: Interviews and Encounters*, Bollingen Series XCVII, Princeton University Press, 1977, pp 324, 276, 256.
35. PLUVINEL, ANTOINE, *Le Maneige Royal*, J.A. Allen, London, 1989.
36. STEIN, H.J., *Kyudo: The Art of Zen Archery*, Element Books, Dorset, 1988.
37. JAFFE, A., *From the Life and Work of C.G. Jung*, Diamon Verlag, Einsieden, Switzerland, 1989.
38. VAN BOREN, A., *Parabola*, Vol. VIII, No. 2, May, 1983.
39. MOYERS, BILL, Interview with Joseph Campbell, *The Power of Myth*, Doubleday and Company Inc., New York, 1988.

BOOK THREE

THE SONGS OF HORSES
Seven Stories for Riding Teachers and Students

CONTENTS

I would like to dedicate this book to the poet A.R. Ammons, one of the greatest teachers from whom I have ever had the honour to learn something.

ACKNOWLEDGEMENTS

The quotation from *The Power and The Myth* by Joseph Cambell and Bill Moyers which appears in the Introduction is copyright © 1988 by Apostrophe S Productions, Inc. and Bill Moyers and Alfred Van der Marck Editions, Inc for itself and the estate of Joseph Campbell. Used by kind permission of Doubleday, a division of Random House Inc.

TEACHING RIDING:
THE CIRCLE COMPLETES

For some thirty years, I have been studying the horse training systems of the world, past and present. This whole process, virtually from the beginning, has been well documented in a variety of media. I have published many articles and produced numerous audio and video tapes which have chronicled my progress, almost every step of the way. My books *Riding Towards the Light* and *Exploring Dressage Technique* are personal accounts of the process. Throughout, I have tried to be honest and to keep to my own experiences – I feel it is the only truly fair way to talk about these things. I hoped that the recordings might be a help or at least a comfort to others. Certainly they were to me.

Concurrently, silently, there was another education going on. It was just as serious, just as frightening, just as rewarding. It was every bit as difficult. It was my attempt to learn how to educate riders and to develop a system to teach riding. It involved many educational experiments. I received help and guidance from many special educators. The development was continuous, bouncing between research, study, experiment, and practice. It broke down into seven distinct phases or systems which covered a span of almost thirty years: from the most traditional of western teaching situations, being a college lecturer and conducting field and laboratory work, to very open alternative forms of education. From large groups to single individuals, from competitions to pure art, successes and failures.

Oddly enough, none of this process has ever been openly chronicled. No one person was with me long enough to know of its complete existence. I have never written about it nor even talked about it – until now. This book, the final one in the trilogy, is about that process. It is about teaching. It is not a book about what to teach: I have written plenty on that subject.

So, if this is not a book about what to teach, then, how do we teach? How do we learn? How do we know something?

First, how do we teach? Many of our lessons come from books. The study of dressage is no different. Many important lessons of the past masters have been documented. In my own education, I have relied heavily on codices like the books of Pluvinel and the Duke of Newcastle. However, it would be a great mistake to think this is how the bulk of teaching has been done. Most of the lessons of horsemanship have never been documented. To some scholars, the ancient Persians were the greatest horsemen who ever lived, but there are no volumes of Persian advice, no lists of their accomplishments. The amazing Islamic horsemen and the far eastern Russians have not written much either. Even the prestigious Spanish Riding School has few written directives.

So how is the bulk of horsemanship passed down? Through word of mouth, through myths, allegories and stories. For example, the mythological connections between humans and horses are rich and deep. Let me quote from the master mythologist Joseph Campbell when asked why anyone should care about myths:

'My first response would be "go on, live your life, it's a good life – you don't need mythology" ... One of our problems today is that we are not well acquainted with the literature of the spirit. We're interested in the news of the day and the problems of the hour. It used to be that the university campus was a kind of hermetically sealed-off area where the news of the day did not impinge upon your attention to the inner life and to the magnificent human heritage we have in our great tradition – Plato, Confucius, the Buddha, Goethe, and others who speak of the eternal values that have to do with the centring of our lives. When you get to be older, and the concerns of the day have all been attended to, and you turn to the inner life – well, if you don't know where it is or what it is, you'll be sorry.

'Greek and Latin and biblical literature used to be part of everyone's education. Now when these were dropped, a whole tradition of Occidental mythological information was lost. It used to be that these stories were in the minds of people. When the story is in your mind, then you see its relevance to something happening in your own life. It gives you perspective on what's happening to you. With the loss of that, we've really lost something because we don't have a comparable literature to take its place. These bits of information from ancient times, which have to do with the themes that have supported human life, built civilizations, and informed religions over the millennia, have to do with deep inner problems, inner mysteries, inner thresholds of passage, and if you don't know what the guide-signs are along the way, you have to work it out yourself. But once this subject catches you, there is such a feeling, from one or another of these traditions, of information of a deep, rich life-vivifying sort that you don't want to give it up.'

(Q: So we tell stories to come to terms with the world, to harmonise our lives with reality?
A: 'I think so, yes.')

So we have been taught by books, and stories, myths and allegories.

How do we learn? Current studies of the brain are just scratching the surface of the subject in terms of understanding the physiology behind learning. Researchers in education have gone far beyond the singular idea of intelligence as being testable in an hour's time with a pencil and paper. Howard Gardner, a professor of education and co-director of Project Zero at Harvard University, has developed a theory in use at hundreds of schools. This theory proposed that people possess different kinds of intelligence which can determine how each person learns. They have defined seven categories of intelligence: linguistic, musical, logical-mathematical, spatial, bodily-kinaesthetic, and inter- and intra-personal.

A truly gifted athlete, for example, may be at genius level in bodily-kinaesthetic awareness, but be more ordinary in linguistic skills. It is a mistake to assume bodily-kinaesthetic intelligence is somehow less intelligent or of less value than another form. The great Canadian ice-hockey player Wayne Gretzky said: 'Nine out of ten people think what I do is instinct. It isn't. Nobody would ever say a doctor had learned his profession by instinct: yet in my own way I've spent as much time studying hockey as a med student puts into studying medicine.'

If teachers teach in too mundane a manner they can miss a learner's real gifts, or special avenues of understanding. We learn in often very different ways. It is easy to see that learning and being taught are creative processes. It is important for teachers and schools to become aware of the vastly different ways in which people learn.

How do we know something? In my searching, I can think of no group of teachers as a whole who have tried more valiantly, or over a longer period of time, to get their students to experience knowledge than the Zen masters. They have tried in creative and sometimes seemingly bizarre ways to guide their students away from the trap of word knowledge into life experience, and the reality of the world of action.

Nuno Oliveira once made the statement that 'books are for people who already know how to ride'. When I heard this, I knew he was referring to the idea that the act of riding is primary. It is the reality. Books on riding can only augment action. They are relatively meaningless by themselves.

On the whole, and over the years, I have developed an affinity with and an admiration for other riding teachers. I see the best of them like Zen masters, driving themselves crazy to get their students to feel something, to do something, to experience something. I could not count how many times riders have asked me for exercises outside riding that they can do to help their riding. I used to concede some advice. Now I simply say that no, only riding will help your riding. Only eating will quell your hunger, only drinking will quench your thirst. Not only is riding the only thing that will help your riding, but it has to be a very specific kind of riding at that.

Campbell said that myths are 'the song of the universe, the music of spheres, that myths were metaphors for what lies behind the visible world .... However, the mystic traditions differ ... They are in accord in calling us to a deeper awareness of the very act of living itself.' The unpardonable sin, in Campbell's view, is the sin of inadvertence, of not being alert, not quite awake.

I wrote *Riding Towards the Light* more than a decade ago; *Exploring Dressage Technique* followed a few years later. During thirty-odd years of riding, things have changed along the way. Once again, Campbell said it so well: 'The Indian yogi striving for release identifies himself with Light and never returns. But no one with a will to the service of others would permit himself such an escape. The ultimate aim of the quest must be neither release nor ecstasy for oneself but the wisdom and power to serve others.'

In my lectures over the years, I have noticed time and time again that when science-like material becomes too dry, and your audience is struggling, you can refresh them with a story. It is an ancient way to teach and to learn the most modern concepts.

So, here are some stories. For me, they are very important stories for they define my riding knowledge, and suggest ways to learn about riding as well as ways I have learned about riding. They are some of the ways I have been taught and perhaps they can suggest some ways to teach riding.

REFERENCES

CAMPBELL, JOSEPH WITH BILL MOYERS, *The Power of Myth*, Doubleday, New York, 1988.
GARDNER, HOWARD, *Frames of Mind: The Theory of Multiple Intelligences*, Basic Books, HarperCollins, 1983.

CHAPTER ONE

THE SYSTEM

Pennsylvania, 1997

A doctor friend of mine used to run a private training stable for disabled riders. One of her pupils, a young man in his twenties, had an incurable congenital condition of the soft tissue, which left his joints and muscles fused or contracted, in some cases non-existent. He weighed just seventy-eight pounds. Through his sheer courage, and some special teaching from my doctor friend, he had won several national awards. He had ridden for the United States at the World Dressage Disabled Championships in Denmark, and was now selected to represent his country again at the World Championships in England.

That particular year, my friend asked me if I would

work with this young man again to help prepare him for these championships. In disabled dressage championships, unlike those for the able-bodied, the rider does not bring his/her own horse. A horse is selected for each individual rider at each site, whether it be Stockholm, Lisbon, or, as in that particular year, London. There is just a very short time for acquaintance and preparation before the combinations are tested in the dressage arenas.

In my stable at that time, we had horses in training at all levels, from three-year-olds being broken to Grand Prix masters. We had but a short time to prepare. At first, my strategy was to help this young man to ride as many different horses as possible in the weeks prior to the championships. This would give him the widest range of experience so that he might be familiar with whatever type of horse he might draw in England.

So we began a series of lessons. My new student's condition had left him with little muscle mass, so, from the beginning, strength was a concern. Arthritis had severely constricted his hands so that normal dexterity and grip to hold the reins were impossible. Instead, my doctor friend had ingeniously rigged sets of wooden dowels which screwed into the reins, leaving a thick peg which my student could wedge between his bent fingers to prevent the reins from slipping. His fingers reminded me of the talons of one of my favourite hunting hawks, wrapping themselves around a wooden perch.

Although I respected such disabilities, I was not intimidated by them. In fact, I felt excited by the challenge of our work, especially by what I thought we could accomplish in our brief time together. However, I soon realised that there wasn't enough time to make complicated, substantive improvements in riding subtleties, which would take even a physically blessed athlete a long time to master.

As we went from horse to horse, an idea began to formulate. The one thing this rider *did* have was a fairly normal skeletal shape. I thought if I could somehow teach him to use his back, he could muster his minimal muscle power to stiffen or relax his body. I knew that this temporary rigidity could turn his body into a lever. I wanted most of all for him to feel how, if he held the reins and engaged his back, a horse could sink and tuck his croup under. Simultaneously the horse could extend and stretch his top line, thus firming up his spine in a big arch, ending with the poll up at the highest point – like a big wave swelling up and over. When the horse was balanced that way, the rider wouldn't need much strength to go into a different movement or make a change. If he could learn to set a horse up, then even if he had only small bursts of energy, these half-halts could re-balance a horse and set up turns or movements. If he ran into difficult horses, he could manoeuvre them without brute strength. If he could learn to use leverage on a horse, to adjust its balance, he could lighten it. He could learn to ride a horse with his bones!

We tried as many horses as I had access to, searching for a way to show him these feelings. However, I soon realised that there was only one horse in my stable that was completely trained to the back and seat, and was sensitive to the weight shifts I was trying to show this young man. This was my own Grand Prix horse who was 17 hands and in his prime, weighing 1450 pounds. He was, and still is, one of the strongest horses I have ever ridden in my life, and he was prone to humiliate riders by ignoring them, deliberately stiffening if they asked too harshly, seemed weak or over-reacted. When he was willing, he could collect all his mass and be as light as a deer.

On this particular day, I saddled this horse and took

him into the indoor riding hall. We started with some simple exercises but soon I felt I was near the same place in trying to explain subtleties of body control with the usual impotent phrases. Moreover, this time we were also strangled by severe time limitations.

If you do something for a long time and you try to practise well, you can become completely comfortable and familiar with your craft. Like a musician, you don't have to think about where exactly you will move your fingers. You just know that if you simply hold the instrument you can express a certain sound or feeling. I suppose that is similar to how I was feeling when I asked my student to stop my horse. Then I did something unusual. I am not sure why, because I had never done it before, but I decided to get up behind him on the horse. I had no idea how the horse would react to my additional weight, especially on his bare back behind the saddle. I didn't know if he would buck us both off. He had never been ridden double in his entire life! Even though I had never tried it before, I thought that if I could ask the horse in the right way, then maybe he would show my student what to look for, what to feel and then what to try. I had them both in front of me. Without any words to get in the way, we went off towards a place I knew so well.

I once calculated that by the time of this incident, I had ridden this horse over five thousand hours. Thus we were going on a very familiar journey – only I had never travelled with anyone else. Even in the countless hours of teaching lessons, the pupil heads off alone, flying solo. But here I was, sitting behind my pupil, like some flight instructor. The immediacy of the guidance and the relinquishing of control seemed strange. The connection, twin-like.

We began to work through some movements. Above

all, I wanted this young rider to feel how a horse could be collected so that he might be able to do it himself. His hands were in front of mine, his legs ahead of mine, his back in the saddle. Of course, I could not see his face, but people watching told me he wore an expression of enchantment as we worked. I could feel the horse doing just what I had hoped for. He moved forward with power but with a comfortable swing in his back. He made smooth, elastic transitions. Perhaps best of all, he settled and sank behind in the same tempo and rhythm. His whole front end seemed to grow up higher and higher in front of my student as the balance tipped back, and then forward again as we moved off. The horse showed him how a rider could control the horse's great strength and balance on command. I could feel when there were four hands on the reins, and when I let mine go to only my student's two. I could feel when I let my legs go, and my student kept riding him. Finally I could feel when I let go of my back, and horse and student were going by themselves.

I never really knew how my student felt, any more than you can know for certain how any person feels. Nor did I know how anyone watching felt. I could, however, feel when my student rode the horse, even if there were moments when he wasn't sure of what he was doing. I knew precisely when he was controlling this 1450-pound horse. It was a beautiful feeling. Those watching said it was a revelation.

When it was all done, I had some strong, but mixed feelings about the experience. I was very proud of my horse, but at the same time (although this might sound odd) I was not particularly proud of myself. I have never told many people about the experience.

To my mind, the incident was too theatrical. I didn't want to be that kind of teacher. I wanted my teaching to stand up to the scrutiny of the old European eye. I wondered how such a display would go down in the great schools I admired so much. How would those great old soldier-teachers react? I wanted to teach a system like theirs. I was unimpressed with my own flamboyance. I admired and respected the old soldiers, not because of some psychological need for their approval, but because I was keenly aware that my beloved dressage came to me because of their iron wills, their abhorrence of frivolity, their life-and-death attention and loyalty to the classical way. So I was not proud of that moment, even though I knew it was monumental. I decided that I would have to work towards a time when I could better understand why.

Thus I continued with my main preoccupation of searching for a system – a more universal approach for all students. And it was in this chasing that I eventually came upon my own enlightenment.

CHAPTER TWO

THE GRAND SILENCE
Somewhere in the countryside near Paris, 1735

It is ironic to say I had *heard* of his great horsemanship, since he was known as the Grand Silence. I had seen him hunting many times in the countryside near Paris, where I once had lived. I have to say that I thought of him then more as the Great Arrogance or the Great Pomposity. It was through the following twist of fate that I met him.

I was hunting an irascible goshawk in the woods not far from some open country where I knew he was hunting peregrine falcons with a member of the royal family. I had just come out of the thick cover when I heard the bells of a falcon. The bird was flying towards the forest carrying off a grouse. My first thought sprang from arrogance: I felt the Great Pomposity must be a better horseman than falconer. The bird was obviously too thin, and instead of staying with his kill until the falconers could retrieve him and the game, he had stolen off with it.

My smugness was to be short-lived. I let my attention falter for a moment and my own hawk, the larger bird of prey, bolted from my fist at the sight of the two-for-one. The peregrine, weighed down by his kill, was travelling slowly. Within seconds my bird struck the pair hard. Loose feathers swirled and floated free of the impact as the knot of birds hung still in the sky for a second before tumbling and cartwheeling toward the ground. When I got to the jumble, the peregrine's talons were locked into the grouse. The goshawk, by luck, had only her hallux (the thickest thumb-like talon) into the peregrine. It took me a whole half hour to sort them out. I kept thinking all the while that the Great Pomposity would ride down upon me and I would be finished. The peregrine must have come a long way with the small grouse because no one from the hunting party came near. No dogs, no horses. No one. The tension was stiffening my whole body. I covered the falcon with the silk scarf that I kept in my bag. I collected all the broken feathers. Under the dark of the silk he quieted and the cloth protected his plumage from further damage. My own hawk remained in a rage, her feathers raised, as I sorted her out from the middle of this scene of carnage. I returned to my horse and took the birds home.

In the days that followed I bathed the wound of the falcon and repaired fourteen broken feathers. I inserted fine wires into the hollow shafts of the feathers and, matching each piece as carefully as I could, I slid the straw-like shaft of the end onto the wire and cemented it with a special wax. Soon the bird would be able to fly well again instead of having to wait a whole year for a new moult.

The falcon ate well for me from the second day, and within two weeks I decided to return him to the Grand Silence.

I had no intention of riding down into his lair among the royalty at the great stables. At a nearby village, I found out where and when he was next hunting. Without knowing what to expect, I rode up to his party. I got close enough to see his face, and while I was giving some disembodied explanation, I was struck by what I saw. His intense, dark eyes were almost too big for his head. He had an inhuman stare, as if the skin around his eyes held his eyes in focus with a muscled grip. All expression in his face waited for orders from his eyes. He actually looked like a falcon.

I soon found that I had underestimated his reputation. He was far beyond arrogance. In order to be arrogant, one would have to entertain the idea of superiority or inferiority. His look suggested that the object of his gaze, namely me, was totally insignificant. I was beneath the realm of even ranking. At least that was how I felt when he looked at me.

When I left, one of his men came after me. He suggested that my riding needed help and if I wanted instruction, I could join Maitre's riding class at the manège of Monsieur Saumont. I thought then it was his way of thanking me.

That is how I started having riding lessons with the Grand Silence.

The first time I rode into the school and saw him out of his hunting clothes and in his riding attire, prepared to teach, he was an impressive sight. He wore a long sky-blue coat. It was tight across his chest, and had two long tails which were split like a swallow's tail lying behind him so as not to interfere with his seat. The coat was edged in golden trim. His wide sleeves were folded back elegantly to show a rich, red lining. Tucked into the wide sleeves were the gauntlets of his riding gloves. Those gloves were as long as a falconer's, but they were thin and soft and made from deerskin. They were the yellowy colour of butter. He wore a three-cornered hat. His long boots were made of supple, thick, dark leather, and they rose well over his knees.

When he rode, it was a revelation. He was the consummate athlete, artist, dancer. Over the roughest ground his great legs kept him steady. In the school, he was all grace, power and delicacy. His students learned by imitation because, above all, he was silent. He was insistent, though, that we learn with our hearts, not just with our eyes.

Someone once suggested that the lessons at Monsieur Saumont's were not on the same level as those when Maitre was working near the palace. I found out this was not so. He was totally incapable of changing his working style. There was not a duplicitous bone in his whole body. He had only one standard for riding, and it was the highest flag on the pole.

It was difficult to know what he was watching for in the practices because he frequently rode in the classes, training one horse or another. He would often stop and watch a single rider and then ride on again. It became painfully obvious to us all, at one time or another, that there was no hope in trying to guess what he wanted to see, or of pleasing him, especially if under his eyes you lost your attention in your own work or your problem at hand. If such a thing happened, he would immediately pick up the reins and ride on. The first steps of his wordless ride would be the equivalent of a screaming exclamation or a mere muttering. No matter where he was positioned in the school, he would turn away from you, and when his eyes broke from you, it seemed there was a perceptible cracking sound. Invariably, he would then execute some of his most brilliant riding. It was as if only the highest form of riding could purify the air from the stench of this ungodly mediocrity, created by these impossible students.

Anyone who thought a pirouette was a pirouette was a pirouette never felt or saw the Maitre turn away from an aggravating student. His turns could convey every minute degree of emotion. His horse might simply revolve in a walk, and effortlessly engage into a trot or a canter. That might mean mild approval. His horse might also turn on the deepest set haunches, fast, high in front, exploding into a caprioling kind of canter – a turn that could not be executed quickly enough to rid his eyes of a most revolting sight of some grovelling pupil. As long as you yourself weren't the object of his silent comments, these incidents were fascinating to watch.

I think he must have hated words; and if he did, he especially hated words that suggested limitation, and he reserved his greatest disgust for the word 'impossible'. The last thing you ever wanted to do, no matter how much trouble you might be in during a movement or practice, was to suggest that the movement was impossible, or worse, that the horse was incapable of it. For he would then ride your horse, in front of you and whoever else might be in the school at the time. He would begin to work on your problem and always he would fix it. It would happen so smoothly, so seemingly effortlessly, so quickly and with such ease. The more he got the impression you thought something was impossible, the greater the ease with which he finished off your tiny protests. At these moments, you didn't know what to do. You would at once wallow in your own self-pity, feeling hopeless, realising the size of the gulf between your own skill and his, and also be mesmerised with inspiration by his incredible gifts.

Sometimes certain students would be wise to the fact that he would ride their problems away if they looked confused. To whine for his attention was a very big gamble. It was almost always a big mistake as he had unbelievable peripheral perception and he would be in the middle of some cyclone of problems when his eye would catch you resting or in a bad position. He was always aware if you were having trouble. Some of us came to realise that it was a compliment if he let you struggle, as long as your struggle didn't demean the horse. On the other hand, if he once categorised you as a slacker, he would patronise you imperceptibly and the course of your instruction would never be of the same standard again. It was practically, if not totally, impossible to break out of this category once you walked yourself into it. I think he took it as a personal insult. It was as if he wasn't a good enough horseman to know what you and your horse were capable of.

Of all the horses he rode, one really stuck out. The great Florido. Florido was a Spanish stallion – white with a translucent softness of marble. There was a glassine quality to his coat, and in different light it could refract like prisms, making him look blue. He was average in size, with a thick mane and tail. He was feline in his disposition. He was at times quiet, almost lazy, and when he intended action, he could be so fast you had to remember his movement. What was most amazing was his almost human intelligence. Together they were a team. It seemed that only on a horse like Florido could the Grand Silence use up all his skill.

Oddly, it was an incident that had nothing to do with their riding together that showed me how connected they were. One of the royal nephews had attempted a courbette on a young stallion. The inexperienced horse bolted with the even more inexperienced rider. In a moment the horse was at full speed rounding the short end of the school. The Grand Silence and Florido were working at the other end. In less than a second, the man slowed Florido and without stopping, he swung his outside leg high over the sinking haunches of his horse. The tails of his blue coat were caught by his leg as he spun in a dismount, stepping from his other stirrup to the ground. The blue coat spread out in a cool blue fan above the blue horse. In the same motion, his gloved hand dropped the reins on top of the neck of Florido. Then, as if in a perfectly choreographed dance, they stepped away from each other. The Grand Silence strode without running, without a word, slicing the distance, cutting off his prey. As the young stallion rounded the corner and began to gallop down the long wall, the Grand Silence was there. Florido stepped in the other direction until man and horse were positioned almost exactly opposite one another on either side of the manège. The Grand Silence stood still, his legs slightly spread, his hands resting at his sides. Florido nickered. It was odd: the man silent, the horse talking.

When the young stallion made the turn heading toward the Grand Silence, it had a choice. Long before it had to face the Grand Silence, it veered away, and ran toward Florido. Then it began to circle Florido as if it were being lunged by the older stallion. Florido nickered again, and the young stallion stopped and carefully approached him, arching his neck like a cautious swan. He never noticed the Grand Silence approaching. Just before the young stallion was about to touch noses with Florido, the gloved hand of the Grand Silence closed its fingers around the rein and held it tight. The gloved fist was raised in the air. Quiet and strong, the way it is offered as a perch for a falcon. The stallion was subdued. It was as if the Grand Silence would never let this impudent renegade actually touch the great Spanish horse.

* * * * *

There was a ride performed by the Grand Silence on Florido which comes to mind as the greatest sustained piece of riding I have ever seen. It is something that I do not say lightly because I have seen some exquisite pieces of horsemanship which may have equalled this event in brilliance or ingenuity, style or power. But there was no equal to that ride as a complete moment. The evening I saw that ride was the first time in my life that I saw a man alter linear time. The man and his horse defeated the science of his day. They went beyond time. No one that I talked to afterwards, even months later, could remember just how long in time this event had taken. Was it an hour? Half an hour? No one took their eyes off man or horse until the Grand Silence and Florido stopped.

This demonstration ride was to take place at a royal party, an occasion which was to feature a heavy equestrian flavour. There was the usual list of socialite guests, but there were also quite a few noted horseman and women. As his riders, the Grand Silence expected us all to work. For all intents and purposes we were, in addition to our riding duties, to serve as waiters for the cognoscenti. It was important to the Grand Silence that the horse people were looked after properly.

The longer I had been around him, the more I admired him. However, I could never understand how he functioned in such a strangling political atmosphere. Was he so socially crafty? How, without words, did he stay ahead of a seemingly million jealous *écuyers*? Maybe he hunted so much and rode so much to stay out of the suffocating tent of gossip and intrigue. He must have had skills outside his riding that we never saw. (Of course, he had political skills we never saw – he had subtle riding skills we never saw!) He seemed indefatigable and yet I wondered what a toll all of this was taking internally. Maybe the brilliance of his riding was the release. One never knew. He was not easy to figure out. Looking back on that evening, I have always felt that the cause behind what turned out to be brilliance but at first seemed like disaster, was sparked by stupidity or jealousy. In that high atmosphere a prank can seem like sedition. I later found out that was how it was treated.

The gala evening had been proceeding as a great success. There were hundreds and hundreds of guests, and several performances of the quadrille. Part of the evening's programme was a solo ride by Maitre on Florido, accompanied by a musical arrangement. The musicians were situated across the riding area, facing the guests, so as to achieve the best acoustics since they were some distance from their audience. I knew this ride would be near perfection. I also knew that Maitre would not upstage anyone, so I was sure the performance would be gracious and short.

Somehow, though I never found out how, the music stopped in the middle of his ride. There seemed to be considerable confusion. I swear I could see the hawk glare of his eyes from where I was near the wall. As can happen with crowds, their collective rhythm stopped, murmurs of conversation quieted, glasses stopped tinkling and faces seemed to wince in irritation. I am sure he felt some embarrassment that the party might lose its ambiance.

Then, from the middle of the hall, he began a passage with Florido that was so exquisite in its cadence that it brought smiles back to the guests. He continued, however, to escalate the rhythm and the height of the steps until the people's expressions clearly changed to amazement. He did not stop and the passage became even higher. It became so high and so cadenced it almost began to frighten some of the guests because it looked as if he were about to leave the ground. There were many members of the audience who could not handle the tension. They did not know what might happen to their minds if he *did* leave the ground. It was all so surreal.

I don't know if Florido was so excited that his coat began to glisten with moisture, but it was as if a beam of moonlight had fixated on him, turning his coat into vibrant silver.

The passage was drum-like. Some of the Spanish men stood up taller, as if about to break into a dance. The Maitre then settled the passage down and, in turn, brought it closer to one group of people after another. There he placed the great horse in a piaffe and raised it to brilliance before moving on. He turned the passage, curved it, circled it, changed its rhythm and intensity. He let the people almost feel the horse. Without one musical note, he began his own concert of motion.

Just when the guests were almost drunk with his powerful cadences and hard lines, he would drop into delicate side-passes and voltes. This amazed me. I knew him as a hunter, as the man's man. Yet he and the stallion moved with as much freshness and femininity as a week-old filly. From there, Maitre went off into gallops so fast and powerful that the audience backed away from the riding area. It was astounding on so many levels.

This remarkable ride was completely commanding yet not at all boastful. I knew he hated showing off. Many times during practices, if someone held a horse in levade too long, the old *écuyers,* who were his lieutenants, would quickly intervene in an effort to shield the student from the Grand Silence. They knew if he saw such a demonstration, the rebuke would be severe. 'Did you think the old *écuyers* were going blind? Did you think we needed to see you work a little longer? Perhaps the old men are going deaf so your riding should shout at them!' The old *écuyers* would remind the riders that humility and modesty of movement showed reverence for your horse. Knowledgeable horsemen could see good work without excessive trappings and flair. Flamboyance has no place among true riders.

The Grand Silence continued to move, it seemed, without effort. He was inventing new movements and patterns that none of us had ever seen before. Sometimes the man and the horse were as a war chant, sometimes a love song. It seemed he was taking movement to such a high form that it trivialised the music that was absent. It is hard to believe but I think that was what he was doing. With silent passion, he was excited by his own anger, but he controlled it. He burned it up like a fuel for his actions. Wherever the ferocity of his energy came from, he somehow got the horse to find it too. Then he married them until there was a motion unlike anything either a man or a horse would be capable of on their own. For good measure, maybe obsessive control or perhaps the pure love of art, he controlled the flame. This flame was the sound, the tempo, the rhythm, the visual juxtapositions. He had taken the simple idea of moving in space on a flat plane from one place to another, and turned motion into emotion. He could make you feel what he was trying to show. This process, this manipulation, of space in space, was his art.

That night, when the music stopped, he was forced to stand up his art and let everyone who wished, see it – naked, amoral, brilliant.

And when he stopped the stallion before the king and saluted, the place went crazy. The party exploded with cheers. I watched him intensely as he accepted the bravos, then politely and tactfully made his way back toward a couple of his lieutenants. I forced my way through the crowd. I wanted to see him closer, to see and hear what he might say to the people.

I got near and heard one of his trusted aides say to him, 'That was some exhibition!' He looked at his aide with a stern face and said, 'That was not an exhibition. I am not an exhibitionist. That was a lesson.'

During the next week, I saw more parts of that lesson, for it was not over. Several familiar faces close to him were no longer to be seen. If he could not trust someone, the cut was made quickly and sharply.

As time went on, and I went travelling, I would often hear the strangest remarks about him. I heard people say that he ran the bloodiest manege in all of France. It was the stupidest, most ignorant of criticisms. He never struck a confused horse or rider. It was not necessary. Wilful riders appeared, but none were a match for his technique and skills. He could dispense with them almost effortlessly. The longer I knew him, the more the force of his character grew, and I saw the gifts of his reflexes from softness to firmness get better and better. Yet there were so many fools who would watch and try to imitate him and his riding without any apparent regard for its difficulty, so some self- destructed. He wasn't going to stop them. Neither would he defend or explain himself. His riding would speak for him. Those who were too ignorant or arrogant to know what he was about, what he was doing, were just that. And he would not tell them otherwise.

I also began to long for some explanation of what he did and when and why. All one ever heard about was his great strength. But I knew enough to know that he was not about riding with strength. How did he know how to shift his intentions? What told him? Why did he pick one course of action over another? How could I learn to understand his vocabulary of motion?

This yearning would not subside. I felt I had to search somewhere else. Feeling like a traitor, I left France and went away from him.

I had already found my own lord.

CHAPTER THREE

THE COUNT

Belgium, 1890

The Doctor was one of the best conversationalists I had ever met. He seemed to know every equestrian personality in Europe. Since his retirement, his competitiveness and rivalries with them had subsided so they were very friendly to him. His guidance was invaluable to me.

We had a silent kind of deal, the Doctor and I. When I was in need of his counsel, I would make a pilgrimage to his home in a small village in the south of Belgium. I would always ask if I could take him to dinner, and each time he would select the same old hotel. To get there we would hire a carriage and travel on a road that cut in and out of a high pine forest. The trees grew right down to the edge of a boulder-strewn river that gave the road its direction. In winter the trip could be unpleasant because the moisture in the valley produced a coldness that could penetrate the heaviest coat or lap robes. Yet it was those winter trips that made the old hotel even more hospitable. Once a castle, the hotel was positioned on the highest ground, which made it look like a small Tibetan monastery.

The hotel was small by grand standards, but it had great charm. The inside was almost entirely finished in oak panels with high walls and sweeping curved and moulded ceilings. Yet the dining rooms were broken off in smaller sizes with burning fireplaces of natural stone in the winter and wide, long, open windows in the summer. You could look straight out into the air above the river valley. The rooms made you feel comfortable and private. We had some special meals there.

This time I wanted to know about a Hungarian Count. People had said that in the old days, the Doctor and the Count were great friends, like brothers, before their families and duties took them in different directions. I knew enough not to ask him for these dossiers right off or he could start on one of his usual tirades of how they were all charlatans and so on. So I waited. We had some wine, and later a brandy or two. Then I felt I could ask him anything. So I brought up the subject of the Count. His lips cracked in a sarcastic but benevolent smile. I told him I felt I needed to work with someone who could ride well, but who also had a real intellectual understanding of riding and training and took that kind of approach. The Count's equestrian writings were encyclopaedic and it was well known that he could also ride. I thought he would be the perfect choice to further my learning of how to ride and teach.

'He is an intellectual,' the Doctor agreed. 'Perhaps one of the most intelligent horseman that has ever lived.'

'He is a scientist,' he continued. This was actually very high praise from the Doctor. 'However,' he said, 'he can be deceitful and political. He is a very clever man. Someday I will tell you about that side of him. If you still insist on going, I will supply you with an introduction.'

It all seemed to go so easily for me. The topic shifted and we shared some very funny stories. When we were about to leave, he stopped. 'There is one thing you need to know about the Count: in spite of his brilliance, which is genuine, horses are not his first love...' I must have looked surprised. He continued. '...women are. Being a young man, you may find it difficult to get his attention.'

I was not unattractive when I was young, and soon after I arrived with my introduction from the Doctor, I was afraid the women there would put too much tension in the air. I couldn't help feeling as if I was some sort of replacement possibility for the young women, who thought of the Count as a grandfather, and the older ones, who were tired of his seductions. However, instead of being jealous, he was amused by all the intrigue and distractions. As always, he was fascinated by women's reactions, especially to different men. It was another chance for him to study women. When his young female assistant, who was also his secretary, and I promptly fell in love, all the workings of the inner sanctum were open to me. She and the Count were very close, and he was captivated with our trying to carry on a love affair and getting all our work done besides.

The Count's stable was in a fairly remote village near the border with Germany. It was an elegantly simple arrangement of stone buildings. The stables, his office, the riding hall, his home, the guest quarters and dormitory were all situated around a cobblestone courtyard. His long office was on the second floor above a section of stables. From there he knew all the comings and goings of guests and students, business or entertainment.

On many evenings, his office lamp, whose light glowed yellow on the irregular stones of the yard, was the last to go out. It was there he kept his library, and did his writing. It was similar to a sculptor's studio, large and spacious, with models of human skeletons and many large bleached bones from horses. It was also like a scientist's laboratory, with mechanical levels and a draftsman's drawing table. At one end was his desk, which always seemed to be covered with opened books and papers except for the small area where he wrote. There were shelves of his beloved books in every language. He spoke and could read five languages. The Count challenged even the most simple assumptions. He was forever measuring everything. He always carried a little measuring tape, like the cloth one of a seamstress, but one that reeled into a tiny canister like a miniature fly-fishing reel. It looked like a silver locket. His over-developed sense of noblesse oblige could tolerate the ignorance of almost any class of students, but nothing could hide his dislike for stupid people, especially stupid men. So we all had to study. But I felt I had to study harder, and I loved it.

Lunchtime at his school was a communal affair where he often expounded on his latest theories or explanations of the day's work or problems. These times were not always the best situations for digestion. He could be combative and testing, and he adored it if you could joust with him. You just had to be careful that you stayed with what you knew or else kept it in question form. If you over-stepped the mark, or were a touch arrogant, you were in trouble. He was too well read, too good a speaker and too cunning. Intellectually he was indomitable, and on the subject of horse, practically divine.

One of the things I liked most about him was his passion for learning, which even he didn't seem to be able to control, and which could be triggered by anything. It was difficult to speculate on all of his motives. However, if, at one of the lunches, something caught his attention, a different application of theory or a question which he couldn't immediately answer, you could see his interest light up. On those occasions his office lamp would be burning deep into the night.

While we were resting or out at some inn, he was moving farther, deeper and deeper into the darkness of his exploration. It seemed to me that no one could ever catch up with him. He was so far ahead. He just could not bear not to understand how something worked, or what someone meant in their writings. He had read so much that it seemed as if he could talk to deceased writers! And doing so, he could draw explanations from ambiguous texts or have clear insight into a vague statement. After he had worked for days or months on a problem, as soon as it was clear, he would write it up. Or he would tell us in us perfectly edited little speech what he had found. He was not in any way selfish with his knowledge. Even if he were critical, I found it hard to dislike him. I always felt grateful.

Not long after I arrived there, a wealthy young couple who had a horse in training with the Count, came out from the city to spend a couple of days and watch their horse's progress. Very shortly after they arrived, they came down to the stables. I think they had no idea the Count's assistant would be a young woman. Before the Count came out they began to treat the assistant in a very condescending way. I wanted to defend her, but I was too new and unless she asked for something, I had to defer to her authority in matters of the stable. I felt helpless, and just as their arrogance reached an unbearable limit, the Count appeared. He instantly assessed the situation.

They had made two mistakes. The first was they didn't know how the Count felt about women. The second was that this particular woman had been with him since she was a young girl, and he thought of her as a difficult daughter, which to him was even more endearing than a well-behaved one. The kind of superiority they displayed had the patronising property of speaking with veiled gentility. It is usually best revealed in language. It can be revealed in dress or action, but without words, this could just be eccentricity. In their case the thickness of the veil was irrelevant because there was no gentility behind it. These people forgot that position is something that is bestowed from a collective consensus. It is done to you. You cannot do it to yourself. It is not the state of an individual's mind. It is more the state of the state's mind. And in this particular little state, the Count's school, the Count was the absolute governor.

Their horse was prepared to be ridden. It was brought out for the Count to ride. He didn't move. Instead, nonchalantly, he informed them that his assistant would ride it. There was a palpable indignation, and silence. A real chess game of innuendo and suggestion began. But the Count would not budge. He just kept talking. They must have thought he was the stupidest man on the earth. No matter how increasingly blatant their opinions became or how lightly disguised their criticisms, he increasingly and completely ignored them. Or worse, when he could sense they were about to say something else, he would start first with counter praise that began to shake their security. The Count had no temper. When you coupled this coolness with his rapier intelligence, he could be verbally devastating. The next day the couple made an excuse and left early.

The school was often visited by owners, and the Count had a way of weeding out the time-wasters. In some cases, when he was courting someone's patronage, he would suffer fools unmercifully. On the other hand, if someone crossed his sense of independence, no matter how much he may have needed the business, they were dismissed, and there was no pardon. After that incident, I have to admit I became a loyal subject.

One of the Count's special talents was his photographic memory. Often, when we were riding in a lesson or practice and he noticed something, he would have you ride the movement over and over as if he were making a series of sequential mental paintings. Then, when he had the entire problem mapped, if the solution was not obvious, he would be able to take his pictures and study the horse or problem at will. Sooner or later he would have an answer or an explanation.

In all the time I spent there I never saw him so excited as when he was working on his famous paper, 'Sympathetic Responses in Horses and Humans'. I was fortunate enough to witness the development of the whole project. I watched him take an idea, test it through theory, and then actually put it into reality. Maybe he was excited because he honestly felt that this particular work was his most important. For him, and others, it became a proof of collection of the horse and a proof of how his forward riding method was the best way to achieve collection. After he wrote this treatise his teaching changed and this work became one of the consistent threads throughout his teachings. In any case I definitely remember exactly where his inspiration came from for this involved piece of research.

The Count had been on holiday in Scandinavia with some of his friends, one of whom was an oceanographer. They had ventured out into the North Sea, where they watched many whales swimming and breaching. The Count was familiar with all the current research on locomotion but there was something fascinating about the particular way in which the whales breached. He was intrigued by the amount of power they could generate to raise their gigantic bodies high out of the water.

When he came back he kept saying that he'd seen whales doing airs above the sea! And that whales could do the best levades and courbettes. That, after all, is exactly what he saw. In the generation of their power they moved their great flukes like horses move their hind legs. Where horses curled their hips under, flexed and pushed off the ground, these great cetaceans brought their flukes under them, and then with a tremendous push against the semi-solid sea water, they came up vertically. He told us how he had asked his friend if any other fish moved like that. His friend told him essentially not. Then he asked his friend if this horizontal fluke movement was a sea-mammal trait. The scientist told him yes, and then reminded him that the mammals of the sea first evolved on land and later moved to the sea. He said that there were still residual small appendages on some whales' pelvises. They were relics from a long time ago when they had legs and moved on land. It was that exchange, the Count later said, that inspired a startling revelation.

One day, soon after his return, we were all at lunch and he brought his small human skeleton to the table. We knew he had been working on something new and pretty important. So we all sat alert. He took the skeleton in his hand and tipped it over so that it was in the position of a person crawling. He looked up at us all half smiling, half very serious. Then, in his challenging teacher's voice, asked, 'What is this?'

I think we all felt trapped, and none of us ventured anything. He waited a little longer than usual for the answer. 'Ah,' he said mocking us. 'You are so young and already you have lost your imaginations. It is a horse!' he exclaimed.

I found it was at times like this that one had to be very fast to keep up with him. The worse thing you could do would be to blurt out a stupid answer, just to relieve the pressure of the silence. That would usually throw him off the rhythm of his little theatre and earn you a sarcastic comment. If instead, you waited and listened, and kept looking at him like you were thinking and almost getting it, concentrating, listening, he would sense your confusion and come around again in another way. If you could bear the pressure of waiting, with each of his passes and explanations, his look of exasperation would get tempered by his fatherly patience. His face seemed to strain under his crushing duty.

If you could stand it, you would get it. He would not give up until he could articulate his idea clearly enough for you to understand. I am not talking about waiting a few minutes. I am talking about sometimes waiting for days before he could find a way, struggling with some of the more subtle or complex riding issues.

That particular day he began to explain things to us by asking: if he put up the skeletal structure of a horse, the skeletal structure of a human and the analogous defining structure of a cockroach, which two would be most similar? Then he asked about a whale, a human, and a snake, and which would be the most different.

He told us how at first he was simply attracted by the whale's movement and the horse's movement. But upon some investigation he realised that the similarity of movement was governed by the similarity of anatomical structure. At first this resonance seemed bizarre because the animals moved in such different mediums. But when his friend pointed out the animals' common evolutionary mammalian past he realised how strong these roots were. The laws of motion were so intrinsic in the bodies of mammals that they were even stronger than the mediums of sea or land. They were stronger than the pressure of any place they might end up. He extrapolated that the same similarities must exist between a horse and a man.

Would that not help explain so many of those mysterious riding position connections? The rider extends his spine, brings his chin in, arches his extended neck, and the horse does the same. This rider's position puts the horse on the bit by teaching the horse through a sympathetic gesture. The horse can easily relate because it has an almost identical underlying anatomical nervous and skeletal structure. If the rider projects the centre of gravity forward, the horse, imitating, moves forward.

In the next days during our riding lessons, we uncovered hundreds of these gestures. Then he showed us a vivid example of how unknowingly this same power backfires in an unintellectual or unsympathetic rider. Sympathetic gestures can be complex, he explained, and they can at the same time work in concert with each other. Or they can be antagonistic. He felt that most riders, whether they know it or not, were often training unconsciously with these gestures.

Then, there is the uneducated rider who tries to drive the horse with his seat bones. This rider curls his hips under, rounding his back, thereby sitting further back on his buttocks and pushing hard down and apparently under. The rider's intention is for the horse to follow – tuck its hips under, sit a little more on the haunches and collect or engage. But the horse does not follow this. So the rider tries harder. The harder he tries, the more he depresses the back of the horse and the horse locks his hind legs out behind. The horse's pelvis tips the opposite way to the rider's intention. The Count said any thinking rider should have been able to figure out why this kind of seat was oppressive and impossible. That even though the sympathetic gestures resonate from a common evolutionary part, different orientations developed over time.

The whale, so similar to the horse, became oriented to the sea and now cannot walk on the land, The horse on the other hand is a quadruped and developed a horizontal orientation towards the effects of gravity. Man developed a vertical orientation. 'You see,' he said, 'it's almost as though the brain is older than the bodies they command. The brain, the memory of common ancestry, is very strong, but things changed. One quadruped moves to the sea and becomes a swimmer. One quadruped remains on land and becomes a great runner. One quadruped remains on land and learns to walk upright, becoming bipedal. The unthinking rider reacts reflexively from common and prehistoric memory. This memory now becomes non-functional. The whale can't walk on land, yet it might remember it in its body's core.' It was his opinion that, as far as he knew, only the THINKING man, of all these animals, could circumvent orientation – and he could do this with his imagination.

The intelligent rider/trainer's greatest attribute is not his body or talent which can be stuck in an orientation whether it be vertical, horizontal or in another certain medium. Rather, it is the rider's mind and therefore the freedom gained from the powers of this imagining tool.

When the Count showed us that human skeleton, tipped over crawling, and asked us to imagine that it was a horse, he was showing us how we could design ways to solve riding problems by trying to understand the complexities of sympathetic gestures. Crude riders are often running into walls because, whether they know it or not, their riding is being controlled by the prehistoric evolution of their bodies. This works a lot of the time because there are a great many evolutionary similarities in mammals. However, there are limitations that have to be addressed outside the physical plane.

The crude rider tirelessly shows the horse how to tip its pelvis, to collect over and over, not realising the horse can't follow the imitation because it is a quadruped with the opposite gravitational alignment. Now if the rider is crude enough, he will persist with so much force, that the horse may try anything to relieve the oppression, in spite of the rider. The thinking rider changes his vertical orientation in his mind to a horizontal one and can invent a way to work in the orientation of the horse, even though it is not his own orientation. In fact, the thinking rider can solve the problem by education with a sympathetic gesture, but a different one. When the rider tips the seat way under, he breaks at the waist. The rider immediately loses the firmness of the elongated spinal line. His body is as useless as a broken lever, no matter how hard he pushes. The truly collected or collectable horse does not imitate just the pelvic tip. It imitates the firm extended spine of a rider in a good position. Once they are sympathetically aligned in firmness, the rider, with the slightest leverage backwards, shows the horse to lower its haunches not lower its back. Sympathetic gestures could be very complex and even contradictory, but they could be revealing and educating as well.

The Count did not want us to get stuck in believing this theory was some kind of game with a certain key for every lock. Most of all he was telling us to use our imagination and minds to step out of the limiting boundaries of our own physical bodies. The freedom in itself could be intoxicating, but it could also yield useful practical results.

This work had a huge effect on me. It was explosively emancipating. On a physical level it clarified so many loose ends for me. It was clear why collection had to come after strong forward riding. Connection, that is firmness, had to come before leverage was possible. If not, you could easily hollow the horse's back and actually force it to evade and be crooked. It all seemed so logical. I realised more than ever how important rider-position was. I saw how lifting the chest of the rider, for example, could lift the chest of the horse. Above all, I felt I really locked on to his message about using one's imagination, using the mind to help the body. I felt I was learning how to learn, and because of that I was learning more about riding than at any time in my life. Some of us felt like we were on top of the whole equestrian world in our little enclave.

* * * * *

Because the farm was remote, the Count's equestrian friends usually stayed in his guest house for a few days whenever they came to visit. These were always festive times with beautiful dinners, and often we were all invited. Always there was the most stimulating conversation. Although he would never admit it, the Count loved gossip and would get excited when his guests updated him on all the equestrian happenings in their parts of the world. Most of his talk would turn up disparaging information about one or another horseman's knowledge or skill. He never minded hearing about a certain horseman's lack of skill, but if he heard about brutality or cruelty this finished off the horseman in his eyes, immediately and forever. And he never forgot them. All in all, I think he was secretly wanting to hear about when and where someone had seen a great horseman. If this did happen he made the visitor carefully recount every detail. It would not take him long, usually a year, before he would somehow make a journey to meet this rider and see the phenomenon for himself. We were so fortunate to hear his first-hand views and opinions of some of the greatest horsemen he had come to know.

Monsieur Etienne Noble, the Count's French friend and a trainer, arranged to visit for a few days. He had unfortunate timing, for the Count was so fresh from his recent discoveries, that it seemed every theoretical point made by Noble could be crushed by the Count's latest thinking. When Noble rode, he had a habit of pricking the horse in the stomach with his spur points. It was his belief that this would lift the back of the horse as the abdominal muscles reacted to the spurs. The Count told him he thought the practice was worthless as an exercise. It was simply a reflex and one could never sustain the position through a whole riding session. He asked how Noble was going to regulate the size or speed of the response if it were mere reflex. He seemed particularly harsh and I was sure he hurt Noble's feelings.

Over the course of two days he systematically presented everything he had found out or been thinking to Noble. When the time came for Noble to leave, they seemed on the best of terms. Certainly Noble did not leave disturbed. After Noble had left, one of the students inadvertently suggested that Noble was stupid. The Count got very sharp. He said Noble had never been stupid. He was ignorant of the new work, and that was the reason the Count argued with him. It was to present his best case to Noble as a matter of honour. It would have been disrespectful to present anything less. He told us one of the reasons they became friends was because, at one time, the Count had been ignorant about Spanish horses. It was Noble who generously taught him all about them.

Through situations like that, the Count continued to grow in my eyes. Coupled with my own romantic endeavours, it was one of the reasons I stayed with him longer than with any other teacher or trainer. I think, though, that this infatuation with his great intellect was also why I failed to see, or failed to want to see, something which may sound strange, but which I came to realise was unfortunately true. The horses at his stable were not progressing in their training. Even horses in training a year or more showed little improvement. He seemed constantly to give up on the physical problems. His famous 'enough for today' became not a slogan of his great patience, as much as an excuse for not pressing with the work if it got too difficult. Whilst he was trying to teach us to move with our imaginations outside the limits of our physical bodies to solve problems, he would often stop there. If he shifted something mentally, corrected a problem, he didn't always feel the need to correct it physically. It almost lost its appeal. This became difficult to ignore the longer I stayed.

It was almost beside the point, but if you added this to what would happen if a beautiful woman came around, almost all substantial work could come to a standstill.

Toward the end of my time with the Count, his assistant and I had fallen out of love and I was feeling edgy, ready for a change. I remember we were all helping the Count prepare for a rather large party he was giving. At one point when everything seemed prepared he sat us all down with some sherry before the guests arrived. I thought he would hold court in his usual fatherly style but he seemed a little softer, more human. He said, 'You will find that five people may know something and then five hundred will read about or hear about it and they will be the type that feel they know it also. Now you may come along and it will look like five hundred and five people know the answer to your inquiry. If you begin asking at random the odds of your finding the one who really knows the answer are very slim. It would be possible for you to go off in hundreds of false starts, blind alleys. It is very possible that in a lifetime with a time limit you could simply make the wrong choices and go through your whole life without ever getting to the one who might hold the answer for you. The one who could truly help you. You have to find a way to cut down those odds. To be able to see through people, or personalities, or situations, faster, more intuitively. Gauge them from a different place inside yourself, use more than just your mind. Above all, don't let the opinions of society or reputation prejudice your own experience.'

Sometimes you hear a public statement that resonates with your mood so strongly you feel the statement was made for you. I thought that. I knew he was right and saw it as the way to find one's teachers. I left the Count on the best of terms. He made me promise to keep him informed of anything interesting that I saw. That could have filled a book, I later discovered.

CHAPTER FOUR

THE RIDING ARTIST
Italy, 1895

I remember the first time I saw her. Some friends of mine had invited me to a small party. They had told me that a woman who specialised in choreographed riding exhibitions would be there, but frankly I hadn't given it much thought.

When she walked into the room, however, it was impossible not to notice her. It would be difficult to describe what she wore as a dress: it was more like a costume – an ensemble in different hues of red, embellished with a fine shawl edged with gold. The shawl looked as if it was from India, and yet it did not.

She was a strking woman with thick, light-coloured hair that caught the colours of her shawl and blended with the colours of her skin. It didn't seem possible that anyone could contrive these dazzling visual effects of clothes and body. I also noticed that her scent somehow evoked the exotic origins of the fabrics she wore. Yet it was hard to believe that the complex way she appeared was just a coincidence.

She was at least fifteen years older than me, but I found her very attractive. Her body was elegant and athletic, and she moved with a kind of trained grace that I found to be an instant magnet.

During the course of the evening I contrived to speak to her, and, of course, our conversation fell into talk about riding. Somehow we got onto the subject of transitions. I felt a little proud of myself because we seemed to be agreeing that transitions were a very important measure of the quality of riding. Then she said something which I thought was odd. It also was intriguing. She told me that if I really wanted to learn about the highest quality of transitions, I should listen to music, and in particular I should especially study a very famous composer whom we both knew. I must have looked at her a little strangely because she continued to explain that this composer was a true master of transitions, of all kinds. She felt that if one could truly study transitions, one would see that a transition is a transition. The knowledge of them could be applied anywhere. I had to ask her to explain more.

'If a person studies one thing very well, and takes it very deep, that person can communicate with other deep students regardless of their respective expert subjects. The process is universal. That is why I contend that the process is more important than the subject. The paradox is that one needs a subject as a kind of password to get into the club. On the other hand, if a person studies many areas, many things, all superficially, that person ends up with a superficial knowledge. He can communicate well with all other superficials, but not with persons of deep knowledge. Superficial learning is too wide and flat for me,' she said. 'It is also limiting.

'In order to arrive at a deep knowledge, there will have to be at least some superficial study. So the deep student can, if he wishes, work in either world. The superficials can only work in one. One good deep student can often help another. That is a little of what I was talking about when we were discussing the genius of the composer's transitions, and the lessons embedded in them.'

She told me she was going to be touring again this year. She presented equestrian exhibitions at various venues throughout Europe. She had several months of practice ahead of her, which she was just starting. In these practices she would design and rehearse the new exhibition. She would then take it on a tour for some nine months before returning to her home in northern Italy. I was fascinated and when she invited me to come, see and be a part of the whole process, I knew I had to go.

My time with her ended up being one of the most important and most difficult segments of my riding education.

* * * * *

I arrived in Italy early in summer. I travelled by train to the village where she rented a small yard. I passed olive groves and poppy fields, the hills growing larger as we came closer to the edges of the Alps. Then, nestled among the steep vineyards with its stone and wood houses, the village appeared. In actual linear miles we were not far from the border with Switzerland.

She had a small complex with some pasture and a compact yard. She had five stallions in work and kept them in a row of boxes, so they stood side by side as they looked out over the half-doors. Near the yard, a small manège with grey sand and river gravel was terraced into a hill side. There on that tiny steppe she trained her horses.

I rented a room with meals from a young woman with two small children. The house was fairly large, one of about a dozen built around the small crossroads that made up the village centre. Nearby was a large communal well and water trough fed by an ever-flowing, clear, cold spring. During the day people came by to collect drinking water. Some women washed clothes. Several times a day small herds of goats were brought to drink. This appeared to be the nerve-centre for the small sprawling farms and cluster of houses that formed the village. In the background the high hills pushed up toward the foothills of forest below of one of the most formidable mountain ranges in the world.

Just living up there in that country was revitalising. It was fascinating to watch the designs for her riding displays come into being and eventually take on more and more definite form. She was a very good trainer and always thought of her horses first. In the beginning she just seemed to be riding and thinking. She would train certain movements on certain horses, and each would be exercised every day, but she seemed to be searching for an idea or a theme. In those first few weeks you could often see her depart from the normal practice routines and try a different pattern or an exercise in an odd place. She might stop on a horse and sit quietly, staring blankly. I found out later she was often thinking of music during those moments.

It was during one of those early sessions that I

remember her saying to me, 'People believe that facts and knowledge will help the world, but it is really *feelings* that will help the world. It is also feelings that will help one ride.' She was trying to explain her work or the differences between it and that of other trainers. But I don't think she realised that that was the whole reason why I was there. I guess she just didn't trust that I would make any sense of those early practices, which did appear somewhat haphazard and vague. The truth was that I most loved to watch it when it *was* so vague and she was brewing her concoctions. She was a riding alchemist, mixing this feeling with that, heating or cooling different expressions. It was exciting to see the smoke puffs of her inspiration swirl like clouds until some would join together gaining mass or form. Then all of a sudden, they would become solid and something recognisable would emerge from her experimentation. It got so I could almost feel it coming.

Sometimes, she would be quiet for a long time. At other times she would start talking right in the middle of her riding as if she were not only trying to explain it to me, but also attempting to verbalise it for herself. It seemed as if the words had to come out right there and then, as if she were a psychic medium.

'You see,' she said to me one day after a beautiful piece of piaffe, 'for so many people all there is to a movement is the anatomy of it. They study the names of bones or muscles, the pattern of the movement, with more and more intellectual explanations, as if they are scientists. If you do this and this you will get the movement. That's all there is to it. For me, movements have feelings first. There are emotional movements and powerful movements. Movements have colours and moods. You have to ride them differently. If you don't ride that way, the performance will look one-dimensional – like an orchestra would sound if it were comprised of only one instrument. I need bass feelings and trill feelings, ranges in emotion.

'A movement like piaffe has its roots in the mating dance of horses. It is a stallion's dance to attract a mare. It has sensual tension. It is about power, excitement, sex. It is not, and never should be, violent, because it is about love.

'If you ride the piaffe or passage without power and with weak mistakes instead of exuberant mistakes, you don't know anything about these movements. Or worse, you don't care. It doesn't matter to me if you know where each foot goes or which muscle does what. You have taken the piaffe out of its natural context. It doesn't make sense any more. It has turned into a parody. What you are doing does not glorify horses. It glorifies yourself, the human, on the horse. I believe you have to touch the soul behind every movement.

'When we take our tour to other countries, you will see riders pulling movements apart and making horses do crazy things. It saddens me, even sickens me, and I want to retreat up here. I want to stay here but I can't. I think those people would ride their horses upside down if they could. They are thrilled with the novelty of what they have created. There is a huge problem, however, because this is all at the expense of the horse's own culture. They mock the language of the horse. The life of the horse, the history of the horse, the movement of the horse. They have no respect for the horse, only an insatiable ambition of their own.'

As the summer wore on, I spent more and more time riding with her. I truly enjoyed it. She would use her training sessions as lessons. She could develop any technical movement from her own view or perspective and then get me to try to express that emotion or feeling.

She hated the practice sessions to be dull and wanted to see real effort and emotion. She once told me, 'If you want to be a soldier, that's fine – join the army. But if you want to be an artist, you have to put feeling and expression in your work.'

Different movements had stories behind them. For her the half-pass had a defensive flavour. 'Imagine a horse trotting down a road,' she said, 'and a wolf leaps out from the side. The horse arches its whole body and bounds forward and sideways. It is more of a feint. If the wolf were to come up from behind, the horse would gallop off using its superior speed. That is an extension – abandonment, almost fearful abandon. But a half-pass must have effort. It should almost startle. It is a graceful dodge.'

In her mind she said she could see the shape of a woman Flamenco dancer: her arms high above her head, her body in one slender long curve from her feet through the smooth arc of her ribs to her stretched arms and fingers, finishing with a sweep into the air. That is how the half-pass could feel to her.

She loved the pirouette most of all. She taught me that the pirouette is like a matador with his cape before him. His body is extended, as the bull, with its thousand-pounds-plus of power, moves into the magic of the thin drape. Just as the matador leads the bull, so the rider must lead the horse, using the lightest of reins and a firm, extended back and open chest. The bull turns the smallest of circles around the feet of the matador as the latter stretches his body line.

'When the pirouette is right,' she said, 'when it climbs high with all the weight collected, then, if at that point you glance down with your inside eye, you will see the inside foot of the horse. It will look like the slipper of a matador. You and the horse, the matador and the bull, will all become one, like a cyclone of power. You must learn to regulate it, to control it. Ask the bull to come in toward you. Close up the distance between you and power, and turn it in a sphere until it becomes a revolution. Get inside the eye of this image, and think. Keep thinking. Ride through every step. Never panic. Go steady. Control it.' I noticed that she always smiled when we were practising the pirouette.

'The shoulder-in', she told me, 'is like herbal tea. It is a potion with medicinal qualities.' She went on, 'When you ride it, let it go slow. Let it steep. Let it brew. You should never rush the shoulder-in. Give it a chance to work its magic. You have to use it every day. Half the value of tea like this is in the careful meditation during its preparation. Take your time preparing the shoulder-in. Then drink it slowly and don't stop using it when you feel better. Use it daily to promote the health of your horse.' To that end she never used the shoulder-in in her exhibitions. It had a more important purpose for her.

As time passed, the tour date was coming closer. I was intrigued by what I might see in other countries – the breaking up of movements, the out-of-control riders, the wild innovations. We talked a lot about what she had observed over the years. She told me she had a unique view of the equestrian world. At this time, it was a world almost completely dominated by men, mostly from the military. In the past there had been the occasional powerful woman, like a Marie Theresa, who had greatly influenced the horse world, but such women were, by and large, the exception.

Her father had been a powerful military man. Even now, long after his death, whenever she travelled to different cities, she usually visited one of his old compatriots, or one of them would feel he had to check on her. 'My military connections have allowed me to see many of the well-known riders and trainers at work,' she told me.

'Moreover, I have been able to observe some of them over a long period of time since I began watching them when I was a young girl.

'People have a habit of seeing a rider once, then filing away their impression in some comfortable place and labelling him that way forever. If you ask them about that rider years later they say, "Oh, yes, he does this or that," dismissing him with a one-sentence description. Certainly some riders do not grow or change, but the good ones do. A lot. It is amazing to see them or talk to them every few years. Their journey can be fascinating.

'There do seem to be two types of riders, though. One is the ambitious type, which seems more prevalent among younger officers, but is by no means restricted to them – there are plenty of older men who also seem obsessed with ambition and victory. When this first type are fighting in wars, they are not a problem. But in peace time, they can't seem to control themselves. They will invent violences. For them, competitions are like that. If things, even on a daily basis, get too smooth, they create pressures. They love to tell you what to do even if they have no control over you. They will show you what it is all about, what *they* can do, not what *you* might be able to do. They *need* you to see them. They need measurement and approval. They are in trouble when they are outside all the didactic support of the rules of the military.

'The other type,' she said, 'was like my father. They have been part of too much violence. They seem to be seeking something for themselves. They might tell you about it but they are not obsessed with showing everyone. This second type seem to be seeking the same thing: beauty. The more violence that has touched them, the more aggressively they seek the antidote in harmony and beauty. Even in this pursuit some of them retain their competitiveness. But all of them work hard. The peace they seek is no sleepy rest. Finding harmony is hard work.

'My father,' she said, 'often said it was a lot harder than war, just as to love is much harder than to hate.'

She felt this grouping into types explained a lot of the developments in riding. I was anxious for the chance to see this for myself, and I felt thrilled that she would be my guide.

As we came closer to the start of her tour, my duties became more involved. Two more horses were brought in so that there would be spares. I was in charge of all the horses' care, the grooms' travel arrangements, the supplies and equipment, etc. More logistical matters were sent my way even though I had no experience in this kind of lengthy travel. I was learning every day. Some days we would catch up with the workload and I would spend a summer evening sitting near the village spring just watching the sun go down. It was as peaceful as any time in my life.

During the practice sessions, the exhibition began to reveal itself. She started to bring in musicians to develop the score behind the whole performance. There were two – a cellist and a horn player. Some days she worked with just one and sometimes they both came. It was fascinating to watch them work together. The sounds of the music, first in short phrases and then in more and more complete pieces, would float into the afternoon or evening air. Sometimes during these practices I would hike over to the opposite hill, from which viewpoint I could barely see her riding but I could hear the horn drift. To me it was exciting to be part of the unfolding, the battling for direction, the nurturing and embellishing of an idea, or a feeling they were working to create. I was beginning to learn to love the work; the opening, the fixing, the hammering and the sawing of the work. She made me work hard, but I loved it. She taught me what she was after and listened to me. She let me be a real part of it. I was thrilled when I saw my humblest suggestions appear as little pieces in the work. She was like so many of the 'good ones'. She just wanted you to be honest – say something honest with all your might.

She had definite ideas as to how the horse and riding should integrate with the music. She would never have the music match any horse's rhythm of gait or footfalls. She felt the riding had to be able to counterpoint the music. There had to even be room for dissonance as well as harmony. 'If you follow the beat of the music,' she said, 'there can be no sophistication or complexity. It ends up looking and sounding like one hundred trombones on the Champs Elysées all playing the same tune. It is a marching band, not an orchestra. You can add more trombones if you wish, but the sound will not get more complex. It will only get louder. The effect is too banal. Furthermore, if you stay too close to the music, the horse ends up as another instrument. Nothing more than an implement of percussion. The music gets bigger than the horse.'

I felt she was exactly right. She would often show the musicians and myself what she meant. If the rhythm of the music and the rhythm of the horse stayed together, one couldn't stand it if the horse got out of sync. She said the audience would always feel that the horse had made a mistake. She was right, of course. It always appeared as if the horse was messing up the music.

She showed me how the counterpoint of the riding need not actually be a counterpoint to the rhythm of the music. It would just be differences in moods – the gentlest music for a powerful pirouette, for example. 'There are no rules,' she said. 'You experiment to see what works for you and for the audience. Never be afraid to challenge people with your art. Even dissonance at times will highlight and amplify harmony without adding more raw volume.

'We have to remember,' she would say quietly so that the musicians could not hear, 'that the music is secondary to our horses. We have to use musicians and their music in order to glorify the horse.'

As the days of the season grew a little shorter, the design began to gel. We were rehearsing the entire show. An odd feeling engulfed me. Everything seemed anti-climactic. We hadn't even started, and I had the strangely sad feeling that it was over. However, I could not afford to feel too much of anything for too long, because the reality of the logistics of travel and the first show had taken over my life. There were venues to formalise, bookings and livery to reserve, train passes to purchase, and so on and so on. We were going to start in Milan, then go to Geneva before the weather got too bad. On to Lyons, then a big stay in Paris. Brussels was next, then Amsterdam. We would go through Germany to Poland and continue east to Kiev. There we would turn south to Budapest, after which we would be starting home, travelling through Vienna and Salzburg. Our last show would be Venice.

And so it began, but much of it was a blur of very long days and nights – and so much to worry about. She was so good at travelling, but I felt I had an overwhelming responsibility to the horses. There was no question that this kind of life was hard on them.

During the tour very little changed. Obviously there was no place for the elixir of innovation. There was a choreography to stick to. Since we couldn't afford to take all the musicians with us, there were often new musicians to teach and fit in in different cities. I know the people loved her work but it was difficult to say how many had any *real* idea of what she was doing. Sometimes I wondered how she kept up her spirits.

Since many people already knew and admired her there were dinner requests and parties after performances. She was always the diva. She never faltered. I know she often had doubts and was discouraged by being asked the same tired questions; and she was dismayed by the often blatant presumptuousness she encountered. Nevertheless she could stay graceful and diplomatic throughout the repetitive onslaughts of ignorance.

I remember an incident one evening in Budapest as we were making our way back home. She opened up to me about herself and her motivations. We were in a café after one of the performances. It was a fairly typical scene but this particular evening seemed less pressurised. It was one of the last shows. I think we all sensed we were nearing the end. We were almost within sight of home.

We stayed late that evening. Everyone in the café was having a good time. In one part of the large room there was a group of workmen who had been drinking pretty heavily. At first, quietly, they began to sing a melancholy folk song. It was one of those typically ethnic national songs that when helped with a little alcohol unleashes the emotions of the most stoic of men. The song spread throughout the café until all the nationals participated. We did not know the words so we were respectfully quiet, although some of us did hum along.

I was sitting next to her and she turned to me and asked, 'Why do you think a song like that works that way?' I had not given it much thought. 'They are usually simple songs,' she continued out loud. 'If you sing them in another country, they won't get any kind of response. Even if you translate them so they would be relevant to another country, you still would not get this kind of reaction.

'Many people assume that there must be something

special in the song. But I have studied this, and it is not the song. Otherwise, the response to the song would be more universal. If you transpose these songs outside their borders, the lyrics can often be almost childlike.' She translated a few lines from some famous songs and out of their context they were powerless; whereas in their particular context, they would often be some of the most powerful music within a society.

'So how does this come about?' she asked me. I told her I wasn't sure. Slowly, with resignation in her voice, she said, 'They were all taught to love that song. From the time they were children,' she went on, 'it was carefully and specifically taught for many reasons, whether to represent love, or feelings of home and family, or of pride, nationalism, patriotism, whatever. That song is a vehicle to transport these often rich and deep feelings. The song can be a trip-wire to an explosion of associations. All those who have been taught this song share a common bond. Only those who have been taught it can participate in the brotherhood and sisterhood of these wealthy emotions. Tonight you and I don't know the song so we can only sit here and enjoy the sight and sounds of this gathering. But we can't be one with them. Any aesthetic ideas take hold or have effect only when the ground has been prepared ahead of time. A song can trigger your love for your homeland, your family, so many things. The song, like any art, can break down inhibitions, huge walls – the emotional fences of strong men and women. The song triggers a camaraderie which escalates beyond the original response. First a man responds to the song, then other men respond to the first, and then they all respond to the song. The magic is what gets involved in the song.' She looked at me with tears in her eyes.

'There is no hope for us if we don't teach all the songs

of the horses. It is not enough just to promote our particular art form. We must teach an appreciation of the horse and all the mythological connections which in the end is all of nature. If we don't succeed,' she said sadly, 'they'll just eat them. We have some obligation to our friends, the horses, if we think they and nature are important. We have to educate people's aesthetic awareness. This is why sometimes I have to move so far away from the technical plan. I don't hate technique, I love it. But it can cloud the issue and make some people look at the wrong thing. Technique will not make these men cry. There isn't a real singer in this whole place. The folk song is not an elaborate composition of technical prowess in music. It is an educated, common feeling. An appreciation.

'There isn't a magic piece of art that affects all people all over the world the same way,' she went on. 'People have to be trained to be hit by art. You train them in the medium you wish them to appreciate, and you train them with the medium you wish them to appreciate. So,' she concluded, 'I am always looking for new ways to catch their attention, enthral them, show them something that they can feel. To show them *why* they should care about horses.'

After that I knew exactly what she was trying to do, and I have never faltered from my belief that she was absolutely right.

CHAPTER FIVE

JANGALA
Maryland, 1960

I had learned to dislike the equestrian press, despite the fact that I myself was both a writer and a contributor. I felt they constantly avoided tough questions and ignored troublesome facts about equestrian personalities who basked in golden reputations. There had been several instances where riders had been arrested and convicted of crimes, and yet the equestrian press had either failed to report these stories or made excuses for those involved. It was the safest kind of journalism. I suppose I was as much at fault because I hated those personality pieces and would have nothing to do with them. Yet I did nothing to rectify the situation.

I was at my defensive best when a magazine sent a young reporter to interview me. I was expecting the usual, banal questions but she threw me off guard when she asked: 'Will you tell me about Jangala?'

'Who told you about Jangala?' I asked.

'Several people. They asked me not to mention their names. They said it was an interesting story.'

'Jangala is dead.'

'I know that,' she said. 'This is important to me. I'll put the notepad down. I won't even write about it if you will just tell me.'

'I don't like to talk about it – not for the reasons you might think. It is not painful or anything, but Jangala is really about the absence of words. I rode Jangala every day for almost twenty years. He was like a seeing-eye dog for a blind person. He took me to places I could never have gone by myself. I feel that talking about it demeans what happened.'

'Please, just a little bit about him. What did his name mean?'

'Jangala is Sanskrit for "impenetrable".'

'How did you get him? Will you at least tell me that much?' she implored.

'It's a long story,' I said.

'I have plenty of time. Please?'

My mind went back to the morning I first met Jangala. I could remember it with no distortion, even though I hadn't thought about it for a long time. Sometimes something would trigger the memory, and I could relive it – the smell, the cold air, the sounds. My recollection of it all was so complete. So I started to tell her about Jangala.

'My wife and I ran a small riding business. I taught riders and trained horses; she managed the yard and agented horses for sale. Our house and stables were close to each other, and near to a small road that wound through horse country and eventually came out onto an important north/south highway. That day, a lorry from a professional shipper from the south was due to arrive in the middle of the night to pick up a horse that my wife had sold. It was nothing unusual. The driver said he would phone when he was fifteen minutes away. He planned to stop, load up the horse, and be off again to return south.

'Around three o'clock in the morning, the phone rang. My wife answered it. I weakly asked if she needed my help, and was ecstatic when she said no. I turned over and went back to sleep. Shortly thereafter I faintly heard the sound of a heavy diesel engine coming down the road, and then idling in front of the stable. I was barely awake, but I could hear the motor running. The transaction seemed to be taking a long time, but what was really annoying was this constant, rhythmic banging. Finally I thought the truck must have some mechanical problem, and the driver was pounding on something to fix it.

'I got up, dressed, and went outside. There was a heavy mist. We lived in a little valley beside a stream, and often in the summer and autumn nights, the fog would build up around us. It felt cold to me, probably because I was not fully awake. As I approached the barn, I could see my wife and the driver talking inside under the yellow lights. I could also see the lorry idling on the edge of the road, shaking with each bang from inside. The source of the noise was now clear – it was a kicking horse. Its banging had not ceased, even for a moment's respite, since the lorry had pulled up and parked there.

'When I went into the barn, they could see by the look on my face that I was perplexed. The driver apologised and told me that, if we didn't mind, he was to rendezvous with another lorry at our farm. He was to unload the rogue that was on his lorry and put it on onto another, bound for New York. The rogue horse was destined for Australia to run with a band of mares. As soon as the switch was made, he would load our horse and be off. He told us that the kicking horse on board was truly a rogue and he thought it might be tricky to switch him onto the other lorry. I became intrigued and asked to look at the horse. "He's boxed in," I was told. I must have looked at the driver oddly.

'When I walked into the large, well-lit box, I couldn't see the horse at first. Then I noticed that the thudding was coming from a small, wooden stall at the back corner of the horsebox. A specially constructed pen was completely sealed to the ceiling on three sides. At the front there was about a foot of space near the ceiling, and inside this wooden-sounding drum was a horse.

'I could see steamy breath coming out the narrow space at the top. I was completely fascinated, and was about to climb on a couple of bales of hay to look inside when I heard the second lorry coming down the road. All the while the pounding was incessant.

'Without seeing the horse I went back out. Our driver talked to the other. Neither was keen on the manoeuvre ahead but they decided on a plan. They were to open the side doors of each truck, and park them as close as possible to one another so there would only be a very small space between them. At that point one of them would dismantle the stall, keeping behind the plywood barrier, and drive the horse from one lorry to the other. Once the horse was on the second lorry, they would move quickly, shut the doors and leave the horse loose inside until they reached New York. I was intrigued as to what they were going to do when they got to New York, but I thought, one step at a time.

'When both men kept hesitating as to who would turn

the horse loose, I volunteered. A certain excitement rushed through me. It was a very odd, very familiar, very good feeling. It invoked one of my earliest memories – the attraction and the excitement of wild animals.

'My family maintain that I am magnetically drawn to animals, and always have been, even before I had any intellect to know why. My mother told me how an angry goose once dragged me around my grandmother's yard when I was two, but it did not phase me. I grew to love birds as one of my favourite animals. At four, my recollections are of animals, not people. And ever since I was a child, I remember that same inexplicable feeling, almost like laughter coming up from way down deep inside me, when encountering a special animal.

'I went in. I planned an escape route and then climbed on a hay bale to look over the partition at the horse. When I saw him, I was at that place from which I want to die. Charged, but quiet. I was where I belonged. It was something I knew I could do. The horse was in a seething rage. His head was held down tightly by two heavy chain cross-ties. He wore a heavy iron muzzle. His eyes rolled back and up as he stared at me. He actually stopped kicking. His eyes transfixed.

'I reached in slowly over the top of the wood partition. It was hot in his stall. I didn't speak to him. I must have sensed that he was not about to respond to words. I gingerly reached to the side of his halter and held the huge snap in my right hand. Quietly I unhooked it.

'I remember thinking it was odd that he hadn't moved a muscle. He stayed frozen, as if he were still hooked up. I moved my arm slowly to the other side. When I carefully took the snap in my hand, he moved his eyes, and I knew I had met a very smart horse. When my hand had been on the first snap, the other chain had prevented his head from going toward me. He hadn't moved until my arm was committed. Now, with my hand on the snap, he simply moved toward the chain, which had slackened. As I attempted to finish my task, he very slowly and very deliberately pinned my forearm to the wall. There was no speed, no fury. He stared at me again. At first I felt the pressure of the steel muzzle increasing. I thought he was going to break my arm. I was wearing a heavy woollen shirt-jacket. Then I realised he was pushing all the space out of the muzzle until his teeth were at the edge. Then, as if he were grazing tenderly on bits of grass, he began to chomp at the fragments of my wool sleeve, pulling more and more material into the wire muzzle cage. He was going to eat my arm, and I couldn't move.

'There was nothing I could reach with my free hand to help me. Finally I worked my left arm up to the top of his stall bars, and as fast and hard as I could, I clapped his ear. That startled him, and for a brief moment he released his grip. I yanked my arm free, but not before I unsnapped the second snap. He was free. As quickly as I could I took off the front wall, and opened his stall. Pulling the partition back with me, and keeping it between him and me, like a huge riot shield, I didn't have to chase him. He saw the opened door and jumped out of his stall right into the second lorry. I followed him and positioned a wooden board to block his exit from the second lorry. The drivers quickly drove the lorries apart so I could close and lock the side doors. As soon as there was space, he knew it and came crashing into my barrier. He knocked me down and onto the road, the board falling on top of me. I could hear his clattering feet on the tarmac surface. He was free. I was stunned. Lying on the road I realised had just shaken hands with Jangala.'

'What happened next?' the journalist asked.

'The first in a series of riddles that lasted for almost

twenty years: he ran a short way down the road, turned, then ran back up the road and into my barn. It was a great old barn with thick stone walls. He ran into one of the back stalls, stood in a darkened corner, and someone shut the door behind him. There was no way anyone was going into that stall. There was a monster in that cave. The lorry drivers made some phone calls, and a little while later they asked me if I wanted the horse. The owner did not want him back. Everyone had had enough. He was clearly dangerous and unmanageable.'

'How did you reach him? I mean, I know you reached him somehow,' she asked.

'Look,' I said. 'It's all rather involved. As I told you, it doesn't fit with words.'

I couldn't hide my irritation with her. I didn't mind that she was curious, but I didn't feel she was really trying to understand the whole perceptual shift – maybe she couldn't. I had been in this situation before, trying to explain a new analogy, using different phrases which all turned out to be completely useless, but there was nothing else, no other perceptions, I could use. I had always known that the essential struggle, the purest struggle, for any teacher is between words and experience. The two will never be the same. Yet I seemed always to be trying to make myself understood – to let someone feel what I had felt and seen.

'Did you treat him with kindness? Is that how?' she went on.

'In the beginning I treated him fairly and with respect. It was not out of some altruistic idea of his worth as a living animal, or some philosophical or moral approach. I treated him with respect because he demanded it. He was dangerous. That stall he was in had three stone walls and one wooden plank one. On one of the first occasions I went into his stall with him, I somehow got behind him.

[71]

I knew it was a mistake. I tried to manoeuvre myself quietly and quickly toward the door, but it wasn't going to work. All of a sudden he started kicking with both hind feet. I immediately crowded his rump so I wouldn't be at the end of his reach where his hooves would hit with full force. I felt him hit one of my knees, but it wasn't too bad. The boards were cracking and splintering behind me. He kept kicking. By a stroke of pure luck I somehow got out the door, and with only a bruise on my knee. I couldn't take him for granted for a minute. You see, he was not interested in kindness. For him, the touch of a stick or a soft hand was equally repulsive. Have you ever been around a couple going through a divorce? Have you ever been in love with someone and fallen out of love?'

She looked a little embarrassed but she admitted that yes, she had. I wasn't sure how deeply she knew this.

'Then you must have seen how touch can change. Touch can be welcome, sought after, exciting. But something happens, and the touch of the same temperature, the same pressure, an identical physical phenomenon can feel heavy, painful, intrusive. I learned so much from Jangala about touch. People are so foolish. They practise touch to seduce, as if your technique will make you be loved. Haven't they ever noticed that some of the most passionate love, that of young lovers, comes from those most inexperienced at touch? Love, and to a lesser degree acceptance of more base pleasures, are based totally on reception. Technique and intention are meaningless without willing reception.'

She interrupted me. 'You know,' she said, 'once when I was very young, I had a dog. I remember that dog as always being with me. One day I reached down to stroke him, and he bit my hand. The bite burned, and my finger was bleeding. I cried and cried. My father thought

[72]

my reaction was completely out of proportion. It wasn't that much of a bite, but I was too young to explain, and maybe I didn't understand or realise why. But what hurt so much was that I felt my friend had betrayed me. It must have been my first recollected experience with what you are talking about. My touch unreceived. Maybe it is base to compare that emotion to the complexities of someone's divorce, and even falling out of love. But I haven't had a clearer feeling of that pleasure/pain all rolled into one quick event.'

'I hope you never know any worse pain, or ever feel any stronger rejection,' I said to her, 'but the odds are great that you will. There is no difference, though. The scale may escalate, the stakes get higher, but the lesson is the same. Think about the ramifications in all ways. Not just if you are or aren't received, but how much you will or won't receive. Because you can respond in many the different ways, you can be like Jangala. He tried to make me afraid to touch him. He taught me so much about reception. Do you give up? Do you turn away? There are infinite ways. Do you make yourself unapproachable, isolate yourself from being touched? On the other hand, you can project and project yourself until your attempts are suffocating. If you touch the same spot over and over again, it becomes irritating, even tortuous. This is a complicated matter, but you have to learn as much as you can about reception. Listen, watch all the time. Become aware. Develop empathy. All the great horsemen and women had keen powers of empathy. If you are in dangerous places, it can save your life. It is also a powerful aphrodisiac.

'Horses are very quiet animals. You will need to learn about and develop empathy. After a long time you can tell by their scars where they have been, and what has happened to them. Like old walruses gouged with scars of battles, horses have these notches inside and out. Little by little, without a single word, you will find out what their experiences have been. You won't need a location. Don't become some silly detective looking for the facts of their lives, what country they are from, who their owners were. This is all meaningless. Everyone is from somewhere else, for God's sake, but what kind of place was this animal from? If he tried to kick your brains out the first time you met him, you can usually assume it was not a good place. But don't trap yourself with even those seemingly obvious observations. Learn to go deeper, and the best way to go deep is to limit your presumptions. Feel your way through. Touch your way through. You see, these are just some of the things about touch that Jangala showed me. This is how he started talking to me.'

'What do you mean he started talking to you?' She looked at me sceptically, but also a little warily, as if the interview were getting a little strange or uncomfortable for her.

'First, let me say that through this touch he escorted me into what was, for me, a new heightening of my senses. Very powerful, very complete.'

'I am not sure I follow you,' she said.

'We need to learn new ways to use our senses. All of our senses. All of the time. That is what I began to learn. I began to increase my powers of perception. This is not as bizarre as it might seem. We all have a passport to this seemingly mysterious level of sensual awareness and existence. You do not have to learn anything new. You have to awaken a gift that you already have! You see, your passport to this learning is the fact that you are also a living animal. You are not a machine. We are incredibly equipped to go on this journey with the horse. But to embark on this journey, you have to do one important thing first, and that is to reduce the dominance of your language, the linguistic monopoly of your senses.'

She looked astonished. 'You don't mean that literally you talked with Jangala – I mean, like you asked him a question and he answered?'

'I don't mean to disturb you, but that is exactly what happened. You are making a big mistake if you think that communication happens only with words. The Zen follower might make the case that it is *because* of words that direct communication often does not exist. The incredible thing is that once I took this step, I began to realise that practically the entire world, except man, communicates and maintains complex relationships of all types without words and sometimes with very little sound. We are making ourselves un-understandable to the rest of the world by insisting and becoming totally dependent on our words. You see, one of the reasons I got tired of talking about Jangala and telling the story of how I met him, is because people love the story. It is like a fable, and what people want from a fable is something mystical. They'd have liked me to have said something divine to him, or to have spoken like Allah, breathing into the nostrils of the first Arabian horse. That would have made it simple, really. They could go home with the tale of Jangala, the horse and the man. What actually happened was even more magical to me, but required years and years of psychological and physical toil on both our parts. How it ends up is the horse is a man, and the man is a horse. Up to this point the Jangala story is fabulous but it is nothing more than the taming of a wild animal. Do you know what the expression *dompteur versus dresseur* means? In classical riding it is the tamer versus trainer. I was the tamer in the beginning, but this horse, more than any other, taught me to be the trainer of a dressage horse.

'I have tamed many animals. I was a falconer. I tamed

irascible goshawks and flighty falcons. I tamed monkeys, a fox and a wolf. Once I tamed a feral dog, and I have even tamed fish. In the end, it was always a man, and a wolf, a man and a hawk, a man and an ape. Only in dressage did the animal and the man merge. We became something more and different from either one of us alone. When you meet a *dresseur* they know that the centaur is no myth.'

'Is it possible to tell me how this starts?' she asked. 'I am stuck on this talking thing. How did he talk to you? I am fascinated as to how this developed?'

'When I eventually led Jangala, then lunged Jangala, then rode Jangala, one of the first awarenesses that came back to me was gravity. This is perhaps *the* most amazing force in our lives, but we often forget about it or take it for granted. For a human the first seduction of a powerful horse is the apparent freedom from gravity he gives us. At least we are released from its powerful limits on our mobility. But all this is very egotistical, very egocentric.

'However, you quickly realise that how you sit on the horse affects how the horse can move. Soon you are forced to appreciate what a burden you are to the horse. You come to an impasse, and you are set up to see that the first step in communication is to listen. If you are in a strange land and its people speak a strange language, you will have to listen first. If you speak first, *they* will have to listen. If they have no interest in you or your language, the process stops. Certainly Jangala had no interest in me. I had to listen, but obviously not for sounds.

'He immediately forced me out of perceptual habits. He was not the first horse I had trained, so I was not totally ignorant of his language. If I had been, he would have been unreceptive to all my points of feeling. My reception had to be heightened, to be trained. He trained me, and in a perverse way he trapped himself. I guess the one thing I can say for myself is that he underestimated my persistence.

'You ask, did he answer questions? If you formulate a question, you are using words. I did things, and he responded. For example, in the simplest sense if I pulled on a rein, maybe he would pull back, maybe he would stiffen a back muscle or a hind leg. He responded to actions of my body with his body. Sometimes he initiated actions with his body, which elicited a reaction from mine. I had to learn what he was doing. I had to learn to feel every part of him in order to make sense of what he was communicating. What was going on might resemble a tennis match at the speed of light. If you filmed a tennis match and tracked the paths of the two players in a graph, placing a dot for the location of each shot and then connecting these dots, the match would look like a weaving. And the thread would weave a story. This graph or garment might be a tangible representation of the tennis match.

'Likewise, we could have made a graph of Jangala's and my interactions, but both would be nothing more than tracks in the sand. They would be past references to something that had already taken place. What actually happens might look like a dance. But in the beginning the interaction is often random, spontaneous, and mostly discordant. When you think about it, this is a description of fighting: two bodies engaged in spontaneous and discordant interaction. The art of riding is to choreograph this movement and to gain control of it by repetition. The art is to make the fight into a dance, and in this case the dance is that of the mythical centaur. The dance is not of one participant or the other. It is something new, and it is a representation of an invisible harmonious action and reaction. The choreography is the visible part, and yet it is meaningless because the real story is the interaction. The centaur represents all the feeling, all of the senses. If you idealise patterned movements, figures and geometric shapes, you will never be a *dresseur*. In other words, instead of being a painter, you would become a collector of paintings. If you talk without listening, you cannot communicate. Jangala made me understand movement, not just the movements of dressage. He taught me the movement in dressage.'

'Can you give me an example?' she asked.

'All right. Let's take a familiar problem and see what he taught me. Have you ever felt how some horses can pull on the left rein and it feels like they have a way to directly pressure the bursa in the point of your shoulder? If you have, you know exactly what I mean. It is a searing pain like a spasm. Sometimes, the horse doesn't have to pull on the rein very hard. It seems to be more the way he pulls – a steady, dull draw. Your arm fatigues, and soon there is this pointed pain. Once it starts, you have to rest the arm, but it seems that the moment you pick up the rein, it comes howling back. I knew I had to loosen Jangala on that rein, and I was persistent. So I held the rein. I found that after the arm spasms and goes numb, one loses a lot of dexterity but the pain subsides. So I held onto Jangala thinking that whoever was more stubborn would win.

'It was too easy for him. He kept his weight shifted a little to the front on that shoulder, and he let me try to hold up the world. He didn't snatch at the rein, but he didn't let go either. I got stronger and probably so did he, but after endless daily battles, all of which I lost, I began to understand what he was doing, and how he was getting to me.

'I started to use my left leg to make him bend around it. If you curve a horse's body the distance from the mouth to the tail decreases. When I could get him to bend from my leg, he momentarily would let go of that rein and therefore also my arm. I began to use my leg with as much determination as my arm. I found that a bigger muscle just takes a little longer to seize, and when it does it hurts more than a little muscle.

'At first, Jangala resisted my leg pressure and leaned into it. I found if I used the leg in conjunction with a turn I could get him off balance and it was easier to move him away from the leg pressure. My success, however, was short-lived. The chess match continued. Once he learned to go sideways away from my leg, he simply slid over and avoided my left leg touch. He then ran away from it fish-tailing sideways. I had to use my other leg to check the overzealous response. Furthermore any relief from my left rein pressure was temporary, because now I had to help my right leg and stop the sideways slide with my right rein. He was back in the hands.

'I decided to block his sideways slide by moving him off my left leg, but along a wall. It worked and I started to get some relief on the heavy left rein, but only as long as we were moving. I had one big problem. I couldn't stop him. So I learned to curve and recurve his body with my legs to induce a curve and control it with the checks and balances of my other leg and the wall. I learned you can't pull a curve in or out with your hands, because the neck will bend easily by itself.

'I could relieve the stiffness of his left side by riding in a curve along a straight line. If I wanted him to move off my leg, he obliged but he kept his balance out on the shoulders. I couldn't tell this until I tried to stop him and then I felt all the weight in front. Of course, I had perceived a sideways or lateral shift of weight and now I was face to face with the world of longitudinal shifts of weight. I started using intermittent tugs of the reins and complete stops to give my arms some relief and to ask him to stop more lightly. If I kept his hind legs active,

[79]

trying especially to push the left hind under, and took tugs on the reins, paying attention not to let him bend his neck too much, he was forced to step into a channel I had created. If I was careful to curve him with my left leg and not pull his head into the turn or curve, then I wouldn't pull him onto his shoulders, and he would scoot his left hind leg up under his body. Then I would get relief in my arm. If he got heavy in the right rein, I simply went the other way.

'Later on, of course, I realised that Jangala had taken me step by step through the historical development of the shoulder-in. The Duke of Newcastle in the 1600s tried to free his horses in the shoulders by side-stepping them in a circle. De la Guerinière came along later and found that if he took the side-step along a straight wall it had the enigmatic effect of collecting the horse and collecting or re-balancing him a little to the rear. That way he could get the shoulders and front end freer than the Duke of Newcastle ever thought possible. Even if you read Guerinière's advice, you will still have to go through the process yourself to learn how to do it.

'Jangala took me through the movement isolating an aid by fatiguing it and thereby making me use something else. Now you can say that is just normal training, and all of this is not unusual, that it is just the exercise working. But Jangala could have stopped me, really **stopped** me at any point in this lesson. He could have reared, which he did later, but not then as it was not in the plan. He blocked me and frustrated me until I mastered another and another muscle nuance. The shoulder-in was a little symphony of muscle movements. He taught me every kind of movement that way. One step after another. My repertoire of muscle, ligament and mental memory accumulated. It was some deal. I saved his life and he taught me everything.'

She questioned me further: 'Did it become easier as you went along? Did he become your friend?'

'Of course, he was my friend, but I never thought of him as a brother. He was a father figure or maybe a great uncle. And no, it never became any easier. He was a great teacher. He was strict and demanding, an absolute stickler for detail every day, every movement. The aid had to be right.'

'And if it wasn't?' she asked.

'He would grab you and go through the hole you had missed and attack your opening. He'd stiffen. Basically he would pinpoint your awareness on your mistake in some dramatic way. As he trained me, he got even more particular. The degrees of strength or speed of reaction became very important. Not enough effort on my part, he'd ignore me. Too much, and he would rebuke me sharply for being crude. I remember, for example, that toward the end of our training he could do a beautiful piaffe pirouette, but it had to be just right. If you tried to rush him and push it around a little too fast, and I mean a little, he would hit the rein as if it were an electric fence, and stand straight up. He never turned over, but you got the message. Lighter, ride lighter. Be more aware!'

'And this lasted for twenty years?!' She seemed amazed.

'Yes.'

'And why in the world did you persist? Are you slightly masochistic?' She looked puzzled.

'No. Don't be silly. The answer to that is easy. You see, of course, I would get sick of his perfectionism, but take that piaffe pirouette for example. When it unfolded correctly, when I did it well enough that he approved, when I earned his respect, we moved in harmony and strange other things would happen.

'I felt concentration like a drug. The rhythm of the movement could become almost hallucinogenic, just as drumming can heighten your senses. I could hear birds very clearly in the middle of the work. For years a mocking bird lived in the trees beside the riding arena, and if he would start his litany of songs, I could hear each song with no other distractions as if it were the only sound.

'Once I heard a different sound very high in the sky, and I saw a perfect skein of snow geese. They are fairly rare for us and the sound is different from the Canada geese, which are plentiful. I heard their muted jazz trumpet improvisations coming straight out of the sky, miles away. Remember, sound is slower than light; nonetheless, a little later, I saw them as they made a slight turn. The sun struck them against the cloudless blue sky. They exploded like diamonds, sound turning to light.

'Other times, I could actually *feel* the consistency of the sand under his feet. I could feel the depth of it, or if the sand was moist and held me well, or if it were too dry and broke away. I knew exactly how deep I was sinking with each step, and I could bounce myself off it on days when its weight was perfect and its texture firm. I knew its temperature and could taste its salty grit. I could feel the ocean where it had come from.

'If we travelled across the grass, there were times when his feet would crush the blades and an almost acidic scent would trail up behind us. On certain days in the spring in the morning when the air was wet and heavy, I could feel movement on my skin. I could feel the power of our motion inside the atmosphere, and some days this atmosphere could be dripping with the perfume of honeysuckle and locust tree blossoms - their distinct sweet jasmine aroma. In this alchemist's reduction, I remember when I fell in love for the first time. Sometimes, later, the scent would change to wild roses and privet blossoms. These sophisticated smells would creep around the piaffe and I could feel all dimensions of space – the air behind me, at the sides and in front of my face. Some days it would change. I swear I often had the strongest sensation of the smell of freshly baked bread floating across the outdoor school. I would have this satisfying feeling of eating warm, moist bread right in the middle of a ride.

'Sometimes I had such acute vision. I could identify insects flying across the arena as if they were in slow motion. I once followed a flying grasshopper for four consecutive fifteen-metre circles. It would land in front of us and then fly up with its dry striped wings, and then land right on the circle track and fly again, around and around until I guess it got bored.

'There were the many, many times when I felt weak or ill and I knew if I could get myself on my horse, I would be OK, and I was. He cured me every time people made me weary. He constantly freed me from the suffocating demands of society. He wouldn't let me become another cultural soldier.

'That is why I did it. To feel deeply, you have to **feel** deeply. When I was a little boy, I went to church every Sunday, confession every Saturday. I knew the biographies of the saints. I memorised long pages of prayer in Latin and in English. My little body vibrated under the tones of the powerful church organs. I served priests and I served nuns. I lit candles and burned incense at weddings, baptisms, funerals – and you want to know something? I never had a religious experience until I rode Jangala, who looked like something contrived by the devil. Jangala was my priest and horses became my religion.'

CHAPTER SIX

JOBAJUTSU
near Kyoto, 1970

In retrospect I realise my time in Japan was not about
fighting, although every aspect of that adventure
concerned fighting. I went in order to learn about an
archaic form of fighting. During that time I felt increasingly destined for an imminent battle, which seemed to
bring me back again and again to a state of agitation or,
rather, confusion. Yet it was not what it seemed at all. It
was one of the most difficult expeditions I could
remember.

It started when a friend of mine who was teaching at a
school in Japan sent me a letter. He told me one of his

fellow faculty members had a son who was one of only two students learning riding from an old Japanese master. He knew how much these things interested me and was sure that I knew a lot more than he did about what this man was teaching. In any case, the old riding instructor seemed to be a genuine master and that in itself was rare because my friend knew of no other riding teachers. Furthermore, horses to ride were quite rare in this part of the world.

He was, of course, absolutely right that these things interested me. I had heard of *Jobajutsu,* the martial art of horsemanship, but it was nothing more than a historical footnote. The idea that it might still be alive somewhere was too much for my curiosity.

Several things had conspired to force me into action, I later discovered, but right then I just had to try to see something that might soon be gone from this earth forever. I asked my friend to explore the possibilities of my having a chance to experience this work. When I received word that I was welcome, I began to make arrangements to go.

After considerable arranging and arduous travel, I found myself approaching the old man's farm. My friend drove me out to meet him. It was a forty-five minute ride from the small city where my friend lived and taught. As we drew closer, the country began to open up to some carefully cultivated hill farms. The old man's little farm complex was situated beside a ravine that dropped steeply in places to a strong-flowing narrow creek. There was a small house and some outbuildings, including a little stable that housed his horse, and a small tea-house that was set close to the brook.

Scattered around were what looked like an odd assort-ment of bonsai trees gone wild. Once carefully pruned and shaped, the trees retained their trained shapes at the bottom, but all the new growth had branched out unattended. It reminded me of forests in which deer populations eat all the tender cedar branches as high as they can reach. Over the years the trees acquire a carefully manicured look up to a uniform distance from the ground, above which the full growth is resumed.

Our first meeting was cordial but rather formal. His two students, polite teenagers, were both there. Everyone respectfully referred to him as Sensei, teacher. He was quite humble and insisted that he had little to offer me, but I was welcome and he would oblige me in any way that he could.

In my time I had seen many schools covering a large range, but this had to be the smallest school of all: one teacher, one horse, two students. Definitely, it was the most basic. He invited me to come out riding the next morning. For my part I tried to be polite, but was careful not to show any feelings one way or the other.

I returned the next day and found him alone. He saddled up his horse, then he looked at me, looked at the horse, looked at me again, and then looked at himself. Then, in wonderful acting as if he were reading my mind, he said, 'Pitiful little school.' With a slight smile on his face he added, 'Just think how pitiful you must be as a student to come half way around the world to this pathetic little place.' We both laughed.

He and I walked the horse up to a long grassy field. After we talked and the horse was warmed up from the walk, he asked me to ride. It was a small horse, with no particularly outstanding characteristics. Certainly, by this stage in my riding experience, it was not the calibre of horse I had grown accustomed to. Although it had a short trot with a little stiffness in the back, I had no trouble sitting to it. The canter was better and the horse was very straight and could go almost perfectly straight with very little guidance. My suspicion was that this had something to do with being able to shoot a bow off its back while galloping, which was a part of Jobajutsu.

I did not want to be presumptuous, so after a brief ride through the field I rode the horse back to the old man to thank him for the honour of letting me ride his horse. I told him his straightness was impressive. I was not prepared for the man's reaction. He began to rave about how well I could sit. I am sure he had never seen a rider from the West, and certainly not someone schooled in dressage. I don't think he realised the countless hours we spend on the lunge line and riding without stirrups. He was so effusive with his praise and compliments that I began to get internally suspicious. Was he setting me up for something? Was he putting me on? He wanted to know who trained me and how we practised. I tried to explain everything. Then he caught me by surprise. He asked me if I would help him to get his students to learn to sit like I did. If I would do that, in return, he would help me in any way that he could.

There was something about him that I quickly grew to like. He seemed both wise and humble. He had a sense of humour, which gave you the feeling that he had a genuine interest in you. He told me if I wanted to learn to shoot the bow I would probably have little trouble since sitting quietly and strong was half the battle. Somehow I doubted this.

We went back to his little tea-house. He built a fire in a small pit in the middle of the room and prepared the tea in a careful ritual. He told me about the sitting position for meditation and the martial arts. Apart from my legs tiring from being bent, I was comfortable in the position. It was similar to sitting on a horse, especially through my back.

He asked me if I had any questions. I had some very

nagging ones, which were part of the reason I had come to learn about warfare and fighting from him. But I couldn't seem to formulate them. So I kept my questions more to the point of my immediate study. I told him that I had read and heard how, especially in archery, the students were instructed to try to *not* hit the target. I asked first how one could get better at something if one didn't try, and secondly why avoid the target?

He smiled slightly at me. 'Whatever gave you the idea that we wouldn't try? All these teachers want their students to try with all their strength to get the form right, not necessarily whether they hit the target. When these teachers talk about not hitting the target, they do not say "try not to hit the target". They say, "don't try to hit the target". There is a big difference. The point is you don't try to hit the target, but neither would you try not to hit the target. The emphasis is to take the student's attention away from outcome.

He went on, 'If you think of ten very successful people and you believe that outcome is an accurate reflection of what goes on before it, then one would say that all ten of those people must be hard workers, intelligent, good people. All would have the qualities which can lead to success. Obviously unless you know very different kinds of people than I do, this is not so. Some people inherit their success without a single day's work. Some steal their fortunes. Some find it, and a very few earn it. The issue of outcome can be a very thorny one which can actually delay or even paralyse the progress of proper practice.'

He told me he knew of one masterful teacher who was so tired of his students worrying about the outcome of their shots instead of their form and the process, that he made huge targets and brought them within a few feet of his archers. It was virtually impossible to miss the target, so his students would have to spend more time focusing on proper technique forms, and their breathing. 'Outcome,' he said, 'is certainly not a fair reflection of effort.'

I told him that in my society the pressures to win at something were very great. Part of the reason I came was to learn to defend myself against these pressures.

'This is not unique to your society,' he told me. 'Since man began chasing woman and woman chasing man, the pressures have been great. Outcomes became important and they were placed on every other aspect of living. But there is more to life than just desires. However, if you must have a winner, you must have a loser. People who think this way begin to divide all life into categories all the time. Life is not so neatly divisible. Nor does outcome necessarily tell you anything about how it came about. So we teach more about the process. And these teachers teach more about shooting the bow, living a life. Let outcomes take care of themselves.'

I felt I was just scratching at the surface, listening to him. I told myself to pay attention. Maybe I could learn how to practise.

After a while I developed a routine. When I arrived in the morning I gave each of the young men a half-hour lunge lesson. Sensei loved to watch these practices, although he rarely said a word. Then we might go to practise shooting the bows. This was not the easiest thing, because these bows had a strong tension and were physically demanding to shoot. Although I knew nothing of archery, I could see he was trying to prepare his students for shooting the bow while riding. I did not know what to do with the bow, but I had an advantage because I had spent years being lunged with hands free or in exercises using my hands in such a way that they would not disturb my seat, or vice versa.

* * * * *

His tea-house, like a lot of Japanese art, paid homage to the irregularities of Mother Nature by deliberately being constructed asymmetrically. It was purposefully set in the woods near the running stream, so that the sound of the water could soothe those inside with a feeling of being deep within a forest.

One day he asked the two students and me to join him for tea. He prepared the brew as always with regular care and ritual. In his odd collection of cups he poured each of us a near-full cup but asked us not to drink yet. He then asked that we sit comfortably but solidly in the sitting position for meditation. This position is almost mechanically identical to sitting on a horse, except that on the floor one's legs are folded up. He often used the term 'riding position' in place of the traditional meditation position, especially with me. He then said he was going to leave and come back, but no matter what happened we were not to let the tea spill on the floor. He looked sternly at his two students. He reminded them that this tea-house was built by his grandfather, and was given by his father to him. He got up and told us to wait until he got back.

There was an air of apprehension when he left. The young students tried to control themselves, but they were nervous. Because I was taller and because of where I was sitting, I could see out the corner of the window of the little house. Quietly Sensei had gone to the stable to fetch his horse. He was leading it toward the tea-house. I could see his face; he was practically giggling. Then he disappeared out of sight. I betrayed no emotion but was still very curious. All of a sudden the whole building shook. In this land of earthquakes, buildings are often built lightly so that if they do collapse, it is better to have a bamboo wall fall on you than one of stone or iron. I saw the students visibly startle. They had no idea what was causing the building to shake.

The teacher backed the horse slowly into the building, bumping the corner again and again. As the horse repeatedly collided with the tea-house, cups started falling. There was considerable movement inside. Each time the building shook, the fire would erupt with a small shower of fine sparks. We all sat as still as possible and during the whole time no one spoke a single word. Each of us tried to keep to the orders of the afternoon. I had no real trouble keeping the tea from spilling, but I attributed this to my addiction of coffee drinking which I did in every location and on every kind of travel mode. The two young men had a terrible time. Both tried hard to hold the cups tightly but both spilled a lot – probably from nerves as much as from the motion. One of them, trying to keep to the master's orders, held his cup over his clothes so that the spilt tea did not hit the floor but instead covered his pants. The other had no chance of even trying to balance the cup in front of him.

Finally the commotion stopped. The building was quiet again. I am sure they thought Sensei was mad. It was obvious that he was behind the disturbance, but they could not tell what he was doing. After a while the master came back and with a stern face examined each of us. He looked at the puddle on the tea-house floor in front of one of his young students. The young man stood silently humiliated. The second student's clothes were stained. The master looked at him less harshly. Then he looked at me. I remember it well because from that moment on he called me 'horseman'.

He said, 'Only the horseman has the hands to shoot the bow. The horseman has not spilled a drop because the horseman knows that to keep the tea still, the hand must move. If you try to keep the hand still, the tea becomes a volcano.' He let his face relax. He told them the spilled

[91]

tea would add character to the house. Besides, he would now have a good story to tell his visitors at tea time. He had relieved most of the tension.

I realised it was a masterful lesson. I had learned this floating hand technique actually from riding, holding the reins. I had learned that in order to affect the bit, to keep it still, or to move it exactly, the hand must have fine control. It is never still or dead, but always is in some kind of searching/feeling action. Even in apparent stillness, there is always motion. Sometimes almost imperceptible motion. The master had seen that from my first ride, and he wanted to find a way for me to help his students. 'Only in death is there stillness,' he had told them.

He went on, 'If you try to shoot the arrow your way, it will be a dead effort – restrictive, dampening, holding back. If one learns to accept movement, all movement, then the movement becomes your master, your friend. Then one can stop trying to hold it in and to stop it. The bow will shoot itself, just as the horse will accept you and let you ride it.

'In life you must learn about movement. Never fear movement, but in essence recognise that you are movement yourself. Take down the barriers,' the master advised.

Later that afternoon, as some kind of reward for me, he asked me to stay after the young men left. He said he wanted to talk. This was his way of letting me ask questions. We walked around the small farm. We passed the irregular bonsai. He told me they had been his wife's and that after she died he could not bear to get rid of them. But neither could he be bothered with all the work that went into them. So as more time passed they became an odd memorial, clearly marking the point when she left and stopped their training.

We went back to his little tea-house near the stable. I wanted to return to my dilemma of riding in competitions and riding outside their sphere. So I started by asking him why he thought I might like to practise more than perform. At first he seemed a little incredulous because it was clear to him that practice was performance. I think he wanted me to explain how I saw them as being different. I said, 'Sometimes I feel uncertain about it. Do you think that I have some subconscious fear of competition?' I didn't honestly feel that that was the case. I can take competitions or leave them. They never meant very much to me. In my culture, if you avoid competitions, people will suggest that you are afraid of them.

He told me he thought that was unfortunate. For one thing, we are always in a competition of sorts. It is the nature of staying alive, as predators in this world of nature. Those who divorce games from life and imbue into them disproportionate importance are paradoxically escaping from the real competition of life. He felt it also unfortunate that I had been made to feel that practice was something less than so-called performances. In Japan practice is celebrated, and practice is believed to be everything. It is lifelong and always changing, but it is also constant since it seems difficult to achieve perfection.

He smiled at me. I wanted to know how practice was going to help me if I didn't prove something with it – if I didn't show someone something. He said that I had to show myself, and that anyone watching, if they wanted to see it, would. He said that practice is unlike work and also unlike play. The right practice will automatically improve one's performance at whatever is one's particular meditation. But this is not the goal. He said that you have to find out what practice can do, and why you want to practise this thing. But you must be careful not to get stuck in practice either. One must not, for instance, only practice alone and only in perfect circumstances. That can be as much a trap as an escape.

A man is not born enlightened. Each of us is born by chance into our individual predicament. The art of living is to work through whatever might be missing in one's balance and development. The right practice at riding very quickly places one face to face with one's own inadequacies. Maybe at first one would feel it is just the body's limitations, like one's arms are short, legs too fat. Soon one goes deeper, and character and mental limitations come into play. Maybe the person has a temper, maybe the person is lazy, too feminine, or too masculine. Every day in practice one gets a concentrated dose, a chance, a time to see these problems and to work on them without the distractions of life, like going to the market, or feeding the dog. Then the person has a rest so he can come back again and again. Every day practice measures the person, and only that person can tell if he is making progress. People can fool everyone but themselves.

The world today pulls us in all directions – materialism, greed, ambition, desires, and pleasures. It is hard to restore or develop balance. In the deep meditations of the right practice, a person will be revealed to himself and given a chance to balance himself. The person will develop. The person becomes a better craftsman. This automatically happens. It is an outcome, yet it is not the reason to practise. That is what is meant by not trying to hit the target. The way you shoot is more important than what you hit. If you learn a way to shoot or a way to ride, you might find a way to live.

Inevitably, in any practice paradoxes occur – dualisms, dichotomies. They can seem irreconcilable and in fact will be irreconcilable. Logic will not yield a satisfactory answer. If you cannot find a way to handle these apparent road blocks, you will be stopped. The right practice gives one repetitive opportunities to learn to handle paradox, to train one's creativity to solve these unsolvable problems. Most people do not want to work that hard day after day. It is a shame because the rewards are great, but they are not the rewards bestowed on you from the outside. Enlightenment is not a prize. As long as you still feel a thrill when you hit the bull's eye or feel dejected by not doing so, you are still looking for external validation. You are not satisfied with who you are. In fact, you may not know who you are. You have to know from inside. You need more work on yourself. Most people just give up. They accept a certain level of performance from themselves. 'That is, after all, who I must really be'... 'I am a thief'... 'I am weak-willed'... 'I can't do that'... 'I've always been this way.' They resign themselves. Resignation is very different from acceptance.

Acceptance may be the honest admission of something, like a shortcoming or flaw. Resignation is acceptance of something plus the feeling of not being able to change that something. In the right practice one year from now you will be able to do things you could not physically or psychologically do at this moment. One must learn all one's weaknesses better than anyone else and then one must develop. One must participate in life.

The person and his horse become a team. Each affects the other. If this were not true, a person could sit on a horse and it would take you wherever it wanted to go. Life would live the person. That's really the choice, isn't it?

It was late. There were a few embers in the dark teahouse. It was time to leave. My luck had not run out. I had found another great teacher.

* * * * *

I had found a place to stay in the small city where my friend was teaching. In the first week I bought a small black and chrome motorcycle. It was almost an hour's ride one way on the little bike, but it cost almost nothing to operate. I began to like the routine of the journey, and no matter what the weather, I made the trip six days a week on my little steel horse. When the weather was fine and in the spring when the flowering cherry trees were in bloom, the ride was nothing less than a sightseeing tour. In my time off I visited museums and martial arts *dojos*. I became fascinated with simple equipment of the Samurai and the unique philosophies of honour. I saw exquisite costumes, foreboding iron masks, and the lightest silken fabrics. Swords and bows, weapons of ferocity often sublimely decorated. Once uncovered, I seemed to see this fighting spirit everywhere and I certainly felt a sense of warfare in myself.

Above all, there were the teachers of martial arts. They were calm but latently ferocious, some with technical wizardry, others with incredible strength. I would be lying if I said I was not comfortable, even pleased, with this potential violence and power. I tried to carefully observe every technique I saw. I know attacks were on my mind a lot. If you have to defend yourself, you should know how to do it well.

When I travelled to the different martial arts training centres, and even when I talked with religious people about the study of Zen Buddhism, the word 'hara' would come up again and again. I felt comfortable with this concept but needed to know more. When my chance to ask questions of the Sensei came up, I knew I had to get him to tell me more about 'hara' and 'tanden', and man's centre. The next time he asked if I had any questions, I was ready.

'Can you tell me about hara?'

'I have to laugh because sooner or later every horseman wants to know about hara, the ocean of energy. I will tell

[96]

you my own experience because you are a rider so you will appreciate it. Hara is a very big concept in the East. It refers to the area below the navel. It is a three-dimensional space. In the West it is referred to as the centre of gravity, but it is much more than that. In the area is a plexus of nerves, the centre of a human being. It is a wellspring for 'ki', the energy of life. Learning to strengthen it and control it and it can send energy to all the extremities. You have seen acupuncture work its healing by unblocking nerve meridians and thus letting energy flow back into an injured area. Well, you might think of it that way.

'If you participate in martial arts or religious meditation you will be taught early on about centring in the hara, or building a strong 'koshi' (abdomen) Some of the very first and most important lessons you will receive are about breathing, learning to breathe from the abdomen, regularly and carefully. This breathing promotes relaxation. Everyone knows that no physical or mental activity of a high order can exist in strangling tension. Breathing becomes very important to settle the mind and body. In our case it is also useful to train someone to locate the tanden, the central point of the hara. At the end of an exhalation, there will be a perceptible tensing of the tanden. One of my teachers had us lie down on our backs and, with the legs straight out, lift them off the floor. At the same time we had to raise our heads up. When we found the place of greatest tension in the lower abdomen, we had found the tanden.'

'Why is there all this training to develop this area and be conscious of it? I asked him.

'For one overpowering reason: to protect oneself from the debilitating effects of gravity. Man, like the insect, is sectional with weakness in the 'hinges'. In the ant, the weak points are between the thorax and the head and

[97]

between the thorax and the tail section. For man, they are in the neck, and between the thorax and the lower cavity – the koshi and hara. If care is not taken to make these areas straight and strong, gravity will cause man to collapse there. People either lean backwards, hollowing their lower backs, or slouch forward, collapsing over their stomachs, thus letting the head fall or tip without carrying balancing strength into the back. In the correct posture, the upper body is relaxed. The koshi is strong; the legs are set slightly apart under the koshi so that a plumb line from the head goes through the hara into the ground between the feet. The force of gravity is stabilised. If the legs are out in front too far, the person is pulled backward by gravity. On the ground, he would fall over backward. In riding, he is held up by the back of the horse. As you know, this is ugly and we both feel this is unethical. Our friend is overburdened, and he is also trying to be in balance.

'Anyway, I was having these breathing and meditation lessons: shoulders down and relaxed, chin slightly in, centre in the hara, letting my legs feel as if they were growing into the earth. Remember, I was being taught in the village, but I was always thinking of my horse, and I admit I was not the best student. I had heard stories of Jobajutsu, the martial art of horsemanship, of shooting a bow from a horse. But there were no horsemanship teachers. So I was always trying to apply this to riding. My teacher used to say "Posture is enough", and over and over "Posture is everything". I wanted to use ki and the forces of the hara for riding, and I experimented. I used to think, "What good is all this sitting in the meditation hall when I could be sitting on a horse? What good was it to learn posture in a vacuum?" I wanted to ride, to move. At least in other martial arts schools, they used ki and koshi (a strength-filled centre) in motion or tanden exercises for control, as in archery. But my teacher was a stickler for posture and kept coming back to "posture is everything".

'At home I was trying to shoot a bow from a running horse. I thought even the Kyudo (archery) teachers couldn't help me because they are all stood so still. I kept at it: extend the pelvis, push the neck to the back of the shirt, knees downward, do not break at the waist, be strong in the abdomen and back. In time I could steer the galloping horse by the projection of ki through the hara, leaving my hands free. It was funny because after a while I would go back to my teacher and almost argue. I don't know why the teacher tolerated me. I was a disrespectful student. I told him what I was doing as if I had finally found a practical use for all his breathing exercises and posture training. I discoursed on ki and its projection. I was an expert. Basically I told him I thought the study of posture without a use was pointless. He was very patient.

'He knew nothing of riding, but one day he asked me if, when I rode, did I have a good position or bad, and did I know if the position was off. I looked at him as if I were further going to prove my point. Of course, without good sitting you cannot ride well. Then I said that posture is everything. We both stopped cold, and he began to laugh. There I was quoting him verbatim. I had gone right around the circle. In that instant I realised what he had been trying to show me all along. Perhaps I am a little dumb and I needed the bigger feelings and motion of riding to teach me the subtle effects in a meditation hall, which I eventually saw were the same.

'This is what I saw in your riding. Someone taught you this way. I could see it in your free hands and deep seat. I realised we were oddly like opposites. I had been raised here among the masters of correct sitting, and should have learned the subtleties of correct sitting. But I had forsaken them, and went to find practical, mundane uses for this skill. But then I realised how practical the subtleties or sitting correctly are. You had controlled breathing, a deep centre, soft shoulders, and obvious control of the hara. But all your ki was just lying dormant. I couldn't believe you didn't realise how much more you could use it. That is why I had you work with my students. Your teaching on sitting was, in a sense, purer than mine because I thought you had no ulterior motives in using your hara. I didn't realise you didn't really know how to do it. So that is why I say it is funny that now you are asking me this. Maybe you are just as greedy as I was.' We both laughed.

'You have to learn to use these forces, but never for ambition or for showing off; but out of respect for nature and our friends, the horses. Balance is ethical. I think in some ways my own teacher did not give me enough credit. I was never going to use this force against nature or the horse or another man. I just wanted to ride the horse better. So I will trust you, and I will tell you all I know. Then you will have to practise for years, and become your own guide as to how you use it, and how far you will go with it.

'The projection of ki is like an awareness to the finest edges of balance – both to receive something, feel something coming toward you, and to issue something, to send a feeling away to someone or something else. I believe it is a very big force, very dramatic. But it took me years to get past this showing off, overdoing it in riding.

'The secret is this: when a horse is in motion and balance, then, as in all things in balance, very little force or weight is needed to tip the scales in one direction or another. Centre yourself in your tanden, but then try to develop a feel for light forces, just enough to guide the purposely unbalanced horse. Your shoulders stay relaxed while your upper body is open and your koshi (centre) is strong. Your legs form a firm base for slight movement or projection of your hara and ki, and send the horse in any direction. For example, in a turn, you don't throw all your weight over to one side of the moving horse. Even if it worked, it would be too upsetting. One finds the balance of the horse quickly, then slight projection of the hips and hara or a steadying. Whatever – the range is infinite. Just remember, no matter what weight is on each side of a scale, if they are in balance a feather will tip the scales.

'The biggest tip I can give you is: do not make hara into a big force. This is unnecessary and can have a reverse effect by desensitising you to subtle shifts. This is what my posture teacher kept trying to tell me. Make hara a small, subtle effect in riding, but make it constant. Concentrate low down in the abdomen and start trying to feel, and then adjust the horse from there first. The horse will let itself be trained if you are in position. Horse and rider start listening carefully to each other. Of course, all these are just words. We need to try this on the horse. That is the only real test and real knowledge.'

The more time I spent with him, the more I came to see how masterful he was at designing action-teaching situations. He disliked explanation with words, although I felt he was very good at it. I know he liked it better when he could orchestrate an incident for the student to feel, or if he himself could act out some drama. His little theatres were always effective. You could not forget the lesson when it came in these forms. I remember once he wanted to get across the importance of the rider's legs as a base of support. The horseman's seat must resemble a stance, the same in any other martial art, or for that matter in any balanced movement. It is a fact that in many martial arts, there is a horseman's stance. He didn't

[101]

want to encourage a stiffening grip, but the leg contact has to be strong and secure to provide stability for the hips and the hara. If there is a weak hinge at the abdomen, just as much care must be taken to firm the bottom of the hinge, the legs, as the top of the hinge, the koshi and the back. If one side of a hinge is firm but the other is not, the joint will still fold in the middle.

There were always further instructions about not hurting the horse's back with what he called 'unethical sitting'. One day he was trying to show all of us, but especially one of the young men, that projection of ki from the hara was impossible without a good stance or seat. There was a heavy, tall stable door at one end of the building where he kept his horse. He asked us one by one to please go and push the door open. He had earlier greased the smooth floor in front of the door, and of course, as anyone pushed on the door, their feet slid away. The harder one attacked the door, the faster the attacker's feet would slide out and the harder he landed when he fell. We all ended up laughing, but the point was well made. Without any grip or friction on the floor, there was no possibility for leverage. Any force exerted forward with the hands and upper body pushing was immediately cancelled out by a backward force exerted at the feet or lower body. Whenever he saw the rider's legs sliding around backward or forward, he would remind them of the lesson of the slippery floor. Guidance would be impossible until the rider had a secure base and that base went down through the legs around the horse, and was not just on top.

I tried to learn to think more like he did, not always in idealised abstractions but through analogous, physical problems that would resonate with the issue or dilemma, thus showing a different perspective.

One day I was flabbergasted when he told me he liked

the paintings of Cezanne. Cezanne, he felt, had no trouble seeing from several perspectives at once. He told me that he preferred to teach with direct actions. It was very hard for him to entertain or present different perspectives simultaneously, with words. One looked at a painting and it was all there in front of you at one. He said it might be different for me, it was just his own preference. Oddly, over time I came to appreciate my Sensei's words more than anything else. It was his wise counsel that I went back for over and over again. He was not without frustrations, but he kept setting up his students to face their own demons. He didn't necessarily send you out alone. You always felt he had one eye on you in case you started drowning, but he would let you go under quite a few times. He had a way of giving his students a warning or a piece of advice, a weapon, so when you were in the midst of a battle you didn't feel completely out-matched.

* * * * *

In many Eastern teaching disciplines there are formal and informal opportunities for the student to ask questions of the master. It's not easy, though, to formulate an important question for your next session. Sometimes you forget what it is you want to ask, or when the time comes to put your question you get shy. You think your question is too trivial, or maybe you feel you should be able to work it out yourself. Like everyone else, it took me a very long time to learn how to formulate respectful and serious questions, and then not be afraid to bring them up when the time came.

As I continued to train with Sensei and study martial arts, I kept having a feeling that I was going to have to use them in some way and this bothered me quite a bit. Finally I went to my master and told him I had been perturbed by something from the day I arrived. I tried to explain that although I wanted to participate in the sport aspects of riding, they were increasingly in direct conflict with the art aspects. It seemed that the business of riding was getting darker and darker. Inhumanities and lack of compassion were becoming more and more common. Some popular public figures had stopped even trying to make excuses for their abusive riding, thereby almost suggesting that extensive and constant force was necessary. Others in national positions of power as teachers and judges were leading completely duplicitous lives, espousing classical principles at conventions, meetings, lectures, while running nothing short of torture chambers at their personal stables, hidden from the public eye.

On two occasions in a five-year period I arrived at two different international trainers' stables to find a tarpaulin covering a horse lying in the school, killed in a so-called riding accident. Also, I rode a horse trained by a famous woman Olympic trainer and found that the unfortunate horse would urinate uncontrollably when asked to piaffe because he had been so terrorised by the trainer's methods. Since these people were in, as I said, positions of power, the press would do nothing but glorify them.

I began thinking of these people as my enemies. My dilemma began to consume more and more of my energy. Finding ways to answer people who would say, 'Don't you think so and so is a marvellous trainer?' took a tremendous amount of strength, so I ended up being silent.

The longer I was in the horse business, the more secrets I knew. The more people I met, the more direct experience I had, not just with isolated mistakes of passionate people, but long-term deliberate systematic abuse and destruction of beautiful animals. I was wanting to fight more and more. I was certain that my training had prepared me for this confrontation. I thought I had been mysteriously groomed to be a fighter worthy of these adversaries. Was my antagonism stirring because in some way I was about to go into battle? How was I supposed to fight? What was supposed to be my part in this struggle?

This was the turmoil I was in. He listened to me very carefully. In fact, the intensity with which he was listening alarmed me. I felt I had to tell him everything. When I stopped, there was a long silence before he started speaking.

'Whenever you have strong reactions that want to turn themselves into stronger actions, you must look deep into yourself. You have to be sure your reactions are not overly sensitised. There is something of a mirror in front of you. To take on the coat of a moral authority is to wear a very heavy garment. This may be your path, but it is a very difficult one.

'Know that once such a choice is made you can never indulge in indiscretions. Everything would have to stay in control. There would be no room for any decadent joy. No matter what injustice might befall you, your rage would have to be contained – no retribution comes from a passionate saint. The life of a saint is lived in a very thick bottle.

'If you choose this life, or it chooses you and you do in fact live it, I myself would bow down before you. You would deserve my respect and admiration, and you would get it. For me, it is hard enough to be an ordinary man. If, however, you fail to live as you preach, then how could I treat that hypocrisy any differently from the hypocrisy of your false horsemen? Even if you decide to step back from the life of a saint, but wish to hold on to your moral authority, there are still strategic problems that come from being a judge or a policeman. You can find yourself in the position of answering rumours, lies, or challenges of your authority. Once you incite a battle, it can become necessary to back it up, to answer every charge against you, your laws and your ideals. Answer every blow with a fiercer one from yourself. It is easy to find yourself in a reactionary place. You can lose your own direction by chasing every true and false scent of your adversaries.

'There is a real truth that no injustice, once committed, can be rectified. No one can take back the pain someone forces on another human or animal. You can get revenge to soothe your own anger, but you cannot go back in time and change what has happened. All your attention must be on the here and now. That is the only way to prevent injustice. Stay in front of it by attending to your own life. Train yourself hard so you will never be a victim or victimise others.

'I want to tell you a little story,' he said. 'There were two very great sword-makers in the time of the Samurai. A man named Maruyama was an apprentice to a legendary sword-maker named Masamune. In time, Maruyama learned everything that Masamune could teach him. His blades were some of the finest any Samurai had ever seen. As you can well imagine, they were highly prized in that time of such violence.

'Maruyama was in great demand. It was said that his blades were so sharp and kept such an edge that to test them swordsmen would take them down to a stream and stand the blade in the water. The edge was so deadly that if a leaf floated gently downstream and ran into it, the leaf would be divided without the slightest friction or hesitation. It was an awful weapon and men feared it. As good as Maruyama was, it was his teacher, Masamune, whose blades went even beyond Maruyama's – almost to divine status. When a swordsman took a Masamune blade down to the stream, it had attained such perfection that leaves floated around it. None would even come near its edge. Masamune blades went beyond destruction.

'I know that your skill,' he said finally to me, 'is now quite formidable, and yet you are nowhere close to being finished. I have no doubt that if you want to do battle, your adversaries will know it. Maybe for you, though, there is something more – more like the difference between Maruyama and Masamune.'

He stopped for a second and looked gently into my eyes. 'You notice I said Maruyama learned everything Masamune could teach him. The last thing Maruyama had to learn by himself, he did not.'

Two weeks after that meeting, Sensei died. He never let on how sick he was. He made excuses for himself on difficult days. At the end he told me with a slight smile that he had much work to do. After all, he had to help get my life in order. I promised him I would never stop trying.

I never went back to the East again.

CHAPTER SEVEN

THE DIRECTIVES

Pennsylvania, 1996

I was returning home on a flight from Europe. Continuing my efforts to complete the philosophical and physical structure of my own riding school, I had visited another well-known riding establishment. I began thinking about an odd thing. Why do so many riding instructors yell at their students?

There are excuses and explanations for this phenomenon. One is that riding is often taught in large buildings or open spaces. The riding instructor must project his or her own voice over long distances and inside some of the poorest acoustical settings. The instructor gets comfortable with shouting. This is an excuse, because what I am talking about is not really a matter of volume. Riders do not complain when their instructor is praising them at the top of their lungs. On the other hand, if the instructor whispers criticism that is vindictive or mean, even if it is constructive but strikes a sensitive spot, the reaction of the student can be that he or she is wounded. I think this emotional change is often brought about by frustration. Sometimes the instructor becomes frustrated by a student's inability to do something for a million of the right or wrong reasons. Sometimes the teacher becomes frustrated by his own inability to make himself understood or the task understandable: 'Don't ask why. Do it because I say so,' is the oft-heard motto of this kind of instruction.

In all fairness to instructors, there are times during the course of learning difficult activities when elements of danger creep in. In such circumstances an instructor may not have time for long explanations. A situation can be so urgent that the elegance of the wording used is irrelevant. If a person is about to step in front of a moving truck, you use any and all the powers of your voice to stop that person dead in his or her tracks.

There is here, though, an enormous responsibility on the part of the instructor not to squander or abuse the student's trust. When the situation merits it, lapses in protocol or manners can be forgiven. If these power-voice situations are used too routinely, they become so inflated in value that they become meaningless to the student. The instructor will lose respect. If the instructor is too regularly frustrated by a student's inabilities, both the student and the teacher have to rethink their work. Teaching is almost entirely about inabilities to do something – that is why the instructor is being sought. In spite of all these explanations, I think we are still talking about excuses for lapses in patience.

There is another case when an instructor will emotionally escalate a situation in order to provide more energy, either his own or the student's, or both, in order to overcome a thorny problem. There is an explanation for this on an elementary, physical level. Inside molecules at the atomic level we can find electrons revolving in an orbit of sorts around the nucleus of an atom. An electron is considered to be at its ground state when it is at its lowest energy level closest to the nucleus of an atom. This is not the only state possible for the electron because it is possible to excite the electron. When that happens it will move into a different orbit. It will change its course, in a sense. In order to do this, it needs a catalyst – more energy. Kinetic energy, heat, for example, can cause this effect.

If a riding instructor can find a digestible kind of energy to infuse into a situation or a student, the orbit of the work can be escalated to a higher level. Maybe this occurs over an impasse in the work. Unless a student has been thoroughly prepared, aimed and schooled, success from escalating a situation will be pure chance. It is probably not worth the risk. Let me give you an example. Suppose you place a person unfamiliar and untrained in computers in front of a complicated set of keyboards which run a powerful industrial task. The person is reluctant to act and will hold still in ground state. You decide to add heat as an additional energy source, and the situation hots up emotionally. Then the person starts pressing buttons and throwing switches at random. The person moves to a new level of action, but is acting without reason and is more likely to wreck the machine or cause a lot of damage than to have a desired positive effect. It would be pure chance that the person would execute the task correctly and with success. The odds of a productive outcome would be very low indeed.

If the student is prepared and trained and an escalation comes about, it can galvanise the situation and provide an impetus to move the practice to a higher level. One of the best examples of this kind of teaching can be found today in some of the more formal teachings of Zen Buddhism, in particular during 'sesshin'. Within the normal day-to-day education of the Zen Buddhist student, there are special times set aside during the course of the year for intense retreats. These might last for a week. The student lives at the Zendo which is the practice hall, or monastery, temple, whatever you wish to call it. These Zendos are often simple places, and even if they are in dramatic places, they are always austere, uncluttered – beautifully simple. Designed to limit distraction and celebrate simplicity, they are also designed to be efficient and practical.

For the time of the sesshin, the student will keep a strict schedule with heavy meditation on their particular 'koan', a riddle of sorts. The student is to try to maintain concentration on the task twenty-four hours a day, even in sleep. Life is a strict schedule of meditating, eating, listening to the talks and all-important one-to-one meetings with the Zen Master, who will quiz and check the students on their progress.

This is no game. Serious monks have been known to meditate on a single koan for years, becoming psychologically and physically taxed to the limit before they 'solve' their koan and move on to the next step. The Master does not make it easy for the student. False interpretations are reproached. Weak effort is insulting to all who have gone before you. If a person falls asleep in the middle of meditation, they must be awakened with a slap on the back with a stick, handled by a wandering proctor. Everything is aimed at crystallising effort and pressure which will help the student reach enlightenment. Personal accounts of years and lifetimes of such work and final enlightenment are wonderful stories of human effort, perseverance, courage, strength, discipline, intuition and joy. The great Zen men of the past and present were masters at infusing energy into a situation. This will serve to train the student to find energy and with that energy they will find the former unsolvable, solvable. It is nothing short of an art form as to how a student is taught to suspend logical rational progressions, or to become comfortable with perceptual shifts, and to handle paradoxes.

I found riding theory and practice to be woven together with frustrating paradoxes. A light seat is a strong and deep seat. Impulsion is and is not speed. These are some of the reasons why I have always been drawn to Zen, and Zen was my first real relief from all the dualisms, unsolvable problems and frustrations. It seemed that I could not grasp these perplexities with standard Western Cartesian thought-processes. I wanted my students to be familiar with Zen and I knew, with it, they would be able to find relief when they fell into riding's inevitable traps. So I began to use it in my teaching.

Over the years I had been continually adapting and learning different systems of teaching so I could glean some of the best methods of the different schools and training systems. For anyone who wondered, this explained my interest in the martial arts. It was the physical concepts, and also the teaching styles and systems that fascinated me. How testing and gradation was and was not deliberately employed was of special interest.

Yet, I was also aware that there is a danger when one takes educational systems out of the cultural context in which they were developed. The more I studied and tried to implement and transplant these different systems the more these cultural clashes, if you will, surfaced. The horticulturist or zoologist who transplants a plant or animal species from one ecosystem to another often does so with dire consequences, usually not apparent until years later. When some exotic species is transplanted to a new area, this is not done in a vacuum. Often it is done at the expense of the native species, which then gets dispossessed. There is something aesthetically and ethically demeaning to the native plants and animals. The natural world is replete with ecological disasters that have occurred because of the blind transplantation of competing species. The delicate balances in the natural world become upset.

I was learning that if I were to build a school, I would have to do it within the native culture of wherever I was. I used to tell my students that we didn't go to work any more in three-cornered hats, but secretly I probably wished we did. I did know that these ideas had to be blended. There has always been a classic dichotomy between the new young school and the traditional old school. The young school is unencumbered by tradition. It can react quickly to changes. It can adapt and isn't harnessed by parochial bias. It can examine all schools of the world and select from all and synthesise. However, because it hasn't had the experience of long testing of theories to codify a set of important or core principles, there is a great risk that it might accept and follow charismatic or fashionable ideas and theories which might prove to be harmful over time. Schools heavy in tradition can become cumbersome in times of change, even resistant to all change. They are intent on holding on to the status quo. The protocol which can be protective becomes strangling. Instead of protecting the school, it can be used to protect the positions of the teachers within the school or the existing bureaucracy. And it does not, therefore, protect the idea of teaching.

* * * * *

The Directives

A short while after I returned from that flight I was back teaching and training at my little school. I had an excellent group of students, some of whom were good instructors themselves, some competition judges, some international competitors, some were nothing short of young artists. I also had a fairly new student who had not been with me very long. She was quiet, almost timid, but she was a natural on a horse. She had beautiful elegant lines even though she was untrained. She could sit on any horse and she had real desire.

When she came to me she had already been searching to learn about riding for years, but with each instructor she had this feeling that she wasn't sure what she was looking for. My instinct was that she was not the competitor type, but that she could become a real artist with horses. I did not feel she was weak, yet people seemed always to jump to that conclusion. I knew she would be lost in the standard equestrian world, precisely because she was of that artist material. I knew there were not many places in the world where she could develop artistically in riding. She probably reminded me of myself when I was her age, so I was especially open to her.

On this particular day she asked to see me. We set up a private meeting. She was nervous. She began by quickly explaining she felt intimidated by the other students because they were special riders. She felt that she was not, and that she was going to leave. I told her this was nonsense. For me, there was no measuring stick other than a desire to learn. I was probably a little patronising. I hoped that if I gave her a little pep-talk we could settle the whole matter, but it was not going to be that easy. She was made of stronger stuff. She told me that I didn't know how imposing I was.

I was reminded of a story an old writer friend told me. A very famous woman poet was giving a reading at an equally famous women's college which my friend attended. Just before the reading, some students were asking the poet questions and discussing their work. One hopeful young woman asked the poet if she thought that the work she was showing her would ever really be poetry. The older woman shot back a definite No! The younger woman was crushed. The poet then dismissed the lot of them and they slunk back to their seats.

The poet began the reading. When she had finished she put her papers aside and talked directly to the group, and in particular to the crushed young woman. She told the whole class what had happened. Then she stopped and looked each person in the audience in the eyes, and said sternly, 'If you cannot make it through the first "no!", then you will never be a poet.' She went on with the reading. Each person in the audience felt they had learned something very important.

So I was about to counter my student's statement very sharply with my most imposing voice, and give my own rendition of the poet's 'no' story. However, something else happened. I don't know if it was because I was exhausted from all the travelling or if something else was involved, but I felt I just couldn't come up with one more psychological ploy. I was tired of listening to others. I was tired of waltzing around sensitive personalities. I was tired of all the diplomatic patiences one must have to teach. I couldn't be aggressive, and I couldn't be soothing. I couldn't patronise nor scold. I felt I didn't want to preach, or push the plan. I didn't want to invite her to leave. I think I didn't want to do anything for her at the moment. Instead, I wanted to do something for me. For myself.

'Imposing,' I said at last, 'of course I had to try to be imposing. Do you have any idea of the opponents I have to face each day? People of fabulous wealth and power all bent on the gratification of their egos. The horses be damned. I have a very dull sword to fight with. Competitors, in some cases the people I actually compete in riding against, and top administrators routinely drug their horses to accomplish what they can't do with skill or hard work. Many use drugs themselves. Judges can judge fairly only until someone they know or have heard of enters the ring. Then no matter what happens in the sand, the score is fixed. Their minds go out of control. They have principles like feathers. At forums where they train each other, the people in power crush dissent like a bad government. They will not go outside their clique to learn anything new.

'The actions of the people in dressage are making a mockery of the great art that I love. I have had to do battle in any way that I could, although I have never underestimated my opponents. I was a realist and often saw my struggle as pathetic as Quixote's, laughable. But like Quixote I could be valiant. So I wanted to try to make my students brave and courageous, but each one had to realise the odds against us. You were going to have to do it for other reasons than actually trying to change anything. Huge corporations were investing large amounts of money in the sport of dressage. Their chosen competitors were their labels, their trademarks. They dominated the press. If you went against them, you had to be prepared for all kinds of fall-out.

'This is not your problem right now,' I told her. 'This is my problem, but someday it might also be yours. You will have to decide.'

My speech ended. It gushed out and it ended. We stood, each disarmed by our own honesty. Silent. I felt I couldn't go any further at the moment. I needed time to think. To think about myself, my school, and if there was merit to her remarks. And if there was, could I do anything about it? I asked her if she would hold off making her final decision for a couple of days. She agreed.

In the days that followed I began to meditate seriously on every aspect of my teaching. My ideas of the school's curriculum, its directives, direction, and its goals. I saw what I was doing in the establishment of my own structures, psychological and physical, as ways to legitimise and formalise my ways of teaching. I envied the great schools of the world, and I knew I was not part of them. I think I needed to make my own. I was not a fool, though, trying to make something to appease my sense of prestige or glory.

No, behind it all was still my child-like excitement of animals, and the fundamental love of horses. I felt a need to repay them. To be useful to them. I felt I needed an authoritative voice. I did not feel I could speak for them, but in a sense I knew what they wanted to say. I meant to be supportive to them, just as you would to a friend. I knew there were great historical examples for what I was trying to do. The great Guerinière was always in poor financial straits mainly because he was on the outside of the popular cliques. There was also La Broue, Newcastle ... the list went on and on, a catalogue of men dying penniless but holding on to their principles. That was the attitude that inspired me.

The next day I gave the young woman a light lesson. I stayed away from contentious points. I let her do the exercises she would be good at. It was safe teaching if it was teaching at all. But I felt I had to stay between her and her learning. It was the kind of teaching I hate.

So I went back to my ideas. I had run into a very old problem: my need to legitimise my teaching by forming a system, a construction, for my school. All of this was really a societal demand. These cultural standards were deeply embedded in me. Partially they had been placed there by a powerful society, partially kept there by my own agreement. These requirements tended to suppress the free-wheeling aspects of my teaching. This kind of teaching did not fit well in the notions of what happens in a good school. On the other hand, there were individuals with standards and requirements who had no rules and who would do anything to get the job done. This is the place where individual creativity lived. This is the place where I could teach anyway I felt I needed to. This, of course, was the reason for so long that I had had mixed feelings about that lesson with my handicapped friend many years ago. There was a long history of my suppressing my impulses. I had had a tendency not to acknowledge them as worthwhile or important. I felt they had no weight. Now I had to learn to balance the two. What an odd situation I found myself in. Was I perhaps at a crystallising moment after years of foment? And what is the catalyst? Not some great indomitable horse, nor some powerful cultural organisation snarling before me, trying to finish me off. No, this moment was crystallised by a diminutive girl-woman who I hardly knew.

On the third day we worked again. The lesson was the same, but I told her I thought I was getting to something important, and we would have to talk.

Things were becoming clearer in my mind. If my school was to be a cultural structure, she was not going to fit in my construction. It looked like I had no choice. Either I had to let her go, or let my system go. Yet, although I had built this system, no one could force me to hold it together. In my admiration of the great schools of the world, I had lost sight of the fact that the Spanish Riding School was a great school because of the great teachers, both horses and men. If they had to move out of the magnificent cultural building in the heart of Vienna, it would still be a great school. The teacher is always the bridge between a student and what is to be learned, not a school or a society. Individual teachers must reach individual students. No matter what cultural laws are imposed, what societal restraints are expressed, this is the way. The curriculum of schools cannot be transmitted without the consent of teachers. Teachers must take the credit or the blame. I began to see the school as a construct of society, to inculcate its laws and restrictions. I saw the teacher and his or her students as representing the individual's pursuit of his or her own path, his or her own freedom. I knew I would have to be the one who must adapt.

So on the third day, I told her it was important to me that I find a way to teach her. I didn't really know how, but I felt certain she would show me. She would have to teach me how to teach her. If what she wanted to know was equally as important as what I wanted to teach, we should be able to work something out. She looked a little unsure but said she very much wanted to learn. I told her we would have to go day by day. She would have to be honest with me if something began to upset her. I would try on my part to be as clear as possible, and patient. If she would talk, I would listen. Above all, we would have to communicate to hear each other, and we would have to learn to invent a way, a new system. It would be one more system in the many.

In the following days I did not feel my school dissolve. Instead I felt an odd and different kind of legitimising. I allowed the creativity which I never could stop anyway, a more acceptable place. I tore down some of my own rules. I didn't start teaching everyone differently. I think I realised I was already doing that to an extent. I was free inside a form, for to teach a discipline to a hundred people, the teacher teaches in a hundred different ways. I honestly did not know where this was leading. The only thing that was clear was that teaching could not be mass-produced. To learn something, the student had to have a teacher.

* * * * *

One evening, not long after this situation, it was very late and all my lessons for the day were finished. My evening ritual of dragging the indoor school to smooth the footing and prepare it for the next morning, had become quite an automatic habit after so many years. My arena is set off by itself, quite some distance from the stables. First I raked down the edges that had got banked up during the day's riding. Then I got my small tractor and dragged a harrow, which dug into the footing and turned it up, smoothing it out. I drove in a precise pattern until the whole arena was printless – all the neat linear grooves like a field ready for planting. My arena had bright lights, and they seemed even brighter when it got dark outside.

The big door through which I had to drive the tractor faced south. Once inside, the difference in the light was so dramatic that you couldn't see anything even one foot away from the doors. Though I knew there was a pond and woods, I could see nothing. It was always a large black square like a giant empty picture.

That night when I began raking the edges as I had done a thousand times, step by step, the same rhythm of the rake hitting the wooden bottom of the kick boards, the same pulling of the footing into the track the horses had created – the process was so mechanical I could look around while I was doing it. In my arena the short wall has mirrors. I found it interesting how certain occupations learn to use mirrors. Dancers, of course, practice with them daily. Hairdressers are so comfortable with them that they often talk to their client through the mirror even though they are only inches apart. They converse through their respective images on a piece of glass. In teaching riding the mirrors are practically miraculous. Once you have become familiar with the angles you become like a billiard player. From all over the riding hall you can see both sides of a horse and rider at once. You can stand behind a horse and rider and also see in front of them.

When I rake the arena at night, I go over the lessons of the day. I remember the glimpse of a certain horse's form. Sometimes I glance up at the prints of the famous engravings on the walls as I work my way around the rectangle. Whether it is cold or hot doesn't matter. It is always so peaceful when everyone is gone.

On this one warm evening I was engrossed in the task – tap, rake, tap, rake. I worked my way around to the mirrors. I thought I heard something outside. All the doors were closed except for the big door to the south. I saw nothing but the framed blackness. I continued – tap, rake, tap, rake. Again, I heard a metal jewel sound, like a bit jingling in a horse's mouth. I looked up and into the mirror and from that angle could see the entire arena. From the blackness a white horse stepped in. My immediate reaction was that my Spanish stallion had got loose. Just as instantly, I realised it was not him. This white horse was being ridden. I kept looking in the mirror. I was so startled. I stood dead still, my heart pounding. The horse was glistening silvery white under the bright lights. The bridle was heavy and ornate and had that dull gloss of gold through it and the reins. As soon as I could make out the image of the rider, I knew immediately who it was.

Almost above the beauty of the horse, and before I could see his face clearly, I saw that long sky-blue coat. There was only one like it, and it belonged to only one man.

The Grand Silence approached me. I couldn't move. The horse walked slowly with high cadenced steps. His long, thick mane bounced softly on his great arched neck. I could see the man's long dark boots. His yellowy deerskin gauntlet gloves. That fantastic coat with the sleeves folded back, showing an almost rosy hue in a shiny, satin-like fabric. Then the blue tight coat with its tails and buttons edged in gold. Finally his hat, one corner with a dark patina from being handled, and the other two trimmed in unusual braid. He walked straight into the middle of the arena. Finally I had to turn away from the mirrors and toward him. I was sure the image would disappear when I broke my gaze from the mirror. It did not. I turned to see him face to face.

He stopped. I was standing in front of the Grand Silence. All I could think about was that this was not in logic or reason, nor was it rational. But, my God, what a presence. Frankly, I was ecstatic to see him. Slowly he looked around my little school. He seemed to pause at each engraving and scrutinise it for a moment, and then his gaze would continue. He nodded his head slightly in approval. In the far corner I had a picture of him and when he got to it, he stopped and very, very quietly shook his head and laughed ever so softly.

My heart was racing. I couldn't explain this. I didn't care to. It was just amazing that he was here. There were a million things I wanted to ask, but this time it was I who was silent. Finally, he spoke: 'I see you have conquered the one and only thing that can stop a teacher.'

'Conquered?' I said. I looked at myself standing before him in all of his splendour: me on the ground with a farmer's rake in my hand, rubber gum-boots on my feet, my forehead beaded with perspiration, my gloves stained with sweat, mine and the horses'.

'I am afraid I don't feel much like a conqueror these

days,' I said. He kind of shrugged his shoulders as if to say it goes like that sometimes. He seemed so much more human to me, so much softer.

'Maitre,' I said, 'what is this one thing that can stop a teacher?'

He looked me in the eyes. 'That he cannot be taught.'

This time I laughed ever so softly.

He turned his white horse and walked toward the black square of the night sky. I stood there with all my questions. I wanted to talk to him for hours, but nothing had come out.

Just before he went through the door, I called out 'Maitre!' I wanted him to wait, let me formulate a question, say something more. He turned his horse halfway around and looked at me. I had nothing more to say and neither did he. He stepped into the dark. There was nothing but a great silence.

EPILOGUE

Very shortly after I finished this manuscript, in the autumn of 1997, and sent it to the publisher, I was helping one of my long-time students through her dressage phase at an Advanced level event. She had, at that time, several Advanced three-day horses. Although I have never really cared about winning or losing, I care a great deal about good riding and although this student, Amanda, was becoming more and more successful, it was the pursuit of good riding that was our common ground. It was not the pursuit of medals.

That particular Friday morning, I was at an event to help her with a brilliant but difficult white horse. This same horse was to leave for Germany in the following week to compete at Achselswang. After the Friday morning dressage phase I had to leave immediately for the airport to teach a clinic in another state. The following afternoon I received a call from my wife, who was competing in the same division as Amanda. She told me Amanda had suffered a freakish but serious fall with another of her horses, and had been rushed to the hospital in a coma.

In the subsequent months she never regained consciousness. Before she passed away, and especially in those last agonising days, I witnessed unbelievable love and heroism from her family and friends. I was asked to deliver a eulogy at her memorial service, which was one of the most difficult things I have ever had to do in my life. I had time to reflect, and I used as a theme the fact that I felt I had learned more from her than I had ever taught her. When I delivered the eulogy, I talked about her final and most compelling lesson.

The teacher is not supposed to out-live the student. When this happens, the teacher has nothing to do. What she showed me was that one's studentship is never over. As a teacher you must continue. You can never hand over the job of learning. You can never give it up and let someone do it for you. She forced me to reconnect myself to learning, to understand that there is no end. I said I thought a passionate life is hard to be around. Not because you can't stand that person's idiosyncrasies, but because they force you to stand on your own feet, to have your own life. You have to become an equal around them. You have to develop your own passion or you won't survive their flame, or their loss if they leave. They do not make you watch them as they attack life. They don't force you to be a part of their risks. But you want to watch them, as painful as it is sometimes. Why? Because they inspire you in the way they experience their life to the fullest.

In the end Amanda's and my last work together revolved around a white horse. The Grand Silence had a white horse. We all must have a white horse. The white horse is a passion. It is light.